Foundations Spanish 1

Second Edition

Cathy Holden

Tutor at the Institute for Applied Language Studies, University of Edinburgh and formerly
Lecturer in Spanish at Manchester Metropolitan University and Staffordshire University

María del Carmen Gil Ortega

Lecturer in Spanish at the University of the West of England, Bristol, and formerly Teaching
Fellow at the University of St Andrews and Tutor in Spanish at the University of Brighton

Series Editor: Tom Carty

Formerly IWLP Programme Leader at Staffordshire University and the University
of Wolverhampton

Review Panel for the Second Edition

Linda Hartley, Lecturer in Spanish, Centre for Applied Language Studies, University of Dundee
Maggi McEwan, IWLP Co-ordinator, University of Portsmouth
Gabriel Sánchez-Sánchez, formerly Tutor in Spanish at the University of Sussex and co-author of *Foundations Spanish 2*
Carmen Catalán Yardley, Tutor in Spanish, Language Centre, Brunel University

palgrave
macmillan

First edition 2001
Reprinted six times
Second edition 2005
Re-issued with CDs 2008
First published 2001 by
PALGRAVE MACMILLAN

Palgrave Macmillan in the UK is an imprint of Macmillan Publishers Limited, registered in England, company number 785998, of Houndmills, Basingstoke, Hampshire RG21 6XS.

Palgrave Macmillan in the US is a division of St Martin's Press LLC, 175 Fifth Avenue, New York, NY 10010.

Palgrave Macmillan is the global academic imprint of the above companies and has companies and representatives throughout the world.

Palgrave® and Macmillan® are registered trademarks in the United States, the United Kingdom, Europe and other countries
ISBN–13: 978–0–230–21726–3
ISBN–10: 0–230–31726–5

This book is printed on paper suitable for recycling and made from fully managed and sustained forest sources. A catalogue record for this book is available from the British Library.

Audio Production: University of Brighton Media Centre. Produced by Brian Hill.

Voices: María Emmerson, María del Carmen Gil Ortega, Ana Martin, Alejandro Salvador, Gabriel Sánchez-Sánchez, Javier García Sánchez, Xavier Ribas, Inés Sal, César Martínez, Adriana Montes

8   7   6   5   4
16 15 14 13 12 11

Printed and bound in China

CONTENTS

OVERVIEW

Unit 7 **En el futuro**	Discussing future plans Using transport, private and public	Future tense Comparatives

Unit 8
Trabajo de
verano
	Ringing up about jobs advertised
	Presenting yourself at an informal
	  interview
	Talking about your experience and
	  what you have done
	Working in a Spanish-speaking
	  country
	Writing letters and postcards
		Perfect tense

Unit 9 **¿Dónde** **estuviste ayer?**	Talking about past events and exchange visits abroad Understanding newspaper reports	Preterite tense (regular and irregular)
Unit 10 **Repaso**	Consolidation and practice Revison of vocabulary in familiar topic areas	

Acknowledgements

The following copyright sources are acknowledged: Helen Bugler pp. 1, 13, 15; María Greco p. 129; Jo Marshall p. 29; Helen Phillips p. 4; Quo, Hachette Filipacchi, S.A. pp. 33, 93, 142; Spanish Tourist Office pp. 2, 6, 20, 28, 44, 55, 85, 86, 103, 112; Esther Thackeray pp. 111, 115.

Every effort has been made to trace all copyright holders, but if any have inadvertently been overlooked the publishers will be pleased to make the necessary arrangements at the first opportunity.

Cathy Holden would like to dedicate this book to Elisabeth Dimock and Jeff Holden.

María del Carmen Gil Ortega would like to dedicate this edition to Antolín Gil Arranz, Encarnación Ortega Guzmán and Nadia Gil García.

INTRODUCTION

Mainly for the tutor

See also the *Mainly for the student* section which follows ...

Foundations Spanish 1 is a course for beginners, principally aimed at students taking a language module on an Institution-Wide Languages Programme (IWLP) or as an option on their degree. In terms of the **Marca de referencia europeo**, overall, it delivers level A2 plus, with several competences at B1. It forms part of the *Foundations Languages Series* which is specifically designed for IWLPs and similar provision. Its structure and content are informed by research and consultation within the HE sector and the authors are experienced tutors on IWLP-style university courses. We keep closely in touch with departments using *Foundations Languages* courses and are particularly grateful to the members of the *Foundations Spanish 1 Review Panel* for their feedback and ideas, which contribute to this second edition. To find out more about the series, visit the dedicated website at **www.palgrave.com/modernlanguages**

Structure

The course is designed to fit the typical university teaching year and assumes two or three hours of class contact per week. There are ten units, structured in the same way (Unit 10 is a revision unit and has a slightly different structure). Extension work, pairwork pages and a private study strand provide flexibility. Grammar and vocabulary are fully supported within each unit as well as in the reference pages.

Element	Pages	Function	Skills*
Core	6	Introduces, practises new material	LSRW
¡Extra!	1	Extension work (e.g. longer dialogues, more demanding reading)	LR
Gramática	2	One page exposition, one page exercises	
Vocabulario	1	Spanish–English, listed by exercise	
Practica en parejas	2	Consolidation	S
Más práctica	2	Consolidation, private study	LSRW

*Skills – L = Listening, S = Speaking, R = Reading, W = Writing

Methodology

The introduction of new material is carefully prepared and dosed. Typically, it builds upon a listening item, most often combined with reading-based exercises on the text of the dialogue, sometimes with questions, wordsearch or matching exercises. Once the input is introduced, follow-up exercises apply and develop it.

To facilitate the use of Spanish in the classroom, the exercises in the unit cores are marked with an icon indicating the linguistic activity or activities involved. They are listed and explained at the end of the 'Mainly for the student' section.

Recorded material

There are two CDs to accompany the course. Digital licences for the download and use of MP3 files are also available. Visit http://www.palgrave.com/modernlanguages/license.asp#Digital.

Mainly for the student

1. Structure (see table on page vii)

There are ten **units**. Units 1–9 have the same clear, consistent structure, which you will soon get used to. (Unit 10 is slightly different because it is a revision unit and doesn't introduce new material.)

The **core** section is six pages in which new material is introduced, then practised and used in various ways. Each unit is divided into numbered items.

The core is followed by a page headed **¡Extra!** This material, while on the same topics as the core, makes extra demands and is that bit more challenging. Two pages are then devoted to the **grammatical structures** you have encountered in the unit, with exercises to practise them. The next page is the **new vocabulary** from the unit. Then come two pages of **partner work**: communication exercises where you are given prompts for half a conversation (Partner A page) and your partner has the prompts for the other half (Partner B page).

Beginning on page 123 there are **supplementary exercises** for each unit. These are for work outside the classroom. Your tutor may sometimes set work from these pages or you can use them as and when suits you to consolidate what you have done from the unit core.

For reference there is a **guide to grammatical terms**, an overall **grammar summary** and a vocabulary list. Also at the end of the book, you will find **answers** to all the exercises.

2. Using the book

Each unit is focused on one or more themes or situations in which the language is used. The short **summary** at the start of the unit tells you what the themes are and describes what you will be able to do with the language once you have completed the unit. That's a key word (*do*): while language-learning requires and develops knowledge and understanding, it above all means developing the capability of using the language in given circumstances.

The **core** contains the input (new language) for the unit as well as a range of tasks designed to help you master it and make it your own. The key inputs come in various forms such as: <u>presentation</u>, when you are given, for example, the numbers or the system for telling the time; <u>listening exercises</u>, especially involving gap-filling; <u>matching exercises</u>, where you are introduced to new words or structures by matching up a word or phrase with a picture, a person with an activity or by questions and answers in a dialogue; <u>reading exercises</u>, where you may, for example, be asked to rearrange the order of a dialogue or narrative; <u>using a model</u>, the best example of which is working on your pronunciation and intonation using the audio.

Whatever the form of input, it is absolutely vital to spend time and effort mastering this material. Be guided by your tutor. He or she will introduce it in class or ask you to prepare it in advance. If there's a word or phrase you're unsure of, turn to the vocabulary page for the unit and check. If a grammatical point puzzles you, refer to the unit grammar pages or the Grammar summary towards the end of the book. If you wonder what a grammatical term means, look it up in the Guide to grammatical terms just before that Grammar summary.

The material introduced in an input exercise flows into exercises in the section(s) immediately following, enabling you to practise, use and master this language. The exercises practising and applying the input material are carefully devised to enable you to progress and consolidate in manageable steps. They are very varied, as the following examples show. They include above all many <u>speaking exercises</u>, typically involving you working with a partner. Here, you are communicating in a controlled situation, using the language introduced in the input sections; there are also <u>listening and reading exercises</u> involving gap-filling, answering questions and re-ordering information or correcting errors, etc.

<u>Grammar exercises</u> develop your ability to deduce rules from examples as well as to recognise and use the structures of Spanish correctly. Grammatical points are highlighted in boxes throughout the core pages of each unit. As to <u>writing</u>, work in the unit core is mostly carefully controlled.

After you have done these exercises in class (or gone over them there, having prepared them in advance), make sure you revise the input material and key structures in your private study time.

The **¡Extra!** page in each unit gives you the opportunity of further developing your Spanish, taking in particular listening and reading skills beyond the confines of the core input material while staying on related topics. The listening material is lively and natural and you have to extract specific information from it. In such exercises, it's important to avoid the temptation to fret over every word: check what information you are being asked for and listen with that in mind.

The **grammar** pages follow. In each unit, the first page gives you a clear overview of the grammar content of the unit, the second provides a set of short exercises so you can test yourself (answers at the back of the book). Don't skip these pages: they simply clarify and check off grammatical structures you have met and used in the course of the unit. This is how you become aware of the language as a system.

The **vocabulary** page gives the new words occurring in the unit item by item. Learn them as you go along and revise them regularly.

The **partner work** material can be used in or out of the classroom to develop communication skills. The scenarios are always based on the material in the unit core, so you are securely in a known context. The challenge is to use the language you have learnt to communicate information your partner needs and to respond to what he or she says.

The **supplementary exercises** give further practice on a unit-by-unit basis and are designed to be used in private study. Answers are given at the back of the book. As the section *Learning a language* stresses, work outside the classroom, both that set by the tutor and that done on your own initiative to meet your own priorities, is an essential part of a taught language course.

Now you have a clear idea of how the book is designed to be used, read the section on *Learning a language* which follows. It gives detailed practical advice which will help you to get maximum benefit from your course.

LEARNING A LANGUAGE

A language-learning programme is essentially workshop-based rather than lecture-based. It involves active classroom sessions and a variety of social interactions, including working with a partner, small-group activity and role-play, as well as answering questions, and working through exercises. Feeding into the classroom sessions and flowing from them is what is called directed study, set by your tutor but allowing you a lot of flexibility in organising your work in ways that suit you. Beyond that there is private study, where you determine the priorities.

Increasing attention is now paid to **transferable skills**, that is skills which are acquired in one context but which can be used in others. Apart from competence in the language itself, successful language learning is also recognised to be rich in skills particularly valued by employers such as communication skills and self-management.

How can you make sure you get maximum benefit from your language course?

1. A practical point first. Check the course or module guide and/or syllabus to see exactly what is required of you by your university or college. In particular, find out how the course or module is assessed. The course guide and assessment information will probably be expressed in terms of the four language skills of listening, speaking, reading and writing. The relative importance of these skills can vary between institutions.

2. Remember this is a taught course – you're not on your own. **Your tutor** is there to guide you. Using the material in the book, he or she will introduce new structures, ensure you practise them in class and then enable you to produce similar language until you develop the capacity to work autonomously. The first rule of a taught language course, then, is to follow your guide.

3. Of course a guide can't go there for you. While your tutor will show you the way, **only you can do the learning**. This means hard work both in the classroom and outside the timetabled hours.

4. **Regular attendance** at the language class is vital. This isn't like a lecture-based course, where you can miss one session and then catch up from a friend's notes or even live with the fact that there is going to be a gap in your knowledge. A language class is a workshop. You do things. Or to put it more formally, you take part in structured activities designed to develop your linguistic competence.

5. But mere attendance isn't enough. Being there isn't the same thing as learning. You have to **participate**. This means being an active member of the class, listening carefully, working through the exercises, answering questions, taking part in dialogues, contributing to group work, taking the risk of speaking without the certainty of being right. It also means preparing before classes and following up afterwards ...

6. ... because what you do **outside the classroom** is vital, too. While new topics will normally be introduced in class, your tutor will also set tasks which feed in to what you will be doing in the next session. If you don't do the preparation, you can't benefit from the classroom activity or the tutor will have to spend valuable time going over the preparation in class for the benefit of those who haven't done it in advance. Classroom contact time is precious, normally no more than two or three hours a week, and it's essential to use that time to the best effect. Similarly, the tutor will sometimes ask you to follow up work done in class with tasks designed to consolidate or develop what you have done.

7. You should also take time to review and reflect on what you have been doing, regularly going over what you have done in class, checking your learning. This will also enable you to decide your priorities for private study, working on areas you find difficult or which are particular priorities for you (see point 9 below).

8. This assumes that you are organised: keep a file or notebook, in which you jot down what you have done and what you plan to do. It's a good idea to work for several shortish bursts a week than for a long time once a week.

9. While a lot of out-of-class work will be done at home, your university or college will probably have a Learning Centre, **Language Centre** or similar facility in the library. Check this out and use whatever you can to reinforce and supplement what you are doing in class and from this textbook. Make sure any material you use is suitable for your level: it will probably be classified or labelled using categories such as Beginners, Intermediate and Advanced.

Possible resources: audio cassettes or CDs, videos, satellite TV, computer-based material, the internet, books (language courses, grammar guides, dictionaries, simple readers), magazines and newspapers, worksheets. Possible activities: listening comprehension, pronunciation practice, reading comprehension, grammar exercises, vocabulary exercises. Computer-based materials and worksheets will usually have keys with answers.

It is possible your tutor will set specific work to be done in the Language Centre or that you will be expected to spend a certain amount of time there, otherwise you should find times during your week when you can drop in. The course assessment schedule may include a **portfolio** for which you choose course work items according to guidelines set by the tutor/course.

10. Don't be afraid of **grammar**. This is simply the term for how we describe the way a language works. Learn it and revise it as you go along. There are boxes with grammar points throughout each of the units in this book, a grammar summary for each unit and a grammar overview for the whole book. You probably feel hesitant about grammatical terms such as *direct object* or *definite article* but they are useful labels and easily learned. There is a guide to such terms towards the end of the book.

11. In addition to listening-based work in class, you should regularly work in your own time on the accompanying audio material. Try to reproduce the **pronunciation and intonation** of the native speakers on the recording. It's easier if you work at this from the start and establish good habits than if you approximate to the sounds of the language and have to correct them later. It's important that you repeat and speak out loud rather than in your head. Why not work with a friend?

12. Always bear in mind that, in learning a foreign language, you can normally understand (listening and reading) more than you can express (speaking and writing). Above all, relax when listening or reading, remember **you don't have to be sure of every word** to get the message and you don't need to translate into your native language.

13. Regular **practice** is the key. Remember *fluency* comes from the Latin for 'to flow': it means speaking 'flowingly', not necessarily getting everything perfectly right. It is also a good idea to dip back into earlier units in the book to test yourself.

14. Universities and colleges are increasingly international and you will almost certainly be able to make contact with **native speakers** of Spanish. Try out your language, get them to correct your pronunciation, find out about their country and culture.

   And cheap flights mean that you can afford to go there …!

15. And finally, **enjoy** your language learning!

Tom Carty, *Series Editor*

El lenguaje de la clase/The language of the classroom

These symbols appear next to exercises and indicate the skill or activity involved.

 Escucha (Listen)

 Lee (Read)

 Habla (Speak)

 Escribe (Write)

 En parejas (Partner work)

 En grupos (Group work)

 Escucha y repite (Listen and repeat)

Also **Busca** (Wordsearch)

El abecedario

Letra	Nombre de la letra	Ejemplo	Letra	Nombre de la letra	Ejemplo
A a	a	Argentina	Ñ ñ	eñe	España
B b	be	Barcelona	O o	o	Oslo
C c	ce	Ceuta, Colombia	P p	pe	Perú
D d	de	Dinamarca	Q q	cu	Quito
E e	e	España	R r	erre	República Dominicana
F f	efe	Francia	S s	ese	Sevilla
G g	ge	Guatemala, Gibraltar	T t	te	Toledo
H h	hache	Honduras	U u	u	Uruguay
I i	i	Italia	V v	uve	Venezuela
J j	jota	Japón	W w	uve doble	Washington
K k	ka	Kuwait	X x	equis	Luxemburgo
L l	ele	Lima	Y y	i griega	Nueva York
M m	eme	Madrid	Z z	zeta	Zaragoza
N n	ene	Nicaragua			

1 Tú y los demás

In this unit you will learn how to give and understand basic information about yourself and others and to ask questions.

1 Saludos/Greetings

a Escucha y lee. Listen and read.

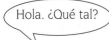

Hola. ¿Qué tal?

Buenos días.

Buenas tardes.

Buenas noches.

Adiós, hasta luego.

b Greet your partner. Then greet two or three other people and say goodbye.

2 Hola, ¿qué tal?

Hola, ¿qué tal?
Me llamo Carmen Salguero Ramírez.
Soy española, de Madrid, pero vivo en Birmingham.
Soy profesora.

– ¿Cómo te llamas?
– ¿De dónde eres?
– ¿Dónde vives?
– ¿Cuál es tu profesión?

– Me llamo Carmen Salguero Ramírez.
– Soy española, de Madrid.
– Vivo en Birmingham.
– Soy profesora.

Buenas tardes. Me llamo Michael Davies.
Soy inglés, de Londres.
Vivo en Nueva York y soy estudiante.

– ¿Te llamas John?
– ¿Vives en Miami?
– ¿Eres escocés?
– ¿Eres de Londres?
– ¿Eres profesor?

– No, me llamo Michael.
– No, vivo en Nueva York.
– No, no soy escocés, soy inglés.
– Sí, soy de Londres.
– No, no soy profesor, soy estudiante.

gramática

¿Cómo te llamas?	**Me llamo …**
What are you called?	I am called …
¿Dónde vives?	**Vivo en …**
Where do you live?	I live in …
¿De dónde eres?	**Soy (española). Soy de (Madrid).**
Where are you from?	I am (Spanish). I am from (Madrid).
¿Eres español/a?	**No, no soy … / Sí, soy …**
Are you Spanish?	No, I'm not … / Yes, I'm …
¿Cuál es tu profesión? / ¿A qué te dedicas?	**Soy …**
What is your job? / What do you do?	I am (a) …

The personal pronouns ('I', 'you', 'he', 'she' etc) are often omitted in Spanish.

3 **Preséntate**/Introduce yourself

Preséntate a tu compañero/a. Take on the roles of Carmen and Michael, and introduce yourself to a partner.

A **Hola, ¿qué tal? … Carmen Salguero Ramírez. … española, de Madrid, pero … en Birmingham. … profesora.**

B **Buenas tardes. … Michael Davies. … inglés, de Londres. … en Nueva York y …. estudiante.**

4 **¿Quién eres?**/Who are you?

Choose a character from the first column. Pick the right nationality and job, making sure the words are in the correct gender for the person you are playing! Introduce yourself to your partner. If your partner thinks you are wrong, s/he will let you know by giving you the correct version.

For example:

A **Hola. Me llamo Antonio Banderas, soy cubano y soy actor.**

B **Falso. Me llamo Antonio Banderas, soy <u>español</u> y soy actor.**

Antonio Banderas	cubano/cubana	pintor/pintora
Joanne Kathleen Rowling	alemán/alemana	cantante
Marie Curie	holandés/holandesa	actor/actriz
Gloria Estefan	español/española	escritor/escritora
Vincent Van Gogh	polaco/polaca	modelo
Claudia Schiffer	inglés/inglesa	científico/científica

Gran Vía desde la calle de Alcalá, Madrid

5 ¿Cómo te llamas?

a Empareja las preguntas con sus respuestas. Match the questions to their answers.

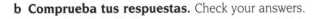

1 ¿Cómo te llamas?   a Sí, soy español.
2 ¿De dónde eres?   b Vivo en Granada.
3 ¿Dónde vives?   c Soy médico.
4 ¿Eres español?   d Me llamo Mario.
5 ¿A qué te dedicas?   e Soy de Alicante.

b Comprueba tus respuestas. Check your answers.

6 Soy estudiante

Ask two classmates the questions below and fill in the table.

PREGUNTA	COMPAÑERO/A 1	COMPAÑERO/A 2
¿Cómo te llamas?		
¿De dónde eres?		
¿Eres español/a?		
¿Dónde vives?		
¿Cuál es tu profesión?		

7 Conociendo a Miguel/Meeting Miguel

Escribe las preguntas en las burbujas. Write out the questions in the bubbles.

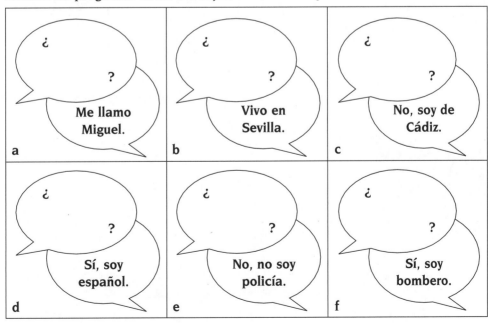

a ¿ ? Me llamo Miguel.
b ¿ ? Vivo en Sevilla.
c ¿ ? No, soy de Cádiz.
d ¿ ? Sí, soy español.
e ¿ ? No, no soy policía.
f ¿ ? Sí, soy bombero.

3

8 ¿Quién es?/Who is s/he?

a Escucha y lee.

Se llama Carmen Salguero Ramírez.
Es española, de Madrid, pero vive
en Birmingham. Es profesora.

Se llama Emilio Gómez y
es colombiano, de Bogotá.
Vive en Edimburgo y es investigador.

Es Ianis. Es griego, de Atenas,
pero vive en Cardiff. Es ingeniero.

Es Krystyna. Es polaca, pero vive
en Dublín. Es abogada.

b Choose one of the people described above. Your partner has to find out who it is
by asking questions. For example:

B **¿Es ingeniero?**	A **No, no es ingeniero.**
B **¿Es española o polaca?**	A **Es polaca.**
B **¿Vive en Dublín?**	A **Sí, vive en Dublín.**
B **¿Es Krystyna?**	A **Sí, es Krystyna. /No, no es Krystyna.**

gramática

¿Cómo se llama?
What is s/he called?
¿Dónde vive?
Where does s/he live?
¿De dónde es?
Where is s/he from?
¿Es español/a?
Is s/he Spanish?
¿Cuál es su profesión?/¿A qué se dedica?
What is his/her job?/What does s/he do?

Se llama …
S/he is called …
Vive en …
S/he lives in …
Es (griego/a). Es de (Atenas).
S/he is (Greek). S/he is from (Athens).
No, no es … /Sí, es …
No, s/he isn't … /Yes, s/he is …
Es …
S/he is (a) …

9 En la universidad

a Escucha y lee.

> ¿Qué estudias en la universidad?
>
> Estudio idiomas.
>
> ¿Qué aprendes en tu curso?
>
> En mi curso aprendo francés y español.
>
> ¿Qué estudia Pepe en la universidad?
>
> Estudia ingeniería.
>
> ¿Qué aprende Pepe en su curso?
>
> En su curso Pepe aprende matemáticas y física.

b **Ordena las palabras.** Put the words in the right order to make correct sentences.

   i la/Estudio/universidad/en/derecho
   ii italiano/Aprendo/la/Roma/de/universidad/en
   iii estudia/María/y/literatura/arte
   iv ¿Qué/su/idiomas/aprende/en/Ana/curso?
   v francés/Yo/empresariales/estudio/con

10 La carta de Marta/Marta's letter

Haz preguntas a tu compañero/a sobre Marta. Contesta también a sus preguntas. Ask your partner questions about Marta. Answer his/her questions as well.

For example: B **¿De dónde es Marta?** A **Es de Venezuela.**

> Soy Marta Serrat. Soy venezolana pero vivo en El Salvador. Soy funcionaria y estudio Relaciones Internacionales. En mi curso aprendo sociología, economía y psicología.

gramática

Yo (I)	Tú (You)	Él/Ella (He/She)
estudio …	estudias …	estudia …
aprendo …	aprendes …	aprende …

11 Los números

0 cero	11 once	22 veintidós	33 treinta y tres
1 uno	12 doce	23 veintitrés	40 cuarenta
2 dos	13 trece	24 veinticuatro	50 cincuenta
3 tres	14 catorce	25 veinticinco	60 sesenta ✓
4 cuatro	15 quince	26 veintiséis	70 setenta ✓
5 cinco	16 dieciséis	27 veintisiete	80 ochenta
6 seis ✓	17 diecisiete	28 veintiocho	90 noventa
7 siete ✓	18 dieciocho	29 veintinueve	100 cien
8 ocho	19 diecinueve	30 treinta	
9 nueve	20 veinte	31 treinta y uno	
10 diez	21 veintiuno*	32 treinta y dos	

*Numbers ending in **uno** lose the **o** before a noun: **veintiún años**

12 ¿Cuántos años tienes?/How old are you?

– ¿Cuántos años tienes?　　　　　– Tengo veinticinco años.
– ¿Cuántos años tiene María?　　　– María tiene cuarenta y cinco años.
– ¿Gabriel tiene treinta y dos años?　– No, tiene treinta y tres.

gramática

		tener	to have	
tengo	I have	BUT	**Tengo X años.**	I *am* X years old.
tienes	you have		**Tienes X años.**	You *are* X years old.
tiene	s/he has		**Tiene X años.**	S/he *is* X years old.

13 Su edad/Their age

a Federico, ___ años　**b** Manuel, ___ años　**c** Alberto, ___ años　**d** Jacinta, ___ años

14 Vamos a contar/Let's count

Practise counting with a partner, one of you taking the even numbers and the other taking the odds.

15 Más presentaciones/More introductions

a Write a few sentences about yourself (name, age, nationality, course, etc).
b Write a few sentences about someone else.

Avenida Gaudí, Barcelona

¡Extra!

 16 **¡Bienvenidos!**/Welcome!

Escucha y rellena el formulario. Listen and fill in the form. Four people want to enrol on a course in a language school in Barcelona.

NOMBRE	Segoshi Tanizaki	Carla Bertolini		Xavier Marchand
NACIONALIDAD				senegalés
PROFESIÓN		diseñadora	periodista	ingeniero
ESTUDIOS		arte y diseño		
DOMICILIO ACTUAL		Llobregat		
DOMICILIO PERMANENTE	Tokio			Senegal

17 **Un par de postales**/A couple of postcards

Querida Eulalia:

Acabo de matricularme en un curso de inglés. Vivo en el centro de la ciudad en una casa grande con 5 estudiantes de la universidad. Trabajo en un hotel para pagar el curso. No está mal.

Un abrazo,

Fernando

Querido Fernando:

Yo también aprendo inglés, aquí en Durham. Vivo con un danés que estudia filosofía y una china que trabaja en la oficina de la universidad.

Hasta luego; un abrazo,

Eulalia

acabo de matricularme	I have just enrolled	**trabajo**	I work
la ciudad	town	**pagar**	to pay for
la casa	house	**también**	also

Contesta a estas preguntas en inglés. Answer these questions in English.

a Give three facts about where Fernando lives.
b What does he do to finance his studies?
c What is Eulalia studying, and where?
d How many people does Eulalia share her house with?
e What nationality are they and what are their jobs?

Gramática

- **Subject pronouns (singular)**

  In Spanish the subject personal pronouns ('I', 'you', 'he', 'she', etc) are frequently omitted. They are:

  yo   I   **tú**   you   **él/ella**   he/she

- **Verbs**

  All Spanish verb infinitives ('to go', 'to have', etc) end in **-ar**, **-er** or **-ir**.

	estudi**ar**	to study	aprend**er**	to learn	viv**ir**	to live
(yo)	estudi**o**	I study	aprend**o**	I learn	viv**o**	I live
(tú)	estudi**as**	you study	aprend**es**	you learn	viv**es**	you live
(él/ella)	estudi**a**	s/he studies	aprend**e**	s/he learns	viv**e**	s/he lives

  As there are often no personal pronouns to help you, you have to look at the endings of the verbs in order to know who the subject is. For example, **estudio** ends in **-o** so it means 'I study'. See page 34 for a full list of personal pronouns.

  Ser 'to be' is totally irregular. It does not follow the same pattern as other **-er** verbs.

(yo)	**soy**	I am
(tú)	**eres**	you are
(él/ella)	**es**	s/he is

  See also page 34.

- **How to ask a question**

  Asking questions in Spanish is pretty straightforward. Take a sentence and put question marks around it (when writing) or raise the intonation of your voice at the end (when speaking).

  Vive en Madrid.   S/he lives in Madrid.   **¿Vive en Madrid?**   Does s/he live in Madrid?

  You can also use question words. For example:

¿Quién?	Who?	**¿Dónde?**	Where?		**¿Dónde vives?**	Where do you live?
¿Qué?	What?	**¿Adónde?**	(To) where?	✓	**¿Quién es?**	Who is s/he?
¿Cómo?	How?	**¿Cuál?**	Which?		**¿Qué estudias?**	What do you study?

- **Nouns**

  All nouns are masculine or feminine in Spanish. Masculine nouns frequently end in **-o** and feminine ones in **-a**. Some, however, look the same for both genders, e.g. **estudiante**, **periodista**.

	singular		plural	
masculine	**el secretario**	*the* secretary	**los secretarios**	*the* secretaries
feminine	**la secretaria**		**las secretarias**	
masculine ✓	**un colegio**	a school	**unos colegios**	*some* schools
feminine	**una academia**	an academy	**unas academias**	*some* academies

Ejercicios de gramática

1 Change the verb forms in brackets so that they agree with the subjects given in English. Except for **ser**, they are all regular and follow the patterns given in the grammar section opposite. The first one has been done for you.

a (I) (Ser) ___**Soy**___ irlandesa y (vivir) _____ en Dublín. (Ser) _____ escritora, (escribir) _____ novelas. También (trabajar) _____ en una universidad y (aprender) _____ turco.

b (You) ¿(Trabajar) _____ en el hotel Bienestar? (Ser) _____ recepcionista y (comer) _____ en el restaurante, ¿no?

c (She) Lola (estudiar) _____ idiomas y (trabajar) _____ mucho. (Vivir) _____ en Toledo y (ser) _____ mexicana.

escribir to write	**trabajar** to work	**comer** to eat

2 What questions could you ask someone in order to fill in this form …

a about himself or herself?
¿Cuál es tu nacionalidad?
¿Cómo te llamas?

b about someone else?
¿Cuál es su nacionalidad?
¿Cómo se llama?

NOMBRE _____

EDAD _____

NACIONALIDAD _____

PROFESIÓN _____

ESTUDIOS _____

DOMICILIO _____

3 Find the appropriate nouns from the list below to fill the gaps and make sense.

Maribel es (**a**) en la universidad y aprende francés. Es (**b**) pero vive en España. Su (**c**) se llama Pierre y es (**d**). Maribel también estudia economía, y su (**e**) se llama Ana, y es (**f**), de Buenos Aires.

profesor/a	**estudiante**	**francés**
francesa	**mexicano/a**	**argentino/a**

Vocabulario/VOCABULARY

1

adiós	goodbye
buenas noches	good night
buenas tardes	good afternoon/evening
buenos días	good morning
hasta luego	see you later
hola	hello
¿Qué tal?	How are you?
saludos	greetings

2

¿A qué te dedicas?	What do you do for a living?
¿Cómo te llamas?	What's your name? (lit. How are you called?)
¿Cuál es tu profesión?	What's your job?
¿De dónde eres?	Where are you from?
¿Dónde vives?	Where do you live?
escocés/escocesa	Scottish
español/española	Spanish
estudiante (m/f)	student
inglés/inglesa	English
Me llamo …	My name is … (lit. I'm called …)
pero	but
preséntate	introduce yourself
profesor/profesora	teacher
Soy …	I am …
Vivo en …	I live in …
y	and

4

actor/actriz	actor/actress
alemán/alemana	German
cantante (m/f)	singer
científico/a	scientist
cocinero/a	cook
cubano/a	Cuban
escritor/escritora	writer
holandés/holandesa	Dutch
modelo (m/f)	model
pintor/pintora	painter
polaco/a	Polish
¿Quién eres?	Who are you?

5

médico/a	doctor

7

bombero (m/f)	fireman
conocer	to meet
policía	policeman/woman

8

¿A qué se dedica?	What does s/he do for a living? / What do you do for a living? (formal)
abogado/a	lawyer
colombiano/a	Colombian
¿Cómo se llama?	What's his/her name? / What's your name? (formal)
¿Cuál es su profesión?	What's his/her/your (formal) job?
¿De dónde es?	Where is s/he from? / Where are you from? (formal)
¿Dónde vive?	Where does s/he live? / Where do you live? (formal)
Es …	S/he is … / You are … (formal)
griego/a	Greek
ingeniero/a	engineer
investigador/investigadora	researcher
¿Quién es?	Who is s/he? / Who are you? (formal)
Se llama …	His/Her name is … (lit. S/he is called …)
Vive en …	S/he lives in … / You live in … (formal)

9

aprende	s/he learns / you learn (formal)
aprendes	you learn
aprendo	I learn
arte (m)	art
derecho (m)	law
empresariales (f pl)	business studies
estudia	s/he studies / you study (formal)
estudias	you study
estudio	I study
francés (m)	French
física (f)	physics
idiomas (m pl)	languages
ingeniería (f)	engineering
italiano (m)	Italian
literatura (f)	literature
matemáticas (f pl)	maths
universidad (f)	university

For more vocabulary turn to the Appendix on p.180.

Práctica en parejas/PARTNER WORK

1 **a** Greet your partner and ask her/him questions in Spanish to find out the following information. Without writing anything down, try to remember the details s/he has given you, as you will have to introduce him/her to the rest of the group.

Name
Age
Nationality
Where s/he is from.
Where s/he lives.
What job (if any) s/he does.
What s/he is studying.

  b Now tell your partner what you remember ('**Eres francés**, **eres profesor**,' etc). S/he will correct you if you are wrong.

  c Your partner will now ask you some similar questions about yourself. Answer in Spanish. S/he has to remember what you say without writing anything down.

  d Check that your partner has remembered correctly the information you gave her/him, and correct her/him if s/he is wrong: ('**No soy argentino**, **soy colombiano**', etc).

2 **a** Answer your partner's questions about Oreste and June in Spanish so that s/he can fill in a table like the one below.
- Oreste Bertona, 21, Italian, lives in Milan, studies sciences and works in a hotel.
- June Thompson, 19, Scottish, lives in Glasgow, studies psychology and works in a hospital (**un hospital**).

  b Ask your partner questions about Iñaki and Elena in Spanish and fill in the table below.

NOMBRE	Iñaki Romero	Elena Fernández
EDAD		
NACIONALIDAD		
DOMICILIO		
ESTUDIOS		
TRABAJO		

Práctica en parejas/PARTNER WORK

1 **a** Greet your partner and answer his/her questions about yourself in Spanish. S/he has to remember what you say without writing anything down.

b Your partner will now check that s/he has your details right. Give her/him the correct information if s/he is wrong ('**No, no soy francés, soy italiano**', etc).

c Now ask your partner questions in Spanish to find out the following information. Without writing anything down, try to remember the details s/he has given you.
Name
Age
Nationality
Where s/he is from.
Where s/he lives.
What job (if any) s/he does.
What s/he is studying.

d Tell your partner what you remember ('**Eres griego, eres estudiante**', etc). S/he will correct you if you are wrong.

2 **a** Ask your partner questions about Oreste and June in Spanish and fill in the table below.

NOMBRE	Oreste Bertona	June Thompson
EDAD		
NACIONALIDAD		
DOMICILIO		
ESTUDIOS		
TRABAJO		

b Answer your partner's questions about Iñaki and Elena in Spanish so that s/he can fill in a table like the one above.
- Iñaki Romero, 22, Spanish, lives in Bilbao, studies economics and works in a bar.
- Elena Fernández, 15, Argentinian, lives in Buenos Aires, studies languages.

La familia en casa

2

In this unit you will add to the personal details you can discuss with others.
You will learn how to describe your family and where you live.

1 La familia

masculine	feminine	plural	
el padre	**la madre**	**los padres**	the parents
el hijo	**la hija**	**los hijos**	the children
el hermano	**la hermana**	**los hermanos**	the brothers and sisters
el marido	**la mujer**	**el matrimonio**	the married couple
el novio	**la novia**	**los novios**	boyfriend and girlfriend
el abuelo	**la abuela**	**los abuelos**	the grandparents
el nieto	**la nieta**	**los nietos**	the grandchildren
el tío	**la tía**	**los tíos**	the uncles and aunts
el sobrino	**la sobrina**	**los sobrinos**	the nephews and nieces
el primo	**la prima**	**los primos**	the cousins

2 El árbol genealógico/The family tree

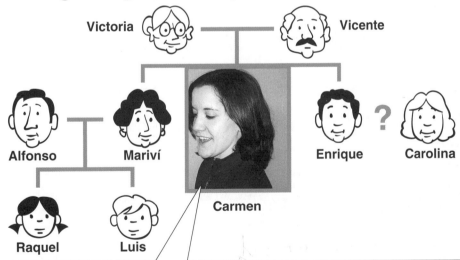

Carmen

> Victoria y Vicente son mis padres. Mariví es mi hermana mayor. Tiene 30 años y está casada. Su marido se llama Alfonso, y tienen dos hijos, Raquel y Luis. Enrique es mi hermano menor. Está soltero, pero tiene novia. Su novia se llama Carolina.

son	(they) are	**está casado/a (con)**	s/he is married (to)
tienen	(they) have	**está soltero/a**	s/he is single
mayor	older	**menor**	younger

> How to say someone or something belongs to you.
>
> Talking about one person or thing   Talking about more than one person or thing
> **mi padre**   my father   **mis padres**   my parents
> **tu hijo**   your child   **tus hijos**   your children
> **su hermano**   his/her/their brother **sus hermanos** his/her/their brothers and sisters

3 La familia de Carmen

a Carmen is being asked some questions about her family. Fill in the gaps in her answers.

– ¿Estás casada?   – No, estoy soltera.

– ¿Cómo se llama tu padre?   – Mi _____ se llama Vicente.

– ¿Cómo se llama tu madre?   – Mi _____ se llama Victoria.

– ¿Tienes hermanos?   – Sí, tengo una _____ mayor y un hermano
                                           _____.

– ¿Cuántos años tiene tu hermana?   – Mi hermana tiene _____ años.

– ¿A qué se dedica tu hermano?   – Mi hermano estudia _____.

– ¿Tu hermano tiene hijos?   – No, pero mi hermana tiene dos _____.

– ¿Cómo se llaman sus hijos?   – Su _____ se llama Raquel y su _____ se
                                           llama Luis.

b With a partner, practise asking and answering questions like the ones above, taking it in turns to be Carmen.

Talking about one person		Talking about more than one person	
Es	**la madre.**	**Son**	**los padres.**
She is	the mother.	They are	the parents.
Está	✓**casada.**	**Están**	**casados.**
She is	married.	They are	married.
Tiene	**dos hijos.**	**Tienen**	**dos hijos.**
S/he has	two children.	They have	two children.
Se llama	**Mariví.**	**Se llaman**	**Raquel y Luis.**
She is called	Mariví.	They are called	Raquel and Luis.
Negative			
No tiene	**hijos.**	**No tienen**	**hijos.**
S/he doesn't have	children.	They don't have	children.

4 La familia de Eduardo

a Dibuja el árbol genealógico de Eduardo. Draw Eduardo's family tree.

Soy Eduardo. Inés e Ignacio son mis padres. Tienen 64 y 59 años. Tomás es mi hermano mayor. Es médico. Tiene 35 años y está casado. Su mujer es inglesa, se llama Sandra, y tienen dos hijos. Sus hijos se llaman David y Dolores. Marta es mi hermana menor. Tiene 20 años. Está soltera, pero tiene novio y viven juntos. Su novio se llama Manolo y tiene 29 años.

gramática

In the following types of sentences with 'apostrophe s' you need to use **de**:
Inés and Ignacio are Eduardo's parents.
Inés e Ignacio son <u>los padres de Eduardo.</u>
Eduardo's sister is called Marta.
<u>La hermana de Eduardo</u> se llama Marta.

b Answer the questions using the possessive **su(s)**. For example:

¿Cómo se llama *el hermano de Eduardo*?   *Su hermano se llama Tomás.*

i   ¿Cómo se llama *la hermana de Eduardo*? _____
ii   ¿A qué se dedica *el hermano de Eduardo*? _____
iii ¿Quién es *el hijo de Tomás y Sandra*? _____
iv   ¿Cuántos años tiene *el marido de Sandra*? _____
v   ¿Cuántos años *tienen los padres de Eduardo*? _____

5 Una encuesta/A survey

Rellena los huecos en la tabla. Fill in the gaps in the table.

Nombre:	Nadia
Estado civil:	
Profesión:	
Profesión del marido:	ingeniero
Número de hijos:	
Número de hijas:	
Edad de los/las hijos/as:	
Número de hermanos:	
Número de hermanas:	
Profesión de los/las hermanos/as:	
Profesión de los padres:	jubilados

6 ¿Quién vive dónde?/Who lives where?

Escucha y escribe el número debajo de la imagen. Listen and write the number under the picture.

el campo	the country	grande	big
una urbanización	housing estate	pequeño/a	small

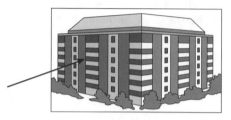

a _____ **un piso**

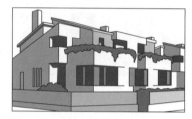

c _____ **un chalet adosado**

b _____ **una casa**

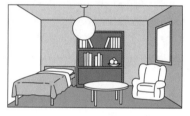

d _____ **una habitación**

 7 ¿Dónde viven?

Rellena los huecos con las palabras del recuadro.

Mariví y Alfonso viven en un chalet (a) _____ y (b) _____ en una urbanización (c) _____ . Victoria y Vicente, los padres de Mariví, viven en el campo. Tienen una casa (d) _____ con dos dormitorios (e) _____ .

grande	pequeño/a	moderno/a	viejo/a
grandes	pequeños/as	modernos/as	viejos/as

gramática

How to describe something or someone.
Adjectives have to agree in number and gender with the noun.

	masculine	feminine
singular	**un piso pequeño**	**una casa pequeña**
	a small flat	a small house
plural	**unos pisos pequeños**	**unas casas pequeñas**
	some small flats	some small houses

Adjectives usually go after the noun they describe. If the singular masculine adjective ends in any letter other than **o**, the feminine form is the same. For example: **un piso grande, una casa grande.**

8 Las habitaciones/The rooms

Rellena los huecos con las palabras del recuadro.

el dormitorio

el cuarto de baño

el salón

el comedor

la cocina

el balcón

el garaje

el jardín

9 ¡Qué error!/What a mistake!

a Escucha y subraya los cinco errores en las transcripciones de estas conversaciones. Listen and underline the five mistakes in the transcripts of these conversations.

Conversación 1

– ¿Vives en una casa o un piso?

– Vivo en un piso.

– ¿Es moderno o viejo?

– Es bastante <u>viejo</u>, muy grande.

– ¿Cuántos dormitorios tiene?

– Tiene tres dormitorios.

– ¿Tiene garaje?

– Hay aparcamiento abajo.

– ¿Tiene jardín?

– No, pero tiene dos balcones.

Conversación 2

– ¿Cómo es tu casa?

– Es muy vieja, y muy bonita.

– ¿Cuántos dormitorios tiene?

– Tiene tres dormitorios, uno muy pequeño.

– ¿Qué más tiene?

– Tiene cocina, dos cuartos de baño, uno arriba y el otro en la planta baja, y salón-comedor. También tiene jardín y garaje.

b Corrige los errores. Correct the mistakes. For example:

El piso no es bastante viejo. Es bastante moderno.

bastante	quite/rather	**bonito/a**	pretty
muy	very	**el aparcamiento**	car park
arriba	upstairs	**la planta baja**	the ground floor
abajo	downstairs	**más**	more/else

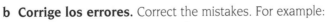

17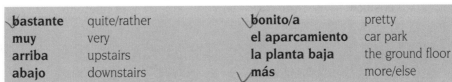

10 En una agencia inmobiliaria/At an estate agent's

Elisa quiere alquilar un piso amueblado. Escucha y contesta a las preguntas en inglés. Elisa wants to rent a furnished flat. Listen and answer the questions in English.

a Describe the one she is offered. **b** How much is it per month?

Quisiera alquilar …	I would like to rent/hire …	**mil**	thousand
¿Cuánto es al mes?	How much is it per month?	**caro/a**	expensive
¿Quiere?	(Do) you want?	**euro**	euro

11 ¿Cómo es el piso?/What is the flat like?

Match the agent's answers to the questions.

1 ¿Cuántas habitaciones tiene el piso?   **a** No, no hay televisor pero hay un estéreo.
2 ¿Hay televisor en el salón?   **b** Son 500 € al mes.
3 ¿Tiene jardín?   **c** Hay un aparcamiento abajo.
4 ¿Cuánto es al mes?   **d** No, está en el centro de la ciudad.
5 ¿Hay garaje?   **e** Tiene dos dormitorios, la cocina y el cuarto de baño.
6 ¿El piso está en las afueras?   **f** No, pero tiene dos balcones.

12 Quiero un piso amueblado

Take on the roles of estate agent and client. The client wants to rent a furnished flat with three bedrooms. The estate agent offers her/him one in the centre of town with three bedrooms, two bathrooms, a kitchen and sitting room, for €1,000 a month.

13 En el salón de Elisa

¿Qué hay en el salón de Elisa?
What is there in Elisa's sitting room?

la ventana	window	☐
la silla	chair	☐
el balcón	balcony	☐
la lámpara	lamp	☐
la alfombra	carpet	☐
la mesa	table	☐
el cuadro	picture	☐
la estantería	shelves	☐
la puerta	door	☐
el sillón	armchair	☐
el sofá	sofa	☐
el televisor	TV set	☐
el estéreo	stereo	☐
el DVD	DVD	☐
el teléfono	telephone	☐

gramática

tiene	s/he has, it has	**¿tiene?**	does s/he have? does it have?
hay	there is / there are	**¿hay?**	is there? / are there?

¡Extra!

14 La familia de Juana

Rellena los huecos.

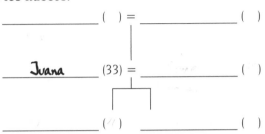

_____ ( ) = _____ ( )

Juana (33) = _____ ( )

_____ ( ) _____ ( )

Nombres
Isabel   Carlos
Juana   Jorge
Roberto   Juan

15 ¿En qué habitación?/In which room?

Read the descriptions below and match them to the rooms in the box.

a Hay una mesa en el centro con cuatro sillas. También hay dos sillones y un sofá. En el suelo hay una alfombra y en las paredes hay tres cuadros.

b Hay una cama grande de matrimonio, un armario viejo y un tocador, viejo también, con un espejo grande. En el tocador hay una lámpara.

c Tiene ducha y bañera. También hay un inodoro y un lavabo con un espejo.

d Hay una mesa con cuatro sillas, una cocina, una lavadora y un frigorífico.

la cocina	el cuarto de baño	el salón	el dormitorio

16 ¿Qué significa?/What does it mean?

Match the Spanish to the English. The descriptions above should help you. Try to use guesswork and a process of elimination rather than a dictionary.

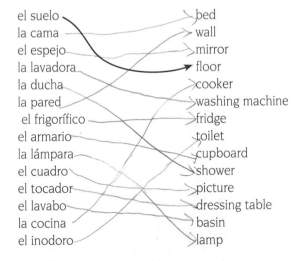

el suelo — bed
la cama — wall
el espejo — mirror
la lavadora — floor
la ducha — cooker
la pared — washing machine
el frigorífico — fridge
el armario — toilet
la lámpara — cupboard
el cuadro — shower
el tocador — picture
el lavabo — dressing table
la cocina — basin
el inodoro — lamp

Gramática

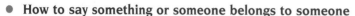

- ## How to say something or someone belongs to someone

One thing owned	More than one thing		Also	
mi	**mis**	my	**La madre de Ana**	Ana's mother
tu	**tus**	your	**Los padres de Ana**	Ana's parents
su	**sus**	his/her/their		

- ## Verbs

Ser and **estar** are not interchangeable, although they are both translated by 'to be' in English. Note how they are used.

Ser is used when someone or something is in a permanent state:

Soy una mujer española. (I am and always will be a Spanish woman.)

Ser is always the verb 'to be' that you use to identify things or people: **Es mi hermano.**

Estar is used when someone or something is in a temporary state:

Estoy casado/a. (I was not born married, and I could get divorced.)

Estar is always the verb 'to be' that you use to say where things or people are:

El piso está en las afueras.

- ## How to talk about more than one person: 'they'

-ar	**estar**	to be	**están**	they are	
	llamarse*	to be called	**se llaman**	they are called	(Reflexive)
-er	**aprender**	to learn	**aprenden**	they learn	
	ser*	to be	**son**	they are	(Irregular)
	tener*	to have	**tienen**	they have	(Irregular)
-ir	**vivir**	to live	**viven**	they live	

*See page 34 for reflexive verbs.

- ## How to describe people, places and things

Adjectives describe nouns and have to agree with them in number and gender. Thus if a noun is masculine and singular, the adjective has to be the same. Most adjectives go after the noun.

	singular	plural
masculine	**un piso moderno**	**unos pisos modernos**
feminine	**una casa moderna**	**unas casas modernas**

Calle Guipúzcoa, Barcelona

Ejercicios de gramática

1 Answer the questions as if you were Diana. For example:

¿Rita es la madre de Lena? _No, Rita es mi madre._

Rita = Pablo

Carmen   Román   Juan   Diana = Andrés

Lena   Laura

a ¿Andrés es el marido de Carmen? _____

b ¿Lena y Laura son las hijas de Román? _____

c ¿Román y Juan son los hermanos de Rita? _____

2 A new friend has written telling you about her family and asking about yours. Fill in the gaps with **mi**, **mis**, **tu**, **tus**, **su** or **sus**.

(a) _____ padres viven en Puerto Rico con (b) _____ hermana menor, pero (c) _____ hermano y (d) _____ mujer viven en Carolina. Tienen una hija y un hijo. (e) _____ hijos son estudiantes en la universidad.

¿Dónde viven (f) _____ padres? ¿(g) _____ familia es grande o pequeña? (h) _____ hermano mayor es abogado, ¿verdad? Y (i) _____ hijos, ¿cuántos años tienen?

3 Use the correct forms of the verbs **ser** or **estar** in the following paragraph.
Elena (a) _____ profesora. (b) _____ muy atractiva y (c) _____ casada con Manolo. Elena y su marido (d) _____ argentinos, de Buenos Aires. Los padres de Elena (e) _____ divorciados y su hermana Rosa (f) _____ separada.

4 Read about Eulalia, and then write a similar short paragraph about Eulalia and her sister Eugenia, making the necessary changes.
Se llama Eulalia y es estudiante. Estudia ciencias y aprende mucho en la universidad. Está soltera pero tiene muchos amigos.
For example: **Se llaman Eulalia y Eugenia y _____** .

5 Change some of the adjectives in brackets in order to make them agree with the nouns they are describing.

Tengo una casa (grande) y (bonito) con tres dormitorios (cómodo). En el salón hay tres (pequeño) ventanas, un sofá (viejo) y unos sillones (moderno). La cocina también es (moderno) pero no muy (grande).

Vocabulario

1

abuelo/a	grandfather/grandmother
familia (f)	family
hermano/a	brother/sister
hijo/a	son/daughter
madre (f)	mother
marido (m)	husband
matrimonio (m)	married couple
mujer (f)	wife
nieto/a	grandson/granddaughter
novio/a	boyfriend/girlfriend
padre (m)	father
padres (m pl)	parents
primo/a	cousin
sobrino/a	nephew/niece
tío/a	uncle/aunt

2

árbol genealógico (m)	family tree
Está casado/a.	S/he is married.
Está soltero/a.	S/he is single.
mayor	older
menor	younger
Son …	They are …
Tienen …	They have …

3

periodismo (m)	journalism
Se llaman …	Their names are … / They are called …

4

juntos/as	together
viven	they live

5

dentista (m/f)	dentist
edad (f)	age
encuesta (f)	survey
estado civil (m)	marital status
jubilado/a	retired
viajan	they travel

6

afueras (f pl)	outskirts
campo (m)	countryside
casa (f)	house
chalet adosado (m)	semi-detached house
grande	big
habitación (f)	room
pequeño/a	small
piso (m)	flat
urbanización (f)	housing estate

7

dormitorio (m)	bedroom
moderno/a	modern
viejo/a	old

8

balcón (m)	balcony
cocina (f)	kitchen
comedor (m)	dining room
cuarto de baño (m)	bathroom
garaje (m)	garage
jardín (m)	garden
salón (m)	lounge

9

abajo	downstairs
aparcamiento (m)	car park
arriba	upstairs
bastante	quite
bonito/a	beautiful
más	more/else
muy	very
planta baja (f)	ground floor
salón-comedor (m)	lounge-diner

10

agencia inmobiliaria (f)	estate agent's
alquilar	to rent
amueblado/a	furnished
caro/a	expensive
¿Cuánto es al mes?	How much is it per month?
euro (m)	euro
mil	(one) thousand
Quisiera …	I'd like (to) …

11

estéreo (m)	stereo
televisor (m)	TV set

13

alfombra (f)	rug/carpet
cuadro (m)	picture
DVD (m)	DVD
estantería (f)	shelves/bookshelf
hay	there is/are
lámpara (f)	lamp
mesa (f)	table
puerta (f)	door
silla (f)	chair
sillón (m)	armchair
sofá (m)	sofa

For more vocabulary turn to the Appendix on p.180.

Práctica en parejas

1 **a** Imagine you are Penélope or Felipe and describe your family tree below. Your partner has to fill in a blank family tree with the details you give. Check that your partner has recorded the information correctly.

Estefanía (66) = Rigoberto (68)   Nuria (62) = Víctor (65)
(jubilada) | (jubilado)   (jubilada) | (jubilado)

Felipe (38)   =   Penélope (34)
(piloto) | (auxiliar de vuelo)

Javier (12)   Trini (10)
(estudiante)   (estudiante)

b Now your partner will describe his/her family tree to you. Fill in the family tree below with the names, ages and jobs of his/her relatives. Check the information with your partner.

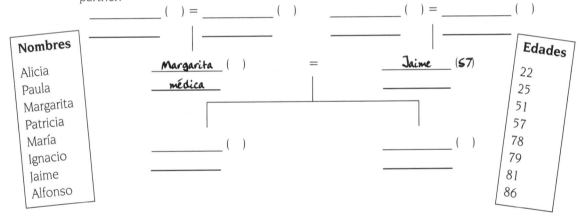

Nombres

Alicia
Paula
Margarita
Patricia
María
Ignacio
Jaime
Alfonso

Edades

22
25
51
57
78
79
81
86

____ ( ) = ____ ( )   ____ ( ) = ____ ( )

Margarita ( ) = Jaime (57)
médica

( )   ( )

2 **a** You are an estate agent and your partner is the client. S/he wants to rent a flat. Describe this one in answer to his/her questions.

> Piso grande, 3 dormitorios, 2 baños, cocina, salón, comedor pequeño, balcón. Centro de la ciudad. Aparcamiento. 700 € al mes.

b You want to rent a flat. Your partner is the estate agent. Find out if s/he has a small flat in town. Ask how many bedrooms it has and if it has a garage and a balcony. Ask how much it is per month.

3 **a** Describe a room containing all the furniture below. Your partner has to draw the items you mention and then tell you what room it is.
● double bed, small chair, lamp, wardrobe, dressing table, mirror

b Draw the items listed by your partner and work out what room they are in.

Práctica en parejas

1 **a** Your partner will describe his/her family tree to you. Fill in the family tree below with the names, ages and jobs of his/her relatives. Check the information with your partner.

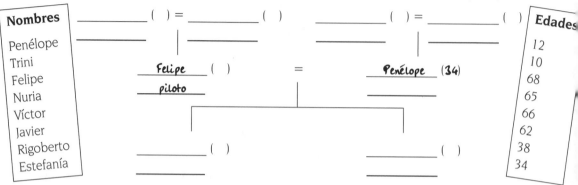

Nombres	**Edades**
Penélope	12
Trini	10
Felipe	68
Nuria	65
Víctor	66
Javier	62
Rigoberto	38
Estefanía	34

_____ ( ) = _____ ( )   _____ ( ) = _____ ( )

Felipe ( )   =   _Penélope_ (34)
piloto

b Imagine you are Margarita or Jaime and describe your family tree below. Your partner has to fill in a blank family tree with the details you give. Check that your partner has recorded the information correctly.

Alicia (78) = Ignacio (81)   Paula (79) = Alfonso (86)
(jubilada) | (jubilado)   (jubilada) | (jubilado)

Margarita (51)   =   Jaime (57)
(médica)   (enfermero)

Patricia (25)   María (22)
(estudiante)   (estudiante)

2 **a** You want to rent a flat. Your partner is the estate agent. Find out if s/he has a large flat in the centre of town. Ask how many bedrooms it has and if it has a garage and a balcony. Ask how much it is per month.

b You are an estate agent and your partner is the client. S/he wants to rent a flat. Describe the one below in answer to his/her questions.

> Piso pequeño, 1 dormitorio, baño, cocina, salón-comedor. En el centro de la ciudad. 500 € al mes.

3 **a** Draw the items of furniture listed by your partner and work out what room they are in.

b Describe a room containing all the furniture below. Your partner has to draw the items you mention and then tell you what room it is.
   ● large table with four chairs, cooker, fridge, washing machine, large window

3 La rutina

In this unit you will learn how to tell the time and describe your own and other people's daily routine. You will also find out how to say what someone is doing now.

1 ¿Qué hora es?/What time is it?

Es la una.

Son las cuatro y cuarto.

Son las cinco y veinte.

Son las siete y media.

Son las ocho menos cuarto.

Son las once menos diez.

gramática

Note: **Es la una** but **Son las dos.**

a **Escribe en números. Por ejemplo:**
Son las dos menos veinte de la tarde. 13:40

i Son las siete y diez de la mañana. _____

ii Son las cuatro y cuarto de la tarde. _____

iii Son las once y veinte de la noche. _____

iv Son las ocho menos cinco de la mañana. _____

de la mañana

de la tarde

de la noche

b **Escucha y subraya la hora correcta.**

i   10:00   10:10

ii 02:10   12:10

iii 16:15   15:45

iv 15:05   14:55

v   12:00   00:20

vi 02:20   09:40

25

2 ¿A qué hora?/At what time?

Rellena los relojes con la hora correcta. Después completa las frases. Fill in the clocks with the right time. Then complete the sentences.

Cada día ...

a Me levanto a las _siete y media._

b Desayuno a las _____

c Salgo de casa _____

d Llego a la universidad _____

e Voy a clase _____

f Como en la cantina _____

g Vuelvo a casa _____

h Ceno _____

3 La rutina de Eduardo/Eduardo's daily routine

a Completa las respuestas.

Carmen	Eduardo
i ¿A qué hora te levantas?	Me levanto _a las 7:45._
ii ¿A qué hora desayunas?	Desayuno _____
iii ¿A qué hora sales de casa?	Salgo de casa _____
iv ¿A qué hora vas a clase?	Voy a clase _____
v ¿A qué hora comes?	Como _____
vi ¿A qué hora vuelves a casa?	Vuelvo a casa _____
vii ¿A qué hora cenas?	Ceno _____

b Ask your partner the same questions.

Los días de la semana

lunes	Monday	**jueves**	Thursday	**domingo**	Sunday
martes	Tuesday	**viernes**	Friday		
miércoles	Wednesday	**sábado**	Saturday		

Days of the week are not written with capital letters in Spanish. All are masculine.

4 El horario de Carmen/Carmen's timetable

a Rellena los huecos en el horario de Carmen.

	9:00–12:00 (por la mañana)	14:00–18:00 (por la tarde)	21:00–00:00 (por la noche)
lunes			
martes		trabajar	acostarme temprano
miércoles	clase de informática	ir al gimnasio	ir al cine
jueves			ir a la discoteca
viernes	libre		cenar con amigos

b Empareja las frases. Match up the sentences.

1 Los viernes por la noche ceno con amigos.

2 Tengo clase de informática los miércoles por la mañana.

3 Los jueves por la mañana estudio en la biblioteca.

4 Los lunes y los martes por la noche me acuesto temprano.

5 El viernes es mi día libre.

6 Los martes y los jueves por la tarde trabajo.

a On Monday and Tuesday nights I go to bed early.

b On Friday nights I have dinner with friends.

c Friday is my day off.

d On Tuesday and Thursday afternoons I work.

e On Thursday mornings I study in the library.

f I have an IT lesson on Wednesday mornings.

c Rellena los huecos.

i Juego al tenis _los lunes por la tarde._

ii Hago ejercicio en el gimnasio _____

iii _____ tengo laboratorio.

iv _____ voy a la discoteca.

v _____ voy al cine.

vi Tengo clase de español _____

gramática

a + el = al
voy <u>al</u> cine
but **voy <u>a la</u> biblioteca**

gramática

Note the difference:
los lunes <u>por</u> la mañana but **la una <u>de</u> la mañana**
los martes <u>por</u> la tarde but **las cuatro y cuarto <u>de</u> la tarde**
los jueves <u>por</u> la noche but **las diez y media <u>de</u> la noche**

5 Concurso para parejas/Game show for couples

a Pepe and Ana are taking part in a game show for couples. How well does Pepe know his wife? **Marca la respuesta correcta.**

Se levanta a las ocho y media. ☐   Vuelve a las siete. ☐

Por la mañana trabaja. ☐   Ve la televisión. ☐

Por la tarde va de compras. ☐   Se acuesta temprano por la noche. ☐

Come en casa. ☐

b Responde a las preguntas.

i ¿A qué hora se levanta Ana? *Se levanta a las ...*

ii ¿A qué hora empieza a trabajar? *Empieza ...*

iii ¿Dónde come a mediodía? *Come ...*

iv ¿A qué hora termina de trabajar por la tarde?

v ¿Adónde va después del trabajo?

vi ¿A qué hora vuelve a casa?

Terrazas en la plaza de la Paz, Castellón de la Plana

6 ¿A qué se dedica?

a Empareja cada descripción con la profesión del recuadro.

i Por la mañana limpia la casa y va de compras.
Luego prepara la comida y trabaja en el jardín.
Por la tarde recoge a los niños del colegio.

ii Trabaja por la noche y duerme durante el día.
Sabe quién entra y quién sale del edificio.

iii Llega a la oficina a las nueve. Escribe cartas por la mañana.
Por la tarde asiste a reuniones. Habla mucho por teléfono.

iv Trabaja mucho. Se levanta temprano, a las seis, y llega al hospital a las siete y
media. Normalmente termina muy tarde, a las once o a medianoche.

secretaria	vigilante jurado	ama de casa	médico

**b Describe cada profesión. Tu compañero/a tiene que averiguar de cuál se
trata. Luego cambiad de rol.**

A **Trabaja en un hospital. Empieza a las seis.**
B **¿Es enfermera?**
A **Sí. Es enfermera. / No, no es enfermera.**

estudiante	jardinero	enfermera	periodista	camarero/a	profesor/a

La universidad de Barcelona

7 ¿Qué están haciendo?/What are they doing?

Rellena las burbujas con las frases del recuadro.

a   b   c   d   e   f

Estoy escribiendo una carta.   Estoy haciendo la compra.
Estoy comiendo un sándwich.   Estamos viendo la televisión.
Estamos escuchando música.   Estoy leyendo un libro.

8 ¿Qué está haciendo Carmen?

Pick a time at random from the pictures below. Your partner says what Carmen is doing at that time today. For example:

A **Son las nueve.**

B **Carmen está desayunando.**

gramática

To describe what someone is doing now, use the present continuous:

estar (to be) + present participle

(hab<u>lar</u>)	estoy hablando	I am speaking
(com<u>er</u>)	estás comiendo	you are eating
(sal<u>ir</u>)	está saliendo	s/he is leaving

Note that the present participle of **leer** is irregular: **le<u>y</u>endo**

9 Ignacio está siempre llamando

Carmen doesn't want to see Ignacio. Listen and complete her excuses. For example:

a El lunes   _Carmen está trabajando._

b El martes _____ comiendo.

c El miércoles _____.

d El jueves _____ la cena.

e El viernes _____ un informe.

f El sábado _____ la tele.

g El domingo _____.

ver   trabajar
comer   escribir
preparar   desayunar
estudiar

10 ¡A comer!/Let's eat!

Empareja las palabras con los dibujos.

la sopa

el café

el vino

las verduras

los cereales

la carne

la cerveza

el zumo

la ensalada

la fruta

el agua

las galletas

el pan

la mantequilla

el bocadillo

la mermelada

el pescado

la leche

(handwritten) arroz   birra

11 ¿Qué tomas?

Haz preguntas a tu compañero/a.

Por ejemplo:

A ¿Qué tomas para el desayuno?
B Como cereales y bebo café con leche.

el desayuno	breakfast
el almuerzo	lunch
la cena	dinner
tomar	to have/to take
beber	to drink

(handwritten) To have a coffee → Tomar

12 Hábitos alimentarios/Eating habits

a Pepe and Ana are comparing eating habits. **Marca la respuesta correcta.**

		Pepe	Ana
i	¿Come carne?	✔	✘
ii	¿Es vegetariano/a?	☐	☐
iii	¿Come muchas verduras?	☐	☐
iv	¿Toma azúcar en el café?	☐	☐
v	¿Bebe vino?	☐	☐

yo sí	I do
yo no	I don't
yo también	so do I
yo tampoco	nor do I

b Compare your own eating habits with those of your partner.
For example:
A ¿Comes carne?
B No, no como carne.
A Yo sí.

13 En el bar

Completa.

a Juana pide _____

b Lucía pide _____

BAR LA PLAYA
Bebidas

vino blanco	sangría
vino tinto	cerveza
jerez	refrescos

Tapas

champiñones	tortilla
patatas fritas	aceitunas
calamares	jamón

14 En el restaurante

a **Rellena los huecos.**

Camarero	¿Qué quiere tomar, señora?
Clienta	Quisiera de primer plato (a) _____ y de segundo (b) _____.
Camarero	¿Quiere algo de beber?
Clienta	Sí, quiero (c) _____, por favor. ¿Qué hay de postre?
Camarero	Hay (d) _____, (e) _____ …
Clienta	No, no quiero (f) _____. La cuenta, por favor.

RESTAURANTE EL SOL
MENÚ DEL DÍA

Primer plato
Gazpacho
Ensalada

* * *

Segundo plato
Paella
Tortilla española
Lenguado
Pollo asado

* * *

Postre
Flan
Helados

de primer plato	for the first course
de segundo plato	for the second course
de postre	for dessert
para beber	to drink
la cuenta	the bill

b Take on the roles of waiter/ress and customers. Practise ordering items from the menu above in pairs or groups.

gramática

To talk formally to a person, use the same verb forms as for *he/she*, or *they*, if you are talking to more than one person. You can omit the word for *you* (**usted/es**) if it is clear you are talking *to* someone:

¿Qué quiere (usted)?	What do you want?
¿Qué quieren (ustedes)?	What do you (more than one person) want?

15 **La buena vida**/The good life

Read this extract from a radio interview with Manuel Ibarra.

a Busca la traducción correcta. Find the correct translation.

> *No hacer absolutamente nada puede ser más sano que trabajar. Los momentos de relax fortalecen el sistema inmunológico, y dormir la siesta todos los días ayuda a reducir el estrés.*

no hacer nada	more healthy
puede ser	doing nothing
más sano	relaxation
relax	can be
fortalecen	to sleep
dormir	stress
todos los días	helps
ayuda	strengthen
el estrés	every day

b Escucha la entrevista y rellena los huecos con los porcentajes.

la entrevista	interview
el tiempo	time
una vez por semana	once a week

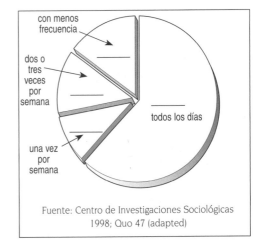

Fuente: Centro de Investigaciones Sociológicas 1998; Quo 47 (adapted)

16 **Cómo evitar trabajar**/How to avoid working

What makes Juan ill once a week?
Contesta a la pregunta en inglés.

Juan no quiere trabajar. Pasa horas en el wáter pensando en cómo puede evitar el trabajo. Hoy le está diciendo al director que tiene demasiado trabajo, y no puede hacer más. En efecto, con el estrés de tanto evitar trabajar se pone enfermo un día por semana.

evitar	to avoid
el wáter	the toilet
pensando	thinking
puede	he can
diciendo	telling
demasiado	too much
tanto	so much
se pone enfermo/a	s/he gets ill

Gramática

- **Present tense: Regular verbs**

	-ar		**-er**		**-ir**	
	Singular					
	estudiar	to study	**comer**	to eat	**vivir**	to live
(yo)	**estudio**	I study	**como**	I eat	**vivo**	I live
(tú)	**estudias**	you study	**comes**	you eat	**vives**	you live
(él/ella/ usted)	**estudia**	s/he studies; you (formal) study	**come**	s/he eats; you (formal) eat	**vive**	s/he lives; you (formal) live
	Plural					
(nosotros/as)	**estudiamos**	we study	**comemos**	we eat	**vivimos**	we live
(vosotros/as)	**estudiáis**	you study	**coméis**	you eat	**vivís**	you live
(ellos/ellas/ ustedes)	**estudian**	they/you (formal) study	**comen**	they/you (formal) eat	**viven**	they/you (formal) live

- **Reflexive verbs**

Reflexive verbs have the normal **-ar, -er** or **-ir** endings, but also have a reflexive pronoun to indicate that the person is doing something to, by or for him/herself.

levantarse   to get up

me levanto	I get up	**nos levantamos**	we get up
te levantas	you get up	**os levantáis**	you get up
se levanta	s/he gets up; you get up	**se levantan**	they/you get up

- **Three irregular verbs**

ser	to be	**ir**	to go	**hacer**	to do/make
soy	I am	**voy**	I go	**hago**	I do/make
eres	you are	**vas**	you go	**haces**	you do/make
es	s/he is	**va**	s/he goes	**hace**	s/he does/makes
somos	we are	**vamos**	we go	**hacemos**	we do/make
sois	you are	**vais**	you go	**hacéis**	you do/make
son	they are	**van**	they go	**hacen**	they do/make

- **How to describe what someone is doing at the moment**

Present continuous

Estar + present participle

Estoy llegando (I am arriving)	**Estamos escuchando** (we are listening)
Estás bebiendo (you are drinking)	**Estáis comiendo** (you are eating)
Está saliendo (s/he is leaving)	**Están escribiendo** (they are writing)

Irregular present participles:

leer:	**leyendo**
dormir:	**durmiendo**
decir:	**diciendo**

Ejercicios de gramática

1 Fill in the gaps with the verbs in the box.

Yo (a) _____ en Pamplona y (b) _____ biología en la Universidad de Navarra.
También (c) _____ francés. (d) _____ a la universidad por la mañana y
(e) _____ en la cantina. Por la tarde (f) _____ en una biblioteca. Después de
cenar (g) _____ la tele o (h) _____ con amigos.

aprendo	estudio	trabajo	veo	vivo	voy
	salgo	como			

2 Change the verbs in brackets into the appropriate form. For example:
¿Dónde (vivir/tú)? ¿Dónde vives?

a ¿Dónde (vivir, tú)?   (Vivir, yo) en Almería.

b ¿A qué hora (levantarse, tú)?   (Levantarse, yo) a las ocho.

c ¿Cuándo (llegar, tú) al trabajo?   (Llegar, yo) al trabajo a las tres.

d ¿Dónde (comer, tú) a mediodía?   A mediodía (comer, yo) en un restaurante.

e ¿A qué hora (terminar, tú) de trabajar? (Terminar, yo) de trabajar a las ocho.

3 What informal and formal questions would you ask to get the following answers?

(trabajar)	**¿Dónde trabajas?**	**¿Dónde trabaja usted?**	**En el banco.**
a (levantarse)			A las siete.
b (comer)			En un bar.
c (terminar)			A las tres.
d (salir mucho)			No.

4 Make at least five sentences by combining items from each column.
For example: **Los niños están escuchando a la profesora.**

Los niños	estoy	comiendo	a la profesora.
Vosotros	estás	mirando	un bocadillo.
Julio	está	saliendo	por la ventana.
Yo	estamos	hablando	con Javier.
Tú	estáis	escuchando	de la clase.
Nosotros	están	escribiendo	en el libro.

5 Write five sentences describing what the people in your class are doing at the moment.

Vocabulario

1

de la mañana	in the morning
de la tarde	in the afternoon/ evening
de la noche	in the evening / at night
Es la una.	It's one o'clock.
¿Qué hora es?	What's the time?
Son las cuatro menos cuarto.	It's a quarter to four.
Son las dos y cuarto.	It's a quarter past two.
Son las tres y media.	It's half past three.

2

¿A qué hora?	At what time?
cantina (f)	canteen
cenar	to dine 进餐
comer	to eat
desayunar	to have breakfast
ir (voy)	to go (I go)
levantarse	to get up
llegar	to arrive
salir (salgo)	to go out (I go out)
volver (vuelvo)	to return (I return)

4

acostarse	to go to bed
amigo/a	friend
biblioteca (f)	library
cine (m)	cinema
clase (f)	class
día libre (m)	day off
discoteca (f)	club
gimnasio (m)	gymnasium
hacer ejercicio	to exercise
informática	IT
jugar al tenis	to play tennis
laboratorio (m)	lab
los días de la semana	the days of the week
por la mañana	in the morning
por la tarde	in the afternoon/ evening
por la noche	in the evening / at night
temprano	early
trabajar	to work

For the days of the week see page 27.

5

después	afterwards
empezar	to start
ir de compras	to go shopping
mediodía (m)	midday
terminar	to finish
ver la televisión	to watch TV

6

ama de casa (f)	home-maker
asistir a	to attend / to go to
camarero/a	waiter/waitress
dormir	to sleep
durante	during
edificio (m)	building
enfermero/a	nurse
entrar	to go in
hablar	to talk
hospital (m)	hospital
jardinero/a	gardener
limpiar	to clean
luego	then
medianoche (f)	midnight
normalmente	usually
periodista (m/f)	journalist
preparar la comida	to prepare meals
recoger	to collect
reunión (f)	meeting
saber	to know
salir	to go out
secretario/a	secretary
vigilante jurado (m)	security guard

7

escribir	to write
escuchar música	to listen to music
hacer la compra	to do the shopping
leer un libro	to read a book
sándwich (m)	sandwich (made with sliced bread)

9

cena (f)	dinner
informe (m)	report
siempre	always

10

agua (f)	water
bocadillo (m)	sandwich (made with French bread)
café (m)	coffee
carne (f)	meat
cereales (m pl)	cereal
cerveza (f)	beer
ensalada (f)	salad
fruta (f)	fruit
galleta (f)	biscuit
leche (f)	milk
mantequilla (f)	butter
mermelada (f)	jam

For more vocabulary turn to the Appendix on p.180.

Práctica en parejas

1 Say the times. Your partner writes them down. You check they are correct. For example:
A 10.00 **Son las diez de la mañana.**

a 10.10 **b** 12.45 **c** 02.20 **d** 14.25 **e** 12.30

2 You want to go out for a drink with your partner. By referring to your diary below, try to find a time when you are both free (**libre**).
For example:
A **¿Estás libre el martes por la tarde?** or **¿Qué haces el martes por la tarde?**
B **No. El martes por la tarde no estoy libre. Tengo clase.** or **El martes por la tarde tengo clase.**

	Por la mañana	Por la tarde	Por la noche
lunes	Trabajo	Trabajo	Teatro con Chus
martes	Trabajo		Cine
miércoles		Trabajo	Trabajo
jueves	Trabajo	Gimnasio	
viernes	Trabajo	Trabajo	Bar con Charo
sábado	De compras		Cine con Pedro
domingo	En casa de mis padres		

3 Mime an activity from the box. Your partner has to say what you are doing.
For example:
A (doing an action) **¿Qué estoy haciendo?**
B **¿Estás escribiendo?**
A **Sí, estoy escribiendo. / No, no estoy escribiendo.**

escribir	pintar
salir	entrar
comer	beber
leer	escuchar
estudiar	hablar

4 Have a conversation in a bar in which you are the customer and your partner is the barman or barmaid. Your partner speaks first.

B _____ A Say, 'I want a beer, please'.

B _____ A Ask what there is. (**¿Qué hay?**)

B _____ A Say, 'I want some olives, please'.

Práctica en parejas

1 Say the times. Your partner writes them down. You check they are correct. For example:
17.00 **Son las cinco de la tarde.**

a 15.10 **b** 16.45 **c** 05.15 **d** 20.25 **e** 02.30

2 You want to go out for a drink with your partner. By referring to your diary below, try to find a time when you are both free (**libre**).
For example:
A **¿Estás libre el martes por la tarde?** or **¿Qué haces el martes por la tarde?**
B **No. El martes por la tarde no estoy libre. Tengo clase.** or **El martes por la tarde tengo clase.**

	Por la mañana	Por la tarde	Por la noche
lunes	Clase	Clase	
martes		Clase	Trabajo
miércoles	Clase	Clase	Gimnasio
jueves	Clase	Clase	
viernes		Clase	Cine con Miguel
sábado	De compras		Bar con Carlos
domingo	En casa de mis abuelos		

3 Mime an activity from the box. Your partner has to say what you are doing.
For example:
A (doing an action) **¿Qué estoy haciendo?**
B **¿Estás escribiendo?**
A **Sí, estoy escribiendo. / No, no estoy escribiendo.**

escribir	pintar
salir	entrar
comer	beber
leer	escuchar
estudiar	hablar

4 Have a conversation in a bar in which you are the barman or barmaid and your partner is the customer. You speak first.

B Say 'Hello' and ask 'What do you want?' A _____

B Ask 'Do you want anything to eat?' A _____

B Say 'There are mushrooms, ham, squid, olives, sandwiches ...' A _____

4 El tiempo libre

In this unit you will learn how to discuss the things you like doing in the evenings and at weekends. You will also learn how to make, accept and reject invitations and to buy tickets for shows.

1 ¿Qué te gusta hacer?/What do you like doing?

Escucha y empareja a la persona con lo que le gusta hacer. Listen and match the person to what s/he likes doing.

a Juana

b Julio

c Miguel

Me gusta ir al cine.

Me gusta salir con amigos.

Me gusta ver la tele.

Me gusta tomar el sol.

Me gusta jugar al fútbol.

Me gusta dar paseos por el campo.

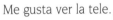
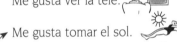

2 ¿Qué le gusta a Julio?/What does Julio like?

a Julio is being asked if he likes certain activities. Write his answers. For example:

¿Te gusta escuchar música?   *Sí, me gusta.*

¿Te gusta jugar al tenis?   *No, no me gusta.*

i ¿Te gusta fumar puros?
_____

ii ¿Te gusta ir de compras?
_____

iii ¿Te gusta hacer ejercicio?
_____

iv ¿Te gusta trabajar?
_____

v ¿Te gusta bailar?
_____

vi ¿Te gusta leer?
_____

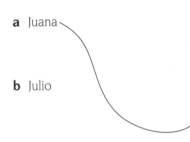

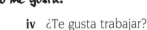
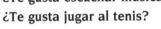
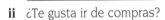

b Haz preguntas a tu compañero/a sobre sus gustos. Por ejemplo:
A ¿Te gusta ver la tele?
B Sí, me gusta./No, no me gusta.

gramática

Me gusta.
I like it (it pleases me).
Te gusta.
You like it (it pleases you).

3 ¿Te gusta el deporte?

a Empareja los deportes con los dibujos.

1   2   3   4   5

canoeing   *bungee jumping*   *horsemanship*   *skating*
a el piragüismo   **b** el puénting   **c** el ciclismo   **d** la equitación   **e** el patinaje
3   5   4   1   2

b Juana wants to know what Miguel thinks of these activities. **Empareja las preguntas con las respuestas.**

Juana	Miguel	
i ¿Te gusta el yoga?	Sí, me encanta.	✓✓✓
ii ¿Te gusta el aerobic?	Sí, me gusta mucho.	✓✓
iii ¿Te gusta la natación?	Sí, me gusta.	✓
iv ¿Te gusta el fútbol?	No, no me gusta mucho.	✗
v ¿Te gusta el tenis?	No, no me gusta nada.	✗✗

c Ask your partner the questions in Section **b** above.

d ¿Qué deportes le gustan a Miguel? Marca la casilla correcta.

	Verdadero (True)	**Falso** (False)
i A Miguel le encanta el fútbol.	☐	☐
ii No le gusta nada el tenis.	☐	☐
iii Le gusta bastante la natación.	☐	☐
iv Le encanta el aerobic.	☐	☐
v No le gusta mucho el yoga.	☐	☐

gramática

Le gusta.
S/he likes (it) (it pleases him/her).
A Miguel le gusta.
Miguel likes (it).

4 Me gustan o no me gustan

Me gusta el vino.

No me gustan las mañanas.

No me gusta el trabajo.

Me gustan las vacaciones.

Haz preguntas a tu compañero/a. Por ejemplo:

¿Te gusta	el vino?
	el curso?
	el trabajo?
¿Te gustan	las vacaciones?
	las clases?
	las mañanas?

gramática

To say someone likes more than one thing:

Me gustan.	I like *them*.
Te gustan.	You like *them*.
Le gustan.	S/he likes *them*.
	You like *them*.
	(formal)

5 ¿Qué les gusta?/What do they like?

a Rellena los espacios en blanco. Fill in the blanks.

	Andrés	Bea	Carlos
le gusta		ir de compras	
le gustan			las clases
no le gusta			
no le gustan	los coches		

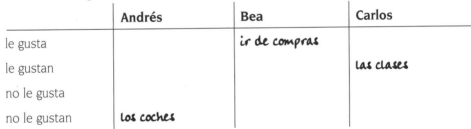

b Who would say the following? For example:

«**A Bea le gusta ir de compras y a mí también.**» _Carlos_

i «A Andrés no le gusta hacer deporte y a mí tampoco.» _____

ii «A Carlos le gustan las clases pero a mí no.» _____

iii «A Andrés no le gustan los coches pero a mí sí.» _____

gramática

To emphasize or specify who likes something: **a mí, a ti, a él, a ella**, etc

A mí me gustan las comedias pero a ti no (te gustan).

I like comedies but *you* don't (like them).

A ella no le gusta la música pop pero a él sí (le gusta).

She doesn't like pop music but *he* does (like it).

6 ¿Quieres venir al cine?/Do you want to come to the cinema?

Juana
¿Quieres venir al cine?
Mar adentro de Alejandro Amenábar.
El viernes.
A las diez.
En la entrada del cine.

Javier
¡Claro! ¿Qué ponen?
¿Cuándo es?
¿A qué hora empieza?
¿Dónde quedamos?
Vale.

7 ¿Y tú quieres salir?/And do you want to go out?

Invita a tu compañero/a a salir. Invite your partner out. S/he must say whether s/he wants to go or not.
For example:
A **¿Quieres venir al cine?**
B **¡Claro! / No, no quiero.**

| el cine | el teatro |
| el bar | el concierto |

8 ¿Qué ponen?/What's on?

a **Invita a tu compañero/a al cine.**
Invite your partner to the cinema.

La mala educación

Dir. Pedro Almodóvar
sábado a las 22:30

A
Ask 'Do you want to come to the cinema'?
Say '*La mala educación* by Pedro Almodóvar'.
Say 'Saturday.'
Say 'At 10.30.'
Say 'In the cinema foyer.'

B
Say 'Sure!', and ask what's on.
Ask 'When is it?'
Ask 'What time does it start?'
Ask 'Where shall we meet?'
Say 'OK.'

b Your partner can now invite you to see *Amores perros*.

Amores perros

Dir. Alejandro González Iñárritu
viernes a las 23:00

9 ¿A qué discoteca deciden ir?

Discoteca	Hora	Música	Entradas
La Boite	23:00	Los Stompers	12 €
Luz de Gas	00:30	Tandoori Lenoir	15 €
El Mojito	00:00	Orquesta sabor cubano	16 €
El Moog	00:00	Los Taxi Boys. Noche Latin-Lover	10 €

10 ¿Qué prefieres hacer?/What do you prefer to do?

Empareja a cada persona con lo que prefiere hacer.

1 Juana   2 **a** No gracias, no quiero salir. Prefiero quedarme en casa y ver la tele.

2 Alex   4 **b** No me gustan las discotecas. Prefiero ir al polideportivo.

3 Lucía   3 **c** No quiero bailar. Prefiero charlar en un bar.

4 Marco   1 **d** No, lo siento, no me gustan los bares. Prefiero ir al cine.

11 ¿Quieres ver la tele?

Pregunta a tu compañero/a si quiere hacer algo. Él/Ella prefiere hacer algo distinto. Por ejemplo:

A ¿Quieres ver la tele? (Escuchar la radio)   B **No. Prefiero escuchar la radio.**

a ¿Jugar al fútbol? (Jugar al tenis)   **b** ¿Hacer gimnasia? (Hacer footing)

c ¿Dar un paseo? (Ir de compras)   **d** ¿Salir? (Quedarme en casa)

12 ¿Qué tienen que hacer?/What do they have to do?

Completa:

a Esther: _«Tengo que ...»_

b Bea: _____

c Carlos: _____

> **gramática**
>
> These are all root-changing verbs
> See page 46.
> **qu<u>ie</u>ro**   I want
> **pref<u>ie</u>ro**   I prefer
> **p<u>ue</u>do**   I can
>
> Irregular in the **yo** form:
> **tengo que** I have to

13 Quiero pero no puedo/I want to but I can't

Invite your partner to do the things below. S/he has to refuse, giving a different excuse each time. For example:

A ¿Quieres venir al cine esta noche?
B Quiero pero no puedo. Tengo que trabajar.

A	B
¿Quieres ...	Quiero pero no puedo. Tengo que ...
venir a la discoteca esta noche?	**quedarme en casa.**
ver una película?	**preparar la cena.**
dar un paseo por el campo?	**estudiar.**
ir al gimnasio?	**ir de compras.**

14 ¿Queréis venir?

Rellena los huecos en las preguntas.

Julio	Lucía y yo vamos a un concierto. ¿Tú y Alex queréis venir?
Juana	¿ (a) _____ vais?
Julio	Esta noche.
Juana	¿ (b) _____ ?
Julio	Manuel García de El Último de la Fila.
Juana	Sí, queremos ir con vosotros. ¿ (c) _____ ?
Julio	Empieza a las diez y media.
Juana	¿Cuánto cuestan (d) _____ ?
Julio	Las entradas cuestan 20 €.

> **CONCIERTO**
> Manuel García, ex-componente de El Último de la Fila toca el 24 de septiembre en la Plaza de Toros de Las Ventas (Madrid). 22:30. Entradas 20 €.

¿Quién toca?	Who's playing?

gramática

nosotros	we	vamos	we go	queremos	we want
vosotros	you (pl)	**vais**	you (pl) go	**queréis**	you (pl) want

15 ¿Y vosotros qué hacéis?

Empareja las preguntas con sus respuestas.

1 ¿Vosotros qué hacéis mañana por la tarde?

2 Ana y yo vamos al cine el jueves. ¿Queréis venir?

3 ¿Podéis venir el viernes?

4 ¿El sábado estáis libres?

5 ¿El domingo?

a El viernes no podemos. Vamos a un concierto.

b El sábado preferimos ir a un restaurante.

c No. El domingo no. Hay un programa muy interesante en la tele.

d ¿Nosotros? Mañana por la tarde estudiamos.

e Queremos pero no podemos. El jueves tenemos que trabajar.

Plaza De Castilla, Madrid

¡Extra!

16 Entrevista con una estrella

Periodista	¿Te gusta la tele?
María Magnolia	La tele, me encanta. La veo todas las noches, sobre todo los culebrones que grabo durante el día en vídeo. También me encantan los dramas psicológicos y las series policíacas – pero no me gustan nada las películas violentas y si creo que me van a dar miedo, apago la tele o cambio de canal.
Periodista	¿Te interesan las noticias?
María Magnolia	Bastante. Pero no me gusta mucho ver las noticias en la tele – prefiero escuchar la radio o leer un periódico para saber lo que pasa en el mundo. Tampoco veo los documentales.
Periodista	¿Y las comedias?
María Magnolia	Me encantan. Me gustan también las entrevistas con los famosos y los concursos.

Rellena los huecos.

a Le encantan _____

b Le gustan _____

c No le gustan _____

la estrella	star
el culebrón	soap opera
el concurso	competition (game show)
las noticias	the news

17 Mi media naranja

Marca con ✓ si la pareja es compatible y con ✗ si no es una pareja compatible.

a Miguel y Bea ☐ **b** Juana y Jaime ☐ **c** Julio y Ángela ☐

18 Algo en común/Something in common

¿Con quién tienes algo en común? Who do you have something in common with? Tell your partner. For example: **A Iñaki le gusta el jazz y a mí también.**

> ¡Hola! Me llamo Iñaki, y me encanta la música – sobre todo el rock duro. El jazz me gusta bastante también, pero no me gusta nada el soul, ni la música clásica tampoco. El tecno me gusta para bailar.

> ¡Hola! Soy Itziar. ¿Qué tal? ¿Te gusta la música? Pues a mí también, sobre todo la música pop y la salsa. No me gusta mucho el rap. Me encanta el flamenco.

Gramática

- **How to say you like something**
  Gustar 'to please'
  To say you like one thing:

(a mí) me gusta	**(a ti) te gusta**	**(a él/ella/usted) le gusta**
I like it	you like it	he/she likes it; you (formal) like it

  To say you like more than one thing:

(a mí) me gusta<u>n</u>	**(a ti) te gusta<u>n</u>**	**(a él/ella/usted) le gusta<u>n</u>**
I like them	you like them	he/she likes them; you (formal) like them

  Because **gustar** means 'to please' and not 'to like', in Spanish you have to say 'X pleases me', rather than 'I like X'. Thus to say you like more than one thing, you need to say 'they please me'. For emphasis you can add **a mí**, **a ti**, **a él**, **a ella** or **a usted**.

- **How to express obligation, desire and ability**
  You need to use two verbs, the second of which is an infinitive.

Tener que	**Querer**	**Poder**
to have to	to want	to be able
tengo que trabajar	**quiero salir**	**puedo jugar**
I have to work	I want to go out	I can play

- **Subject personal pronouns (plural)**

vosotros/as	you (informal)	**ustedes**	you (formal)
nosotros/as	we	**ellos/ellas**	they (male/female)

- **Root-changing verbs**
  These have a vowel in the 'root' of the verb which changes in all parts of the present tense except for the **nosotros** and **vosotros** forms.

Qu<u>e</u>rer		P<u>o</u>der	
qu<u>ie</u>ro	queremos	p<u>ue</u>do	podemos
qu<u>ie</u>res	queréis	p<u>ue</u>des	podéis
qu<u>ie</u>re	qu<u>ie</u>ren	p<u>ue</u>de	p<u>ue</u>den

  Tener and **venir** are root-changing verbs which are also irregular in the **yo** form:
  tengo (I have); **vengo** (I come).

Ejercicios de gramática

1   Fill in the gaps in the sentences with the words from the box.

me	te	le
	gusta	
	gustan	

 – A mí (a) _____ _____ las novelas policíacas.
   ¿Qué tipo de novelas (b) _____ _____ a ti?
 – A mí no (c) _____ _____ leer. Prefiero ver la tele.
   ¿Cuáles son los programas que (d) _____ _____ a ti?
 – Los programas que a mí (e) _____ _____ más son las noticias.
   A Julieta (f) _____ _____ los programas de entrevistas, ¿verdad?
 – Sí, pero a ella también (g) _____ _____ los programas concurso.

2   Turn down the following invitations for the reasons indicated in brackets.
   For example:
   ¿Quieres ir al campo? No, no quiero. Prefiero ir a la ciudad.

 a ¿Quieres ir al cine?   (preferir) … (al teatro)

 b ¿Quieres jugar al fútbol?   (querer) … (al tenis)

 c ¿Quieres salir?   (tener que) … (estudiar)

 d ¿Quieres ver la película en la tele?   (preferir) … (las noticias)

3   Complete the table.

estamos	we are	**estáis**	you are
_____	we want	**queréis**	_____
_____	_____	_____	you prefer
_____	we have	_____	_____

4   Change the verbs in brackets to the correct forms. For example:
   Lo siento. (Querer) pero no (poder).   Lo siento. Quiero pero no puedo.

 a ¿(Querer, tú) _____ venir al cine mañana? (Preferir, yo) _____ ir al teatro.

 b Juan no (poder) _____ venir al cine. (Tener) _____ que lavarse el pelo.

 c ¿Cuándo (ir vosotros) _____ al concierto?

 d Bea y yo (querer) _____ ir, pero no (poder) _____ , (tener) _____ que estudiar.

Vocabulario

1

dar paseos	to go for walks
ir al cine	to go to the cinema
jugar al fútbol	to play football
Me gusta …	I like …
por el campo	in the country
salir con amigos	to go out with friends
Te gusta …	You like …
tomar el sol	to sunbathe
ver la tele	to watch TV

2

bailar	to dance
fumar puros	to smoke cigars
leer	to read
trabajar	to work

3

aerobic (m)	aerobics
ciclismo (m)	cycling
deporte (m)	sport
equitación (f)	horse-riding
fútbol (m)	football
Le gusta …	S/he likes …
natación (f)	swimming
patinaje (m)	skating
piragüismo (m)	canoeing
puenting (m)	bungee-jumping
tenis (m)	tennis
yoga (m)	yoga

4

vacaciones (f pl)	holidays

5

coche (m)	car

6

cine (m)	cinema
¡Claro!	Sure! / Of course!
entrada (f)	entrance
¿Qué ponen?	What's on?
quedar	to meet (by arrangement)
querer (quiero)	to want (I want)
Vale.	OK.

9

entrada (f)	ticket
discoteca (f)	disco

10

charlar	to chat
polideportivo (m)	sports centre

preferir (prefiero)	to prefer (I prefer)
quedarse en casa	to stay at home

11

footing (m)	jogging
gimnasia (f)	gym
radio (f)	radio

13

película (f)	film
poder (puedo)	to be able to (I can)
tener que (tengo que)	to have to (I have to)

14

concierto (m)	concert
¿Quién toca?	Who's playing?

16

apagar	to switch off
cambiar	to change
canal (m)	channel
comedia (f)	comedy
concurso (m)	game show
culebrón (m)	soap opera
dar miedo	to frighten
documental (m)	documentary
drama (m)	drama/play
estrella (f)	star
famoso/a (m/f)	celebrity
grabar	to record
Me encanta …	I love …
mundo (m)	world
noticias (f pl)	news
periódico (m)	newspaper
policíaco/a	detective
psicológico/a	psychological
serie (f)	series
tampoco	neither
vídeo (m)	video
violento/a	violent

18

flamenco (m)	flamenco
jazz (m)	jazz
música clásica (f)	classical music
música pop (f)	pop music
rap (m)	rap
rock duro (m)	hard rock
salsa (f)	salsa
sobre todo	above all / especially
soul (m)	soul
tecno (m)	techno

Práctica en parejas

1 a Find out if your partner likes the following activities:

canoeing   cycling   dancing   bungee-jumping   football

b Your partner will ask you for your opinion on types of music.

2 Your partner wants to know what your friend, Ana, likes to eat and drink. Answer his/her questions.

For example:

B **¿Le gusta a Ana el café?**   A **Sí, le gusta el café.**

● Ana likes coffee and green vegetables and she doesn't like wine or ice cream.

3 a Invite your partner to the events below.

Ask 'Do you want to go to the sculpture exhibition?'

Say when it is.

Say 'It is free.' **(Es gratis)**.

Ask 'Do you prefer to go to a concert?'

Say 'It is a concert by the Vienna Symphony Orchestra.'

Say what the tickets cost.

Exposición de escultura
(31 obras de artistas del siglo XX)
Gran vía Marqués de Turia (Valencia)
Miércoles
Entrada gratis

Viena en Valencia
Concierto por la orquesta sinfónica de Viena
Auditorio Regional (Valencia)
Entradas 12 € – 21 €

b Your partner wants to invite you out. S/he speaks first.

Ask 'When is it?'

Ask 'How much are the tickets?'

Say 'No, I don't want to go.'

Say 'Yes', and ask what's on.

Ask how much the tickets cost.

4 Someone you don't like is going to ask you out. With your partner think of as many excuses as possible in three minutes.

Práctica en parejas

1 a First answer your partner's questions about your sports interests.

b Then find out if your partner likes the following types of music:
rap   classical   salsa   hard rock   pop

2 Ask your partner what his/her friend, Ana, likes to eat and drink.
For example:
B **¿Le gusta a Ana el café?**   A **Sí, le gusta el café.**

- You want to know if she likes coffee, wine, green vegetables and ice cream.

3 a Your partner wants to invite you out. S/he speaks first.

Ask 'When is it?'

Ask 'How much are the tickets?'

Say 'No, I don't want to go.'

Say 'Yes.' Ask what's on.

Ask 'How much do the tickets cost?'

b Invite your partner to the events below.

Ask 'Do you want to go to the Planetarium?'

Say when it is.

Say 'It is free.' **(Es gratis)**.

Ask 'Do you prefer to go to the Visual Theatre Festival?'

Say 'It is an exhibition: *The Monster's Smile*.'

Say what the tickets cost.

Planetario Observación con telescopios
(para ver la luna, Júpiter y Saturno)
Parque Tierno Galván, Madrid
Viernes, Entrada gratis.

Festival de Teatro Visual
Exposición: *'La sonrisa del monstruo'*
Centro de Cultura Contemporánea
Jueves, Entrada 5 €

4 Someone you don't like is going to ask you out. With your partner think of as many
excuses as possible in three minutes.

5 El dinero

In this unit you will learn how to spend money on clothes and presents. You will also learn how to talk about holidays and what you are going to do.

1 ¡Voy a viajar por el mundo!/I am going to travel round the world!

a Ramón is being interviewed after winning the lottery. In English, give five ways in which he plans to spend his fortune.

Periodista ¿Qué vas a hacer con el dinero?
Ramón Voy a viajar por todo el mundo y voy a comprar una casa grande en el campo.
Periodista ¿Vas a comprar un coche nuevo?
Ramón Voy a comprar un avión, un yate de lujo, ¡y muchos coches!
Periodista ¿No vas a ahorrar un poco?
Ramón No, no voy a ahorrar. Voy a gastar todo el dinero, y voy a empezar inmediatamente – ¡cava, por favor!

ahorrar	to save
empezar	to start
gastar	to spend
cava	Spanish sparkling wine

gramática

To say what you are going to do:
Ir (to go) + **a** + infinitive.

Voy a gastar mucho dinero.	I am going to spend a lot of money.
Vas a viajar por el mundo.	You are going to travel round the world.

To remind you: **Ir** (to go)

voy	I go
vas	you go (sing)
va	s/he goes; you go (formal sing)
vamos	we go
vais	you go (pl)
van	they go; you go (formal pl)

b You are the lucky lottery winner and your partner is interviewing you.
B Ask 'What are you going to do with all the money?'
A Say 'I am going to travel round the world.'
B Ask 'Are you going to buy a big car?'
A Say 'I am going to buy a plane, a yacht and a lot of cars.'
B Ask 'Aren't you going to save a little?'
A Say 'No, I'm not going to save. I'm going to spend all the money immediately!'

2 Más números

a Escucha y repite los números.

100	cien	500	quinientos/as	100.000	cien mil	
120	ciento veinte	600	seiscientos/as	500.000	quinientos/as mil	
131	ciento treinta y uno	700	setecientos/as	1.000.000	un millón	
200	doscientos/as	800	ochocientos/as	9.999.999	nueve millones	
300	trescientos/as	900	novecientos/as		novecientos/as noventa y	
400	cuatrocientos/as	1.000	mil		nueve mil novecientos/as	
450	cuatrocientos/as cincuenta	1.500	mil quinientos/as		noventa y nueve	
		2.000	dos mil			

b Escribe estos números en cifras. Por ejemplo:

i   Ciento uno   <u>101</u>

ii Doscientos cincuenta   _____

iii Quinientos cuarenta y cinco   _____

iv Mil novecientos noventa y cinco   _____

v Tres mil ochocientos ochenta y seis _____

vi Siete millones, setecientos treinta   _____
    y tres mil, quinientos setenta y uno _____

> **la cifra**   figure

3 ¿Cuánto vas a gastar?/How much are you going to spend?

Take the roles of Ramón and a friend. Look at
Ramón's accounts and talk about how
much he is going to spend on each item.
For example:

A (friend) **¿Cuánto vas a gastar en los
coches nuevos?**

B (Ramón) **Voy a gastar 850.000 € en los
coches nuevos.**

A **¿Cuánto vas a dar a tus amigos?**

B **Voy a dar … etc**

Coches nuevos	850.000 €
Amigos	300.000 €
Casa grande	450.000 €
Familia	400.000 €
Yate de lujo	375.000 €

4 Ramón viaja por el mundo

¿Cuándo va a estar en cada lugar? Rellena los huecos con los meses del año.

a Argentina   <u>en agosto</u>   **e** Australia   _____

b Estados Unidos _____   **f** India   _____

c Rusia   _____   **g** África   _____

d China   _____   **h** España   _____

Los meses del año			
enero	**abril**	**julio**	**octubre**
febrero	**mayo**	**agosto**	**noviembre**
marzo	**junio**	**se(p)tiembre**	**diciembre**
la fecha	the date:	**lunes 24 de diciembre de 2032**	

5 ¿Cuándo?/When?

These three people are also off on holiday. **Rellena los huecos en la tabla.**

NOMBRE	DESTINO	SALIDA	VUELTA
Señor Cid	Marruecos	10 de octubre	
Juana la Loca	Lisboa		
Pepe Botella	París		

6 De vacaciones/On holiday

Tu compañero/a se va de vacaciones. Haz preguntas a tu compañero/a sobre sus vacaciones. Luego es tu turno para contestar.

Granada
Salida 11/4
Vuelta 10/5

Barcelona
Salida 28/1
Vuelta 14/2

La Coruña
Salida 19/7
Vuelta 20/8

Por ejemplo:

A
¿Adónde vas a ir?
¿Cuándo vas a salir?
¿Cuándo vas a volver?

B
Voy a ir a Granada.
Voy a salir el 11 de abril.
Voy a volver el 10 de mayo.

7 La carta de Juana

a Contesta a las preguntas en español.

i ¿Cuándo termina el curso?
ii ¿Adónde van a ir Juana y Miguel durante las vacaciones?
iii ¿A quién van a ver en Colombia?
iv ¿Cuánto tiempo van a pasar viajando en total?
v ¿Quién va a reservar los billetes? ¿Cuándo?

> Querida Lucía:
>
> El curso termina en junio y Miguel y yo vamos a viajar por Sudamérica. Primero vamos a ver a mis amigos en Colombia. Luego ellos van a acompañarnos a Ecuador y Perú. Vamos a pasar tres meses en total viajando por todas partes.
>
> Miguel va a reservar los billetes mañana. ¿Y vosotros? ¿Qué vais a hacer tú y Julio este verano?
>
> Un abrazo
>
> Juana

b Reply to Juana's letter, including the information below.

This summer you and Julio are going to see some friends in Tanzania. Then you are all going to visit Kenya. You are going to spend two months in total travelling around Africa. Julio is going to book the tickets on Wednesday. Ask Juana what she and Miguel are going to do this Christmas **(estas Navidades)**.

8 Os vais de viaje/You are going on a trip

a With your partner, agree when and where to go on holiday. For example:
¿Adónde vamos a ir de vacaciones? ¿Cuánto tiempo vamos a pasar allí?

b Now ask another pair about their plans. For example:
¿Adónde vais a ir de vacaciones? ¿Cuándo vais a salir? ¿Cuándo vais a volver?

9 Comprando ropa/Buying clothes

Empareja cada prenda con el dibujo adecuado. Match each item of clothing with the right picture.

El hombre	La mujer
el traje	el vestido
los pantalones	la chaqueta
los zapatos	el monedero
el abrigo	el bolso
la camisa	las botas
la corbata	la falda
la cartera	las medias

La mujer   El hombre

10 ¿Cuál es su talla?/What size are you?

Rellena la tabla.

Cliente	1	2	3
Prenda	una falda		
Talla		44	

11 Los colores

Empareja los colores en inglés con su equivalente en español.

rojo   negro   amarillo   azul   naranja   verde   blanco   morado   gris

blue   white   red   yellow   black   grey   orange   green   purple

12 ¿Qué color quiere?

Rellena los huecos.

a – ¿Qué color quiere?

– Me gusta esta falda _____ .

b – ¿Le gusta este traje _____ ?

– Prefiero el traje _____ .

c – ¿De qué color?

– Me gustan estos pantalones _____ .

d – Estas botas _____ están muy de moda.

– Prefiero las _____ .

13 ¿Cuánto cuesta?/How much does it cost?

Haz preguntas a tu compañero/a. Por ejemplo:

A **Me gusta esta camisa morada.**
¿Cuánto cuesta?

B **Esta camisa cuesta 25 €.**

purple shirt (25 €)
orange suit (285 €)
brown coat (195 €)

yellow shoes (68 €)
white tights (5 €)
grey jacket (90 €)

Centro comercial 'La Vaguada', Madrid

> **gramática**
>
> **est<u>e</u> vestid<u>o</u> roj<u>o</u>**
> this red dress
> **est<u>a</u> camis<u>a</u> roj<u>a</u>**
> this red shirt
> **est<u>os</u> zapat<u>os</u> roj<u>os</u>**
> these red shoes
> **est<u>as</u> bot<u>as</u> roj<u>as</u>**
> these red boots

14 Esta camisa es demasiado grande/This shirt is too big

Corrige el error en cada frase.

a «Esta falda es demasiado pequeña.»

b «Estos pantalones son demasiado caros.»

c «Este abrigo es demasiado barato.»

d «Estas botas son demasiado grandes.»

caro/a/s	expensive
barato/a/s	cheap
grande/s	big
pequeño/a/s	small

15 ¿Te gusta esta camisa?

Your partner is very difficult to please. S/he finds something wrong with each of the items in the box. For example:

A **¿Te gusta esta camisa roja?**

B **No, no me gusta. Es demasiado cara.**

A **¿Te gustan estos pantalones negros?**

B **No, no me gustan. Son demasiado grandes.**

| red shirt |
| black trousers |
| white boots |
| yellow suit |
| green shoes |

16 Vamos a comprar regalos

a Empareja a cada persona con el regalo que le corresponde. Escribe los precios en los huecos.

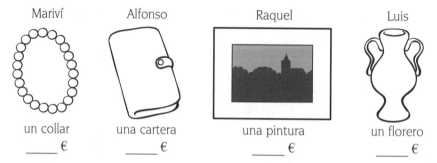

Mariví	Alfonso	Raquel	Luis
un collar	una cartera	una pintura	un florero
____ €	____ €	____ €	____ €

b Escucha otra vez la conversación de Ramón con Carolina y contesta a las preguntas en inglés.

   i What does Carolina say is wrong with each of Ramón's suggestions?

   ii What does he end up buying?

17 Pagos en efectivo

Contesta a las preguntas en español.

a ¿Cuánto es?

b ¿Cuál es el problema?

How to pay	Cash only
¿Puedo pagar con un cheque?	**Pagos únicamente en efectivo.**
¿No aceptan ustedes tarjetas de crédito?	**Hay que pagar en metálico.**
	Sólo dinero en efectivo.

18 ¡Fiesta!

a Haz preguntas a tu compañero/a sobre la fiesta de Ramón. Por ejemplo:

   A **¿Cuántas personas van a ir?**   B **Van a ir 600 personas.**

¿Cuántas personas van a ir?	(600)
¿Cuánto dinero va a costar la fiesta?	(10.000 €)
¿A qué hora va a empezar?	(11.00h)
¿Cuántas cajas de cava va a comprar Ramón?	(75)
¿Vais a ir, tú y tus amigos?	(Sí, o No)

b You are organising a party. Write down all the details. For example:

A mi fiesta van a ir 40 personas, va a costar 80 € ...

¡Extra!

19 **Lotería y juegos de azar**/Lottery and games of chance

Este año cada español va a gastar 186 € en juegos de azar; 117 € de ellos en la lotería. ¿Por qué nosotros los españoles gastamos tanto en sueños e ilusiones? Porque es una forma de evadirse de la realidad. La sociedad actual tiende mucho hacia valores materialistas y el consumismo, pero la ilusión, los sueños no van a desaparecer nunca.

a How much will each Spanish person spend this year on
  i games of chance
  ii the lottery?

b Why do people spend so much on hopes and dreams?

el sueño	dream
la ilusión	hope
evadirse	to escape
nunca	never

20 **¿Qué va a hacer cada uno para ahorrar dinero?**

Juana and Miguel are broke. What are they each going to do to save money? Who says what? **Subraya el nombre correcto.**

a Yo voy a tirar mis tarjetas de crédito. — Juana /Miguel
b Yo voy a pagar siempre en efectivo. — Juana /Miguel
c Antes de ir de compras voy a hacer una lista de lo que necesito y no voy a comprar nada más. — Juana /Miguel
d Vamos a comer en casa. — Juana /Miguel
e Tú vas a dejar de fumar, ¿no? — Juana /Miguel
f Tú no vas a salir todas las noches, ¿verdad? — Juana /Miguel
g ¿Cuándo vamos a empezar? — Juana /Miguel

tirar	to throw out	**a menos que**	unless
elevado/a	high	**dejar de**	to stop
menos	except	**no hay prisa**	there's no hurry
salvo	except	**la semana que viene**	next week

21 **Cómo ahorrar dinero**

Rank these money-saving ideas in order of the amount of money they would save you.

Comprar de segunda mano
Dejar de beber alcohol
Pagar en efectivo
Utilizar el transporte público

Dejar de ir al cine
Arreglar tu vehículo tú mismo
Vivir más cerca de la universidad
Llamar por teléfono los fines de semana

Gramática

- **How to talk about the future**

  1 Use the present tense to express the future:

Te llamo mañana.	I'll call you tomorrow.
Empieza a las cinco.	It starts/will start at 5.

  2 Use **IR** + **A** + infinitive to say what you are *going* to do:

voy a ir	**vamos a llegar**	
vas a salir	**vais a viajar**	With a reflexive verb:
va a volver	**van a venir**	**voy a quedarme** or **me voy a quedar**

- **How to specify a particular object or person**

	masculine	feminine
this	**este**	**esta**
these	**estos**	**estas**

- The personal '**a**'

  When the direct object of the verb is a person:

  Voy a ver a Juan.

- **How to describe people and things**

  In Unit 2 you saw that adjectives have to change according to the number and gender of the noun they are describing:

una camisa roja	**un abrigo rojo**
unas camisas rojas	**unos abrigos rojos**

  Some exceptions:

  Adjectives ending in **-e** change only in the plural, when you must add **-s**:

una corbata verde	**un vestido verde**
unas corbatas verdes	**unos vestidos verdes**

  Adjectives ending in a consonant change only in the plural, when you must add **-es**:

una falda azul	**un traje azul**
unas faldas azules	**unos trajes azules**

- **How to ask 'How much?' or 'How many?'**

  ¿Cuánto/a? means 'How much?'

¿Cuánto es la falda?	**¿Cuánto son los pantalones?**

  ¿Cuánta comida llevas a la fiesta?

  ¿Cuántos/as? means 'How many?'

¿Cuántos coches tienes?	**¿Cuántas personas van a venir?**

Ejercicios de gramática

1 Fill in the gaps in the conversation with the appropriate part of the verb **ir**, as indicated in the brackets. For example:

¿Qué (a) __vas__ a hacer durante las vacaciones?

(b) __Voy__ a viajar por Europa.

¿Con quién (c) (**tú**) _____ a ir?

(d) (**yo**) _____ con Charo.

¿Cómo (e) (**vosotros**) _____ a viajar?

(f) (**nosotros**) _____ a viajar en tren.

¿Cuánto tiempo (g) (**vosotros**) _____ a pasar en Europa?

Un mes, pero Charo (h) (**ella**) _____ a volver más temprano porque sus padres (i) (**ellos**) _____ a venir a su casa.

¿Dónde (j) (**vosotros**) _____ a quedaros?

(k) (**nosotros**) _____ a quedarnos en hostales.

2 Write out the following dates in Spanish. For example:

   a Mon 14 July 2005 ___lunes 14 de julio de 2005___
   b Thurs 16 September 2007 _____
   c Fri 22 May 1999 _____
   d Sat 30 March 2020 _____
   e Sun 1 January 2009 _____

3 Write out the following numbers in full. For example:

263 **doscientos sesenta y tres**

263   554   6.689   17.777   43.167   122.943

4 Put the correct form of the adjective into the spaces. For example:

   a (Este/a/os/as) **Esta** camisa es demasiado __cara__ (caro/a/s).

   b (Este/a/os/as) _____ zapatos son demasiado _____ (pequeño/a/s).

   c (Este/a/os/as) _____ botas son demasiado _____ (grande/s).

   d (Este/a/os/as) _____ traje no es muy _____ (barato/a/s).

Vocabulario

1

ahorrar	to save
avión (m)	aeroplane
cava (m)	sparkling wine
coche (m)	car
comprar	to buy
de lujo	luxury
dinero (m)	money
gastar	to spend
hacer	to do/to make
inmediatamente	immediately
nuevo/a	new
poco (m)	bit
todo/a	all
viajar	to travel
yate (m)	yacht

2

For numbers 100–1,000,000 see page 52

4

fecha (f)	date
los meses del año	the months of the year

For the months see page 52

5

destino (m)	destination
Marruecos	Morocco
salida (f)	departure
vuelta (f)	return

7

acompañar a	to go with
billete (m)	ticket
primero	first
reservar	to book

9

abrigo (m)	coat
bolso (m)	handbag
bota (f)	boot
camisa (f)	shirt
cartera (f)	wallet
chaqueta (f)	jacket
corbata (f)	tie
falda (f)	skirt
hombre (m)	man
medias (f pl)	tights
monedero (m)	purse
mujer (f)	woman
pantalones (m pl)	trousers
prenda (f)	item of clothing
talla (f)	size

traje (m)	suit
vestido (m)	dress
zapato (m)	shoe

11

amarillo/a	yellow
azul	blue
blanco/a	white
color (m)	colour
gris	grey
morado/a	purple
naranja	orange
negro/a	black
rojo/a	red
verde	green

12

de moda	fashionable

14

barato/a	cheap

16

collar (m)	necklace
florero (m)	flower vase
pintura (f)	painting

17

aceptar	to accept
cheque (m)	cheque
crédito (m)	credit
en efectivo	in cash
en metálico	in cash
pagar	to pay
pago (m)	payment
tarjeta (f)	card
únicamente	only

18

caja (f)	box/case
costar	to cost
fiesta (f)	party

19

año (m)	year
cada	each/every
consumismo	consumerism
desaparecer	to disappear
evadirse	to escape
forma (f)	way
hacia	towards

For more vocabulary turn to the Appendix on p.181.

Práctica en parejas

1　**a**　Congratulations! You have won €1,000,000 on the lottery. Your partner wants to know what you are going to do with the money. Answer her/his questions.

　　b　Now your partner is the lucky winner. Find out how much money s/he has won and ask her/him at least three questions like the ones below:

　　How much money do you have?
　　What are you going to do with the money?
　　Are you going to save a little (**un poco**)?
　　Are you going to travel around the world?
　　Are you going to buy a house in the country / a big car / a luxury flat?
　　Are you going to give a little to charity (**a la caridad**)?
　　Are you going to give me (**vas a darme**) a little?

2　**a**　Ask your partner what s/he is going to do in the holidays. Find out where s/he is going, when s/he is leaving and when s/he is getting back.

　　b　Your partner wants to know about your holiday plans. Tell her/him that you are going to travel round South America. You are setting off on 16 September and you are coming back on 17 October.

3　Play a variation of B*ingo*! with your partner. Write down six numbers between 540 and 560. Your partner will try to guess them. Cross them off when s/he says them. Then your partner will write down six numbers between 770 and 790 and you will guess them.

4　Tell your partner the following dates in Spanish. S/he must write them out in figures. For example: 5/8/1977. You will say '**cinco de agosto de mil novecientos setenta y siete**', and your partner will write **5/8/1977**.

　　5/8/1977　　10/10/2000　　1/2/2016

5　Practise buying clothes with a partner, each taking one of the roles below.

Cliente	Say 'I like this yellow shirt.' Ask how much it is.
Dependiente/a	Say it is €22. Ask 'What is your size?'
Cliente	Say it is 44.
Dependiente/a	Say this shirt is too big. It's size 48.

Práctica en parejas

1 **a** Your partner has won the lottery. You want to know what s/he is going to do with the money. Ask at least three questions like the ones below:

How much money do you have?
What are you going to do with the money?
Are you going to save a little (**un poco**)?
Are you going to travel around the world?
Are you going to buy a house in the country / a big car / a luxury flat?
Are you going to give a little to charity (**a la caridad**)?
Are you going to give me (**vas a darme**) a little?

b Now you are the lucky winner of €3,500,000. Answer your partner's questions.

2 **a** Your partner wants to know about your holiday plans. Tell her/him that you are going to travel round Africa. You are setting off on 30 June and you are coming back on 28 August.

b Ask your partner what s/he is going to do in the holidays. Find out where s/he is going, when s/he is leaving and when s/he is getting back.

3 Play a variation of B*ingo!* with your partner. S/he writes down six numbers between 540 and 560. You have to guess them. S/he crosses them off when you say them. Then you write down six numbers between 770 and 790 and your partner will guess them.

4 Tell your partner the following dates in Spanish. S/he must write them out in figures. For example: 19/6/1959. You will say '**diecinueve de junio de mil novecientos cincuenta y nueve**', and your partner will write **19/6/1959**.

19/6/1959   3/7/2012   17/8/2016

5 Practise buying clothes with a partner, each taking one of the roles below.

Cliente	Say 'I like this yellow shirt.' Ask how much it is.
Dependiente/a	Say it is €22. Ask 'What is your size?'
Cliente	Say it is 44.
Dependiente/a	Say this shirt is too big. It's size 48.

6 En la ciudad

In this unit you will learn how to say where things are, give directions and instructions and find your way round a town and within office buildings.

1 ¿Dónde está el banco?

Escucha y busca los edificios del recuadro en el plano. Find the buildings on the map.

el banco	Correos	la estación de trenes (la RENFE)
la farmacia	el museo	la universidad

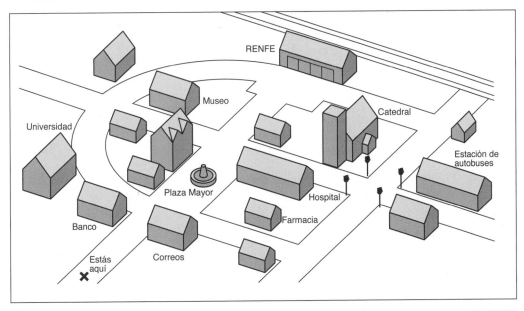

RENFE

Museo

Universidad

Catedral

Estación de autobuses

Plaza Mayor

Hospital

Banco

Farmacia

Estás aquí

Correos

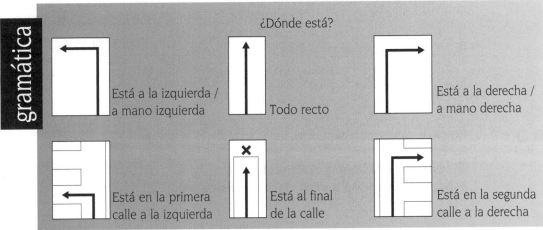

gramática

¿Dónde está?

Está a la izquierda / a mano izquierda

Todo recto

Está a la derecha / a mano derecha

Está en la primera calle a la izquierda

Está al final de la calle

Está en la segunda calle a la derecha

2 ¿Dónde están?

a Write in the letter for each building on the map in Section 1 (page 63).
  i **Galería de Arte Moderno** (G)
  ii **Oficina de turismo** (O)
  iii **Comisaría** (police station) (C)
  iv **Ayuntamiento** (town hall) (A)

b Test your partner. Using the map in Section 1 (page 63), give the exact location of a particular building. Your partner must work out which one it is. For example:
  A **Está en la primera calle a la derecha, a la izquierda.**
  B **¿Es la universidad?**
  A **No. Está en la primera calle a la <u>derecha</u> …**
  B **¿Es la farmacia?**
  A **Sí.**

3 Y la universidad, ¿está lejos?/And the university, is it far?

Empareja cada frase con el dibujo.

a Está a 20 minutos en coche.

b Está a 15 minutos en autobús.

c Está a 25 minutos en bici.

d Está a 40 minutos andando / a pie.

e Está a 10 minutos en tren.

f Está a 10 minutos en metro.

4 ¿Está lejos?

a **Rellena los huecos en la conversación.**
  i – ¿La universidad está lejos?
    – No, está muy **cerca** , a 5 minutos a pie.
  ii – ¿Está cerca de aquí el centro comercial?
    – No, está muy *lejos* . Está a unos *treinta* minutos en coche.
  iii – ¿Hay una farmacia cerca de aquí?
    – Hay una bastante *cerca* , a unos *diez* minutos a pie.
  iv – ¿Está lejos de aquí el polideportivo?
    – No, no muy *lejos* . En autobús está a unos *quince* minutos.

> **Está <u>a</u> 5 minutos.**
> It's 5 minutes away.
>
> **a <u>unos</u> 5 minutos**
> <u>some</u> 5 minutes away
>
> **Está cerca de aquí.**
> It's near here.

b **Practica con tu compañero/a.** Use the buildings in the box. For example:
  A **¿Está lejos de aquí la biblioteca?**
  B **No está lejos. Está a unos cinco minutos a pie.**

> library
> sports centre
> canteen
> laboratory

5 Al lado del polideportivo

a Work out the meanings of the underlined words.

    i La piscina está <u>al lado del</u> polideportivo.   <u>**next to**</u>

    ii El polideportivo está <u>enfrente del</u> parque.   _____

    iii El polideportivo está <u>entre</u> la piscina y el colegio.   _____

    iv El colegio está <u>en la esquina.</u>   _____

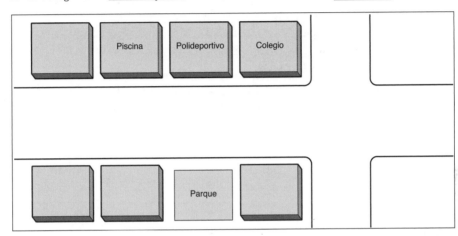

b Practica con tu compañero/a. Por ejemplo:
    A **¿Dónde está el polideportivo?**
    B **Está al lado de la piscina.**

c These places have been left off the diagram in Section **a**.
Decide where they are and describe their locations to your
partner, who has to fill them in.
For example:
    A **¿Dónde está el cine?**
    B **El cine está en la esquina, enfrente del colegio.**
(A writes **cine** where s/he thinks it is on the diagram.)

el cine
el restaurante
el bar
el supermercado

6 En la primera calle a la derecha

Escucha y rellena los huecos.

    a La mezquita está en la _segunda_ calle a la _izquierda_.
       Está _en_ la esquina.
    b El centro comercial está en la _tercera_ calle a la _derecha_.
       Está _enfrente_ la catedral.
    c El campo de fútbol está _al lado de_ la piscina,
       en la _quinta_ calle a la _izquierda_.
    d La iglesia de Santa María está _entre_ la biblioteca y la librería,
       en la _tercera_ calle a la _derecha_.

1°	primero/a
2°	segundo/a
3°	tercero/a
4°	cuarto/a
5°	quinto/a

7 Ve todo recto

Escucha y coloca estas instrucciones en el orden correcto. Listen and put these directions in the correct order.

Dobla a la izquierda	_2_	Sigue todo recto	_4_
Ve todo recto	_1_	Coge la primera calle a la derecha	_3_
Dobla a la derecha	_6_	Coge la segunda calle a la izquierda	_5_

ve go	**dobla** turn	**sigue** continue	**coge** take

8 Desde la estación

Using the map in Section 1 (page 63), follow these directions from the railway station (RENFE) and put a cross on the map where you end up.

> Desde la estación ve todo recto hasta el cruce.
> Dobla a la izquierda y sigue hasta los semáforos.
> Dobla a la derecha y coge la primera calle a la derecha.
> Ve todo recto y coge la segunda calle a la derecha.
> En el cruce dobla a la izquierda.
> Sigue todo recto y hasta el final de la calle.

desde	from
hasta	to
el cruce	the crossroads
los semáforos	the traffic lights

9 Sigue mis indicaciones/Follow my directions

Using the map on page 63, send your partner on a wild goose chase round the town.

10 Coge el autobús

a Escribe el número del autobús y dónde hay que subirse y bajarse. Write down the number of the bus and where to get on and off.

	número	súbete en …	bájate en …
i	19	el centro comercial	La Plaza Nueva
ii	12	La Plaza Nueva	Hospital
iii	13	La Plaza Mejor	Biblioteca

bájate	get off
súbete	get on
la parada	the bus stop

b Practica con tu compañero/a. Por ejemplo:

«Coge el autobús número 10. Súbete en el cine y bájate en la calle Calella.»

i No 11 – on at supermarket – off at Parque Santa Eulalia

ii No 21 – on at Plaza Real – off at football stadium (**el estadio de fútbol**)

iii No 42 – on at museum – off at Plaza España

iv No 14 – on at Avenida de la Constitución – off at cathedral

gramática

To give directions to friends and young people you can use the imperative (see Grammar Section).

| (to one person) | **dobla** | turn | **sigue*** | continue |
| | **coge** | take | **ve** | go |

*Root-changing

11 ¡No hay pérdida!/You can't miss it!

> Hola, ¿Qué tal?
>
> Voy a dar una fiesta el sábado 24 de junio, para celebrar el fin de curso. ¿Quieres venir?
>
> Te voy a decir cómo llegar a mi casa: Coge el autobús número 19 que sale de la parada que está enfrente de la universidad. Baja en la Plaza Colón y ve todo recto hasta los semáforos. En el cruce dobla a la derecha. Coge la segunda calle a la derecha. Sigue todo recto, y mi casa está a mano izquierda. ¡No hay pérdida!
>
> Hasta luego; un abrazo,
>
> Julio

a Marca en el plano dónde está la casa de Julio.

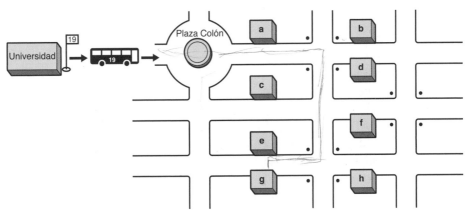

b Give your partner directions to another house on the map above. Did s/he make it to the right one?

c Tell your partner how to get to your house from where you are now, and how long it takes.

12 Una entrevista de trabajo

a Carmen has a job interview with the manager of the Excelsor company.

Contesta a las preguntas en inglés.

i Where is Reception?
ii Where is the lift?
iii Where is the secretary's office?
iv Where is the manager's office?

en un edificio:	in a building:
la recepción	Reception
los servicios	the toilets
el ascensor	the lift
el despacho	the office
el pasillo	the corridor
el piso	the floor

b Haz preguntas a tu compañero/a en español. Por ejemplo:
A **¿Dónde está el departamento de Marketing?**
B **Está en el segundo piso, al final del pasillo a la izquierda.**

Marketing Department	2nd floor; at the end of the corridor, on the left.
Secretary's office	4th floor, next to the lift, on the right.
Manager's office	5th floor, opposite Reception, on the left.
IT Centre (**Centro de informática**)	2nd floor, between the toilets and the lift.

13 Siéntate/Sit down

a Escucha y coloca estas instrucciones en el orden correcto.

b Empareja cada frase en español con su significado en inglés.

Español		Inglés	
Escribe tu nombre.	_____	Come in.	**1**
Siéntate aquí.	_____	Wait a moment.	_____
Espera un momento.	_____	Close the door.	_____
Pasa.	**1**	Write your name.	_____
Dame tu currículum.	_____	Sit down here.	_____
Cierra la puerta.	_____	Give me your CV.	_____
Rellena este formulario.	_____	Fill in this form.	_____

c You are the secretary and your partner is the interviewee. S/he has to follow your instructions. For example:
A **Rellena el formulario.** (B fills in a 'form')
A **Abre la puerta.** (B opens the door)

¡Extra!

14 En mi buzón de voz/On my voice mail

Jorge has left this message on your voice mail. **Contesta a las preguntas en inglés.**

a Where is he inviting you to go? *Cinema Rex*

b How does he suggest you get there? *Bus, city center, No17, 20 mins approximately*

c What directions does he give you? *Go off on Plaza Mayor, 5 mins walking*

d How long will it take you? *25 mins*

e When and where does he say he'll meet you? *9.45, in front of the cinema*

15 ¡Fiesta el sábado!

> ¡Hola!
>
> Voy a dar una fiesta el sábado, ¿quieres venir? Es en mi casa y empieza a las once. Ven con tus amigos y trae algo para comer o beber.
>
> Mi dirección es: c/Calella, 3, 2º Dcha. *numero 3, segundo derecha* Para ir desde la universidad coge el metro y bájate en la Plaza Colón. Ve por Los Reyes Católicos hacia el centro. En el cruce dobla a la izquierda - ésta es la calle Calella. Mi casa está enfrente del Hostal Bienestar. Sube hasta la segunda planta y mi piso está a la derecha.
>
> ¡Hasta luego!
>
> Carmen

Contesta a las preguntas en inglés.

a When does the party start? *11*

b What and who does she ask you to bring? *Friends, food and drinks*

c What means of transport does she suggest you use? *Underground*

d Where in her building is her flat? *2nd floor on the right*

traer	to bring
algo	something
por	along

Gramática

- **How to describe where something is**

  <u>a</u> la izquierda/derecha   <u>al lado de</u>l cine   <u>al final de</u> la calle

  <u>en</u> la esquina   <u>enfrente de</u>l bar   <u>cerca de</u> aquí

  <u>entre</u> el bar y el café   <u>lejos de</u> la comisaría

  Some prepositions have more than one equivalent in English:

a	'to' or 'at'	**de**	'from' or 'of'
Voy al centro.	I go to the centre.	**Soy de Cádiz.**	I am from Cádiz.
Voy a las tres.	I go at 3 o'clock.	**Un libro de arte.**	'A book of art.' (an art book)

  Estar (to be) is the verb used to describe where something or someone is.

estoy	I am	**estamos**	we are
estás	you are	**estáis**	you are
está	he/she/it is; you are	**están**	they/you are

- **How to give instructions and directions**

  In most cases you can use the simple present tense. See page 34.

  The imperative (below) is only used when addressing a person or people informally. To give formal instructions the subjunctive is used, which is beyond the scope of this book.

	Talking to one person:		Talking to two or more:
dob<u>l</u>ar	**dob<u>la</u>**	turn	**dob<u>l</u>ad**
cog<u>er</u>	**cog<u>e</u>**	catch/take	**cog<u>e</u>d**
sub<u>ir</u>	**sub<u>e</u>**	go up	**sub<u>id</u>**

  With root-changing verbs the vowel only changes when talking to one person.

s<u>e</u>guir	**s<u>i</u>gue**	continue	**seguid**

  Some verbs are irregular in the singular form, i.e. when talking to one person.

salir	**sal**	leave	**salid**
ir	**ve**	go	**id**

  With reflexive verbs the reflexive pronoun is attached to the verb and the **d** in the plural forms is omitted.

subirse	**súbete**	get on	**subíos**
sentarse	**siéntate**	sit down	**sentaos**

Ejercicios de gramática

1 Write the following in Spanish:

My house is next to the church, opposite the park. On the left there is a small hotel. At the end of the road between the swimming pool and the sports centre there is a large cinema.

2 a Tell your friend how to get to your house by changing the form of the verbs in brackets. For example:

Coge **el autobús número 16.**

i (Coger) _____ el autobús número 16.   **iv** (Ir) _____ por la calle Mola.

ii (Subirse) _____ en el cine.   **v** (Doblar) _____ a la derecha.

iii (Bajarse) _____ en el centro deportivo.   **vi** (Seguir) _____ todo recto.

  b Give two other friends the same instructions by changing the verbs again. For example:

Coged **el autobús número 16.**

3 a You are the secretary in an office. A job applicant has come to see the manager. Tell him/her what to do by using the imperative form of the appropriate verb.

sentarse	esperar	pasar	escribir	cerrar	rellenar

i Hola, … .   **iv** … aquí. ¿Quieres café?

ii … la puerta, por favor.   **v** … el formulario.

iii … un momento.   **vi** … tus datos aquí.

  b Two applicants have turned up at the same time. Give them the instructions above.

4 Make a command with each of the verbs in brackets by combining it with one of the sentence endings on the right.

(abrir)	el teléfono.	(leer)	leche.
(escuchar)	de la cama.	(beber)	de la casa.
(levantarse)	la ventana.	(salir)	verduras.
(coger)	música.	(comer)	el libro.

71

Vocabulario

1

a la derecha	on/to the right
a la izquierda	on/to the left
a mano derecha	on the right hand side
a mano izquierda	on the left hand side
al final de	at the end of
autobús (m)	bus
banco (m)	bank
catedral	cathedral
coger	to take/catch
Correos (m)	post office
estación (f)	station
farmacia (f)	chemist
museo (m)	museum
perdone	excuse me
primero/a	first
RENFE	railway station
segundo/a	second
todo recto	straight on
tren (m)	train

2

ayuntamiento (m)	town hall
comisaría (f)	police station
galería (f)	gallery
oficina de turismo (f)	tourist office

3

a pie	on foot
andar	to walk
en autobús	by bus
en bici	by bike
en coche	by car
en metro	by underground

4

a cinco minutos	five minutes away
cantina (f)	canteen
centro comercial (m)	shopping centre
cerca (de)	near
lejos (de)	far (from)

5

al lado de	next to
colegio (m)	school
delante de	in front of
enfrente de	opposite
en la esquina	on the corner
entre	between
parque (m)	park
piscina (f)	swimming pool
polideportivo (m)	sports centre
supermercado (m)	supermarket

6

campo (m)	ground/pitch
cuarto/a	fourth

iglesia (f)	church
librería (f)	bookshop
mezquita (f)	mosque
parada (f)	stop
quinto/a	fifth
tercero/a	third

7

doblar	to turn
seguir (sigue)	to continue (continue)
ve (ir)	go

8

cruce (m)	crossroads
desde	from
hasta	as far as
semáforo (m)	traffic light

10

bajarse	to get off
parar	to stop
subirse	to get on

11

celebrar	to celebrate
dar	to give
decir	to tell
fiesta (f)	party
fin (m)	end
que	which
salir	to leave

12

ascensor (m)	lift
departamento (m)	department
despacho (m)	office
edificio (m)	building
pasillo (m)	corridor
piso (m)	floor
recepción (f)	reception
servicios (m pl)	toilets
subir	to go up

13

cerrar	to close
currículum (m)	CV
esperar	to wait
pasar	to come in
sentarse	to sit down

15

dirección (f)	address
metro (m)	underground
planta (f)	floor
por	along

Práctica en parejas

1 a Your partner will ask how far away these places are. Give the approximate time it would take her/him to get there. For example:

B **¿Está lejos la Plaza Mayor?**
A **No, está muy cerca, a unos 10 minutos andando.**

The police station	5 mins	walking/on foot
The hospital	25 mins	by car

b Now ask how far away the cinema and the cathedral are.

2 Using the map in Section 1 (page 63), give your partner directions from the train station to these places – without saying where you are directing her/him. Did s/he make it?

> the hospital
> the bank
> the museum

3 a In Spanish, describe a street to your partner, using the model below. Your partner has to put the buildings you mention in the correct places in the street.

The Gallery of Modern Art is on the corner next to the sports centre. The post office is opposite the Gallery of Modern Art. My house is between the post office and the bar on the corner. The chemist's is opposite the bar.

b Listen to your partner describing a street and put the buildings s/he mentions in the correct places.

		AYUNTAMIENTO

4 a You are your partner's own personal fitness trainer. Give him or her instructions to help him or her get into shape. Use some or all of the suggestions below, and if s/he doesn't understand at first, demonstrate what you want your partner to do, without explaining anything in English. For example: A **Levanta la pierna izquierda tres veces … toca la pierna derecha con el brazo izquierdo… etc**

(levantar) el brazo cinco veces
(bajar) el brazo
(correr) por la clase dos veces
(tocar) la pierna derecha
con el brazo izquierdo

levantarse	to stand up
sentarse	to sit down
levantar	to lift
bajar	to put down
correr	to run
tocar	to touch
el brazo	the arm
la pierna	the leg
cinco veces	five times

b It is now your partner's turn to get her/his revenge. Do as s/he says.

Práctica en parejas

1 **a** Ask how far away these places are.
The police station?   The hospital?

b Your partner will now ask about the places below. Give the approximate time it would take her/him to get there. For example:

A **¿Está lejos la Plaza Mayor?**
B **No, está bastante cerca, a unos diez minutos andando.**

The cinema	10 mins	by bus
The cathedral	15 mins	walking/on foot (or 5 mins by car)

2 Using the map in Section 1 (page 63), give your partner directions from the train station to these places – without saying where you are directing her/him. Did s/he make it?

> the bus station
> the post office
> the chemist's

3 **a** Listen to your partner describing a street and put the buildings s/he mentions in the correct places.

		GALERÍA DE ARTE MODERNO

b In Spanish, describe a street to your partner, using the model below. Your partner has to put the buildings you mention in the correct places in the street.

The Town Hall is on the corner next to the Italian restaurant. The park is opposite the Town Hall. My house is between the park and the bank on the corner. The swimming pool is opposite the bank.

4 **a** Your partner is your own personal fitness trainer. S/he is going to give you some instructions to help you get into shape. Do as s/he says.

b Time for you to get your revenge. Use some or all of the suggestions below, and if your partner doesn't understand at first, demonstrate what you want her/him to do, without explaining anything in English.

(levantar) la mano
(bajar) la mano
(correr) hasta la puerta tres veces
(tocar) el pie derecho
   con la mano izquierda

levantarse	to stand up
sentarse	to sit down
levantar	to lift
bajar	to put down
correr	to run
tocar	to touch
la mano	the hand
el pie	the foot
cinco veces	five times

7 En el futuro

In this unit you will learn another way of discussing future plans. You will also learn how to find your way around by various forms of transport, private and public.

1 ¡Qué será, será!/What will be will be!

Ordena las frases. Arrange the following sentences chronologically.

_____ El año que viene hablaré español muy bien.

__I__ Mañana iré a clase.

_____ El próximo verano viajaré a un país extranjero.

_____ La semana que viene cenaré con amigos en un restaurante indio.

_____ Dentro de 40 años seré abuelo/a.

el año que viene	next year	**hablaré**	I will speak
mañana	tomorrow	**iré**	I will go
el próximo verano	next summer	**viajaré**	I will travel
la semana que viene	next week	**cenaré**	I will have dinner
dentro de 40 años	within 40 years	**seré**	I will be

2 La adivina/The fortune-teller

a Carmen visita a una adivina y le hace unas preguntas sobre su futuro. Rellena los huecos con las expresiones del recuadro.

Carmen	¿Cuándo viajaré a la India?
Adivina	Viajarás a la India (i) _____.
Carmen	¿Cuándo conoceré a mi hombre ideal?
Adivina	Conocerás a tu hombre ideal (ii) _____ en el supermercado.
Carmen	Mmm ¿y cuándo me casaré?
Adivina	Te casarás (iii) _____.
Carmen	¿Cuándo ganaré la lotería?
Adivina	No ganarás la lotería (iv) _____, pero ganarás mucho dinero en tu trabajo y serás millonaria (v) _____.

> dentro de cinco años
> pronto
> el invierno que viene
> pasado mañana
> nunca

gramática

viajarás	you will travel	**te casarás**	you will marry
conocerás	you will meet	**ganarás**	you will win/earn

b Take on the role of a fortune-teller and, following the model in Section **a** above, answer your partner's questions about his/her future.

3 Eduardo viaja a Sevilla

a Escucha y contesta a las preguntas en español.

Eduardo
- La semana que viene iré a Sevilla.
- Llegaré el martes día seis.
- Alquilaré un coche.
- Me quedaré en un hotel.
- Volveré en dos semanas.

Alicia
- ¿Qué día llegarás?
- ¿Cómo irás desde el aeropuerto al hotel?
- ¿Dónde te quedarás?
- ¿Y cuándo volverás a Madrid?

i ¿Qué día llegará Eduardo? <u>Llegará el ... .</u>

ii ¿Dónde se quedará? <u>Se quedará en ... .</u>

iii ¿Cómo irá al hotel? _____

iv ¿Cuándo volverá? _____

gramática	
llegará	s/he will arrive
irá	s/he will go
volverá	s/he will return

b You are going to Madrid next week, arriving on Wednesday 13th and returning three weeks later. You will hire a car and stay in a hotel. Have a conversation similar to the one above, with your partner.

4 En el aeropuerto

a Rellena los huecos en las respuestas de Eduardo.

Alicia
¿A qué hora sale tu vuelo?
¿Cuánto tiempo dura el viaje?
¿Cuándo llega?
¿Cuál es el número del vuelo?
¿De qué puerta sale?

Eduardo
i _____ .
Dura una hora, aproximadamente.
ii _____ .
iii _____ .
iv _____ .

VUELO	DESTINO	SALIDA	LLEGADA	PUERTA	OBSERVACIONES
1B1919	SEVILLA	13:55	15:00	2	ÚLTIMA LLAMADA
1B2417	CARACAS	14:45	23:50	8	ÚLTIMA LLAMADA
1B1560	ROMA	15:20	17:45	6	RETRASO DE 55 MINUTOS
BA3479	LONDRES	17:40	20:30	3	CONTROL DE PASAPORTES
BA9211	NUEVA YORK	19:30	02:00	7	CONTROL DE PASAPORTES

b Haz preguntas. Por ejemplo:

A **¿A qué hora sale el vuelo de Caracas?**   B **Sale a las ... .**
A **¿A qué hora llega el vuelo de Londres?**   B **Llega a las ... .**
A **¿Cuánto tiempo dura el viaje?**   B **Dura ... .**

5 Nos veremos en el bar

Eduardo sent this e-mail to his colleague Jesús in Seville.

> Querido Jesús:
>
> Llegaré el miércoles 10 de octubre a las seis. Alquilaré un coche en el aeropuerto, así que nos veremos en el hotel Sol enfrente del ayuntamiento.
>
> Me quedaré allí la primera noche y te llamaré por teléfono desde el hotel. Si quieres, tomamos una copa en el bar a las ocho o las nueve.
>
> Hasta luego
> Eduardo

Contesta a las preguntas en inglés.

a Where does he suggest they meet up?
b Where will he stay the first night?
c How will Eduardo contact Jesús?
d What does he suggest they do, and when?

6 Eduardo alquila un coche

a Escribe las preguntas en español.

Eduardo	Empleado
Quisiera alquilar un coche pequeño, por favor.	Tenemos un Nissan Micra, un Peugeot o un Ford Fiesta.
Quiero el Peugeot.	¿Para cuántos días?
Para cuatro días.	

el seguro	insurance
lleno	full
el permiso	licence
las llaves	the keys

i ¿ _Cuánto es por día_ ? Son 42 € por día.

ii ¿ _____ ? El seguro es 9 €.

iii ¿ _____ ? Sí, está lleno.

iv ¿ _____ ? Súper sin plomo.

v ¿Acepta usted _____ ? Sí. Su permiso de conducir, por favor. Firme aquí. Aquí están las llaves.

b Your partner works for a car hire firm in Spain. Arrange to hire a car using the details provided.

Car	Ford Fiesta
Per day	€40
Insurance	€8
Petrol	Super unleaded (full tank)

7 En la estación de trenes

Escribe los detalles del viaje.

¿Adónde va? _Sevilla_

¿De ida (sólo) o de ida y vuelta? _____

¿De primera o de segunda clase? _____

¿Fumador o no fumador? _____

¿Cuánto es? _____

¿A qué hora sale? _____

¿A qué hora llega? _____

¿Hay que hacer transbordo? _____

¿De qué andén sale? _____

de ida (sólo)	single
de ida y vuelta	return
hay que	you need
hacer transbordo	to change
andén	platform

8 Para ir de Granada a Barcelona

Tren	Andén	Granada		Linares-Baeza			Barcelona
		Salida		Llegada	Salida		Llegada
Rápido	10	09.15	____	12.06	____	12.25	____	22.30
Talgo	12	15.15	____	17.52			
Interurbano	2	18.05	____	21.20	____	21.58	____	09.00
Expreso	5	23.15	____	02.18			

You are travelling from Granada to Barcelona. Ask your partner for information about the trains above. S/he has to answer your questions by looking at the timetable.

For example:

A **¿Hay un tren para Barcelona esta mañana?**

B **Sí, el Rápido.**

A

Ask 'Is there a train for Barcelona this morning?'

Ask 'What time does it leave?'

Ask 'What platform does it leave from?'

Ask 'When does it arrive in Barcelona?'

Ask 'Do I need to change?'

B

Answer.

9 En el andén

Contesta a las preguntas en español.

a ¿Adónde va Juana?

b ¿Adónde va Miguel?

c ¿Cuándo sale el tren?

d ¿De qué andén sale?

10 Iré a Barcelona

Juana sent this letter about her trip to Barcelona to Lucía.

En junio iré a Barcelona. No viajaré en coche – cogeré el tren, porque será más fácil, ¡y más ecológico! Pasaré unos cuatro días allí y me quedaré en un hostal barato. Veré la casa de Gaudí y la Sagrada Familia.

Take the role of another friend and ask your partner questions about Juana's trip. For example:

A **¿Cuándo irá Juana a Barcelona?**

B **Irá en junio.**

¿Cuándo irá …?
¿Cómo viajará?
¿Dónde se quedará?
¿Cuántos días pasará …?
¿Qué verá?

> **gramática**
>
> The future tense
> Add **-é, -ás, -á, -emos, -éis, -án**
> to the infinitive:
>
> | | |
> |---|---|
> | **iré** | I will go |
> | **irás** | you will go |
> | **irá** | s/he will go |
> | **iremos** | we will go |
> | **iréis** | you will go |
> | **irán** | they will go |

11 En el tren

a Juana y Miguel se encuentran en el tren de Barcelona y entablan una conversación.

Miguel	Juana
– ¿Tienes amigos en Barcelona?	– No, pero mi amiga Lucía llegará mañana desde Zaragoza y pasaremos unos días juntas.
– ¡Que bien! ¿Cuánto tiempo os quedaréis allí?	– Estaremos cuatro días en Barcelona, luego yo volveré a Granada y Lucía cogerá un avión para Londres.
– ¿Qué haréis en Barcelona?	– Visitaremos la casa de Gaudí y la Sagrada Familia.
– ¿Iréis a las Ramblas?	– Sí, también pasearemos por Las Ramblas y el Parque Güell.
– ¿Dónde os quedaréis?	– Esta noche buscaré un hostal barato cerca del centro de la ciudad.
– Llegaremos bastante tarde a Barcelona, ¿sabes? Esta noche, si quieres, podrás quedarte en casa de mis padres y mañana iremos juntos a recoger a tu amiga Lucía de la estación.	– ¡Estupendo! ¡Eres un sol! Nunca olvidaré este detalle.

b Escribe las frases en español.

i   We'll spend some time together.
ii How long will you spend there?
iii Tonight I'll look for a cheap hotel.
iv You're a star!
v   I'll never forget.

12 Ana va en el 'Bus Turistic'

Escucha y contesta a las preguntas de Ana.

¿Dónde está la parada para el 'Bus Turistic'?   Está en …

¿Los autobuses son frecuentes?   Vienen cada … minutos.

¿Para en el Park Güell?   Sí/No …

¿Cuánto tiempo tarda para ir desde Cataluña
hasta la Sagrada Familia?   Tarda … minutos.

13 Ir en autobús es más barato

Miguel	Quiero alquilar un coche. Ir en coche es más cómodo que ir en autobús.
Ana	Yo prefiero viajar en autobús. Es más barato y contamina menos que el coche.
Miguel	No es verdad. Viajar en autobús contamina más, además, el coche es más práctico.
Ana	No estoy de acuerdo. Es muy difícil aparcar en Barcelona, por lo tanto, ir en coche no es tan práctico como ir en autobús.

¿Verdadero o falso?

	Verdadero	Falso
a Miguel piensa que viajar en coche es más cómodo que viajar en autobús.	☐	☐
b Juana prefiere viajar en autobús.	☐	☐
c Juana cree que viajar en autobús contamina menos pero es más caro.	☐	☐
d Para Miguel viajar en autobús es más práctico.	☐	☐
e Es muy fácil aparcar en Barcelona.	☐	☐

¿Con quién estás de acuerdo? Who do you agree with?

gramática

Ir en autobús es <u>más</u> barato <u>que</u> ir en coche.	(more than)
Ir en coche es <u>menos</u> barato <u>que</u> ir en autobús.	(less than)
Ir en autobús es <u>tan</u> rápido <u>como</u> ir en coche.	(as … as)

14 Pero ir en bici es más ecológico

Weigh up the relative merits of the forms of transport below. The words in the box might help you. For example:

A **Ir en bici es más ecológico que ir en coche.**

B **Sí, pero ir en coche es más cómodo que ir en bici.**

¿en bici o en coche?   ¿en tren o en coche?   ¿en moto o en coche?
¿en metro o en coche?

barato	cómodo	rápido	divertido	fácil	mejor	seguro
caro	incómodo	lento	aburrido	difícil	peor	peligroso

15 La contaminación

Eduardo is listening to a programme on his car radio.

a What is the programme warning about? Underline the five problems mentioned.

i	la lluvia ácida	**iv**	el calentamiento global	**vii**	la contaminación
ii	el tráfico	**v**	los cambios del clima	**viii**	los incendios en los montes
iii	la basura	**vi**	las selvas tropicales	**ix**	las emisiones de CO_2

b Tick the measures which are mentioned by the speaker.

Para solucionar el problema del tráfico:

i Aumentarán los impuestos sobre la gasolina.

ii Los empleados que van en el tren recibirán descuentos.

iii Se producirán automóviles eléctricos.

iv Los conductores pagarán multas por el daño ambiental.

v Conducirán coches con motores ecológicos de bajo consumo.

impuestos	taxes	**descuentos**	discounts
multas	fines	**daño**	damage

16 Por venir

Empareja las descripciones con los inventos del recuadro.

1 La compañía petrolera BP instalará células solares en sus gasolineras. De esta forma reducirá en 3.500 toneladas al año las emisiones de CO_2.

2 La 'Rowbike' es una bicicleta sin pedales que se moverá con la fuerza de los brazos. Permitirá ejercitar los brazos.

3 La empresa Car Cosy comercializará una vitrina de microfibra que se abrirá y cerrará electrónicamente y servirá como garaje para cualquier coche.

4 Daimler-Chrysler será la primera compañía en alimentar un vehículo con un combustible diésel sintético que tiene pocas emisiones contaminantes.

5 Las batallas aéreas estarán dominadas por el 'Eurofighter Typhoon'. Alcanzará velocidades supersónicas y dispondrá de sistemas de infrarrojos.

> **a** Un garaje portátil
> **b** Combustible para el coche del futuro
> **c** Gasolineras al sol
> **d** El avión del siglo XXI
> **e** Una bici con remos

Gramática

- **Future: Use**

There are three ways of expressing the future in Spanish. The second two in particular are often interchangeable.

1 Present tense   for scheduled events: **El tren sale a las 3.**
2 **Ir a** + infinitive   for intentions and plans: **Voy a salir esta noche.**
3 Future tense   for predictions: **En julio iré a África.**

- **Future: Form**

Add the endings **-é, -ás, -á, -emos, -éis, -án** to the infinitive.

llegaré	I will arrive	**llegaremos**	we will arrive
llegarás	you will arrive	**llegaréis**	you will arrive
llegará	s/he will arrive	**llegarán**	they will arrive
	you will arrive		you will arrive

Irregular verbs have the same endings, but the root of the verb changes:

salir: **saldré, saldrás,** etc   **tener:**   **tendré, tendrás,** etc
poder: **podré, podrás,** etc   **venir:**   **vendré, vendrás,** etc
hacer: **haré, harás,** etc   **decir:**   **diré, dirás,** etc

Reflexive verbs have the pronouns at the beginning, except in the infinitive:

quedarse: **me quedaré**   **nos quedaremos**
             te quedarás   **os quedaréis**
             se quedará   **se quedarán**

- **Comparatives**

más ... que	more ... than	**El coche es <u>más</u> caro <u>que</u> la bici.**
		The car is more expensive than the bike.
menos ... que	less ... than	**La bici es <u>menos</u> cara <u>que</u> el coche.**
		The bike is less expensive than the car.
tan ... como	as ... as	**El tren es <u>tan</u> cómodo <u>como</u> el autobús.**
		The train is as comfortable as the bus.

With numbers:

más or **menos** + <u>de</u>:   **Tiene más <u>de</u> cinco años.**
                            He is more than five years old.

Ejercicios de gramática

1 Write the questions in Spanish. For example:

¿A qué hora llega el tren?   **El tren llega a las seis.**

a ¿ _____ ?   El tren llega a las seis.

b ¿ _____ ?   El autobús sale a las cuatro menos veinte.

c ¿ _____ ?   El viaje dura dos horas.

d ¿ _____ ?   Llega a París a las ocho y diez.

e ¿ _____ ?   El tren sale del andén número cinco.

f ¿ _____ ?   El vuelo sale de la puerta número siete.

2 These are the things Juana wants to do after her university course.
Change all the verbs to the **yo** form of the future tense. For example:
Después de la universidad _iré_ de vacaciones …

Después de la universidad (a) (ir) de vacaciones. (b) (Levantarse) tarde todos los días porque ¡no (c) (tener) que ir a clase! (d) (Salir) todas las noches y (e) (ver) a todos mis amigos. (f) (Hacer) muchas cosas: (g) (escuchar) música y (h) (aprender) a bailar salsa, por ejemplo. Después de uno o dos meses, (i) (buscar) un trabajo …

3 Itziar and Iñaki want to do exactly the same as Juana. Change the verbs in the above text to the **nosotros** form of the future tense. For example:
Después de la universidad _iremos_ de vacaciones …

4 Ana's father is asking her what she thinks she will do after her course. Change the verbs to the **tú** form of the future tense. For example:
¿Adónde _irás_ después de la universidad?
a ¿Adónde (ir) después de la universidad?
b ¿Cuándo (volver)?
c ¿Qué (hacer) todos los días?
d ¿Cuándo (empezar) a buscar trabajo?

5 Iñaki's and Itziar's parents ask them the same questions. Change the verbs to the **vosotros** form of the future tense. For example:
¿Adónde _iréis_ después de la universidad?

6 Rellena los huecos con <u>más … que</u>, <u>menos … que</u> o <u>tan … como</u>.
a Viajar en avión es **_más_** seguro **_que_** viajar en coche.
b Un Ford Fiesta es _____ caro _____ un BMW.
c El campo es _____ peligroso _____ la ciudad.
d El japonés es _____ difícil _____ el español.
e El tren es _____ lento _____ la bicicleta.
f Los hoteles son _____ baratos _____ los hostales.

Vocabulario

1

dentro de	within
el año que viene	next year
extranjero/a	foreign
indio/a	Indian
mañana	tomorrow
próximo/a	next
verano (m)	summer

2

casarse	to get married
ganar	to win/to earn
hombre (m)	man
pasado mañana	the day after tomorrow
pronto	soon

3

alquilar	to hire/rent

4

aterrizado	landed
destino (m)	destination
durar	to last, take
llamada (f)	call
llegada (f)	arrival
observación (f)	remark
pasaporte (m)	passport
procedencia	from
puerta (f)	gate
retrasado/a	delayed
retraso (m)	delay
salida (f)	departure
último/a	last
vuelo (m)	flight

5

allí	there
así que	so (that)
copa (f)	drink

6

conducir	to drive, driving
firmar	to sign
gasolina (f)	petrol
llave (f)	key
lleno/a	full
permiso (m)	licence
plomo (m)	lead
seguro (m)	insurance

7

andén (m)	platform
clase (f)	class

de ida (sólo)	single
de ida y vuelta	return
fumador	smoking
hacer transbordo	to change (trains)

8

Expreso (m)	express
Interurbano (m)	Intercity
Rápido (m)	fast train
Talgo (m)	high-speed train

10

ecológico/a	environmentally friendly
fácil	easy
hostal (m)	guesthouse

11

¡Estupendo!	Great!
juntos/as	together

12

frecuente	frequent

13

además	moreover
aparcar	to park
cómodo/a	comfortable
contaminar	to pollute
difícil	difficult
por lo tanto	therefore
práctico/a	convenient

14

aburrido/a	boring
divertido/a	enjoyable/interesting
bici(cleta) (f)	bike (bicycle)
incómodo/a	uncomfortable
lento/a	slow
mejor	better
moto(cicleta) (f)	(motor)bike
peligroso/a	dangerous
peor	worse
rápido/a	fast
seguro/a	safe

15

ambiental	environmental
aumentar	to increase
automóvil (m)	automobile
bajo/a	low
basura (f)	rubbish

For more vocabulary turn to the Appendix on p.181.

Práctica en parejas

1 **a** Answer your partner's questions about what you will do at the end of this course.

b Ask your partner at least four questions about what s/he will do at the end of this course. For example:

¿Qué harás después de la universidad? **¿Buscarás un trabajo?**
¿Viajarás por el mundo? **¿Te casarás?**

2 **a** You are going on holiday to Jamaica for two weeks. Answer your partner's questions using the information below.

	FECHA	HORA	LLEGADA
IDA	10/5/03	10.20	21.50
VUELTA	24/5/03	12.10	23.00

b Ask your partner where s/he is going for the holidays, how long s/he is staying, when s/he is leaving and coming back, and how long the journey takes.

3 You want to take the train from Barcelona to Seville. Ask for the departure and arrival times and if you need to change, and the price of a second class return. You are a non-smoker.

4 You want to go on holiday by plane, but your partner wants to travel by train. Use the adjectives in the box to persuade him/her. For example:
Viajar en avión es más rápido que viajar en tren.

> rápido   práctico   cómodo

Jardín Tropical- Atocha, Madrid

Práctica en parejas

1 a Ask your partner at least four questions about what s/he will do at the end of this course. For example:

¿Qué harás después de la universidad?   **¿Buscarás trabajo?**
¿Viajarás por el mundo?   **¿Te casarás?**

b Answer your partner's questions about what you will do at the end of this course.

2 a Ask your partner where s/he is going for the holidays, how long s/he is staying, when s/he is leaving and coming back, and how long the journey takes.

b You are going on holiday to India for two weeks. Answer your partner's questions using the information below.

	FECHA	HORA	LLEGADA
IDA	21/7/03	12.40	20.55
VUELTA	05/8/03	02.10	10.25

3 Give your partner the information s/he asks for about the train service below.

Barcelona	Valencia	Sevilla		Sencillo	De ida y vuelta
0700_____	1100 _____	1940	1ª clase	100 €	150 €
			2ª clase	80 €	120 €

4 You want to go on holiday by train, but your partner wants to travel by plane. Use the adjectives in the box to persuade him/her. For example:

Viajar en tren es más barato que viajar en avión.

barato	divertido	seguro

Jardín
Tropical-
Atocha,
Madrid

8 Trabajo de verano

In this unit you will learn how to ring up about jobs advertised, to present yourself at an informal interview and to talk about your experience and what you have done. You will also learn some useful language for working in a Spanish-speaking country.

1 Buscando trabajo/Looking for a job

A

HOSTAL ARIAS
c/ Córdoba, 39, León

Se necesita camarero/a con buena presencia para trabajar en el bar.

Interesados ponerse en contacto con la Sra Ibáñez
Tel (987) 42 37 89

B

Se necesita
MOZO/A DE CUADRA
con experiencia,
land

Diríjanse a CORTIJO
KUPANDA
Cta de Torre
Tel (950) 24 43 34

C

¿Quieres trabajar en un campamento de verano?

Si eres una persona con entusiasmo e iniciativa, y te gusta trabajar con niños de 7 a 15 años, llámanos.

Tel (949) 35 71 20

a Mike quiere un trabajo de verano en España. Escribe los detalles de su experiencia laboral en inglés.

– Hostal Arias, ¿dígame?
– Hola, buenos días. Quisiera hablar con la señora Ibáñez, por favor.
– Sí, soy yo.
– He visto su anuncio en el periódico, y quisiera solicitar el puesto de camarero.
– ¿Tiene experiencia?
– He trabajado en un bar y en un restaurante en Escocia, pero no he trabajado nunca en España.
– ¿Qué hace actualmente?
– Soy estudiante.
– Venga mañana por la mañana a las diez.

b Escribe las frases en español.
  i I have seen your advert in the paper.
  ii I'd like to apply for the post of …
  iii I have worked in a bar …
  iv … but I have never worked in Spain.
  v What are you doing at the moment?
  vi Come tomorrow morning …

c Ring up about the other jobs, taking turns as the employer and the student. Ask to speak to the manager (**el encargado**) and say 'I have worked in my country but never in Spain'.

2 He visto su anuncio/I have seen your advertisement

With a partner, take on the roles of Juana and Mike. Ask and answer questions about his job search.

Juana

¿Has visto el anuncio en el periódico?

¿Has decidido solicitar el puesto?

¿Has llamado al hostal?

¿Has hablado con la encargada?

¿Has escrito tu currículum?

Mike

Sí, he visto el anuncio.

Sí,

_____

_____

_____

gramática

To express what someone has done: perfect tense

	-ar verbs	
he	**hablado**	I have spoken
has +	**trabajado**	you have worked
ha	**llamado**	s/he has called

-er and **-ir** verbs

decidido   decided

Irregular:

visto   seen

escrito   written

3 Referencias

Which of the jobs in Section 1 would suit these students? **Escribe a, b o c.**

Juana ha trabajado en una escuela de equitación en Almería. Ha terminado el segundo año de su carrera universitaria y quiere trabajar durante el verano. Le gustan mucho los animales y es una persona trabajadora y responsable. _____

Mike ha trabajado a tiempo parcial en un bar y en un restaurante en Escocia para pagar sus estudios universitarios. Es una persona inteligente con muy buena presencia y buenos modales. _____

Julio es una persona imaginativa e independiente con entusiasmo e iniciativa. Ha completado el primer año de su carrera y ha trabajado de ayudante en una academia de idiomas.

4 Mi experiencia laboral/My work experience

Tell your partner about the jobs you have done. For example:

A **¿Qué trabajo has hecho?**

B **He trabajado de dependiente en una tienda de ultramarinos.**

5 Escribiendo una referencia

Write a reference for your partner and give it to the teacher. Look up any words you need which are not here. When s/he reads out some of the references for the people in the class, guess who they are for.

6 El currículum/The CV

Escucha la entrevista e identifica los errores en el currículum.

7 Te llamaremos mañana

¿Por qué no consiguió Dolores el trabajo? Why didn't Dolores get the job?

Habla con tus compañeros.

CURRÍCULUM VITAE

Michael Marshall
Fecha de nacimiento: 12 de febrero 1986

Dirección: Avda. de la Hispanidad nº 8, 28041 Madrid
Tel: 918749273

Estudios

Napier University	2001 – 2005
Licenciatura en Ciencias	
Empresariales	

Experiencia Profesional

Marco's Bar	1999 – 2003
Barman (tiempo parcial)	
Dispatches Restaurant	1999 – 2000
Camarero (tiempo parcial)	
Napier University	2000 – presente
Técnico en informática	
(tiempo parcial)	

---

8 La entrevista

Tick the best answers to the questions below. Then interview your partner for one of the jobs in Section 1. Would you give her/him the job?

1 ¿Qué haces actualmente?
 a Estudio Ciencias en la universidad de Leeds.
 b Nada.

2 ¿Tienes experiencia en este campo?
 a No.
 b Sí, he trabajado de camarero/a en un restaurante pequeño.
 c No, pero estoy dispuesto/a a aprender.

3 ¿Por qué quieres trabajar en esta empresa?
 a Porque quiero adquirir experiencia en este sector.
 b Porque necesito el dinero.
 c Porque la empresa tiene muy buena fama.

4 ¿Sabes trabajar en equipo?
 a Prefiero trabajar solo.
 b A mí me gusta trabajar solo o en equipo.

5 ¿Estás dispuesto/a a hacer horas extras?
 a Si es necesario sí, pero también tengo que estudiar.
 b No, de ningún modo.
 c Sí, haré todas las horas necesarias.

6 Pagamos 4 € por hora. ¿Está bien?
 a No. Exijo por lo menos 10 € por hora.
 b Sí. Necesito este trabajo.
 c Lo siento, no. Eso no es suficiente.

9 La reserva

a Dolores did eventually get a placement in a hotel, as a receptionist. Spot the mistakes she made on the hotel register when booking in Señor Serrat.

Estimado señor:

Quisiera reservar una habitación doble con baño y balcón, si es posible. Mi mujer y yo llegaremos por la tarde el lunes, 21 de junio y quisiéramos quedarnos cuatro noches hasta el jueves 25. Quisiéramos pensión completa para dos personas.

Le saluda atentamente

Joan M Serrat

NOMBRE	FECHAS	HABITACIÓN DOBLE / INDIVIDUAL	PENSIÓN MEDIA / COMPLETA	BALCÓN	BAÑO/DUCHA
SERRAT	12-15 junio	individual	media X 2	no	ducha
PONS					

b Could you do better? Señora Pons wants to make a reservation. **Rellena la tabla.**

c Practise this conversation, then change the items underlined to the ones in brackets.

A **Quisiera una habitación, por favor.**
B **¿Para cuántas noches?**
A **Para <u>dos noches.</u>** (a week)
B **¿Doble o individual?**
A **<u>Individual.</u>** (double)
B **¿Con baño o ducha?**
A **Con <u>ducha</u>.** (bath)
B **¿Media pensión o pensión completa?**
A **<u>Media pensión.</u> ¿Tiene <u>televisión</u>?** (full board; balcony)
B **Todas las habitaciones tienen <u>televisión</u>.** (balcony)
   Firme aquí, por favor.

10 La recepcionista se ha equivocado/The receptionist has made a mistake

a Rellena los huecos con las letras de las frases del recuadro.

Sr Serrat	Buenas tardes. (1)__a__ a nombre de Serrat.
Dueño	¿Para esta noche?
Sr Serrat	Sí. (2)____
Dueño	Sí, sí, pero (3)____ con la reserva. (4)____ una habitación doble con baño y balcón, y pensión completa, ¿no?
Sr Serrat	Sí. Para cuatro noches.
Dueño	Muy bien; firme aquí.

> **a** He reservado una habitación
> **b** Usted ha reservado
> **c** ¿No ha recibido mi carta?
> **d** la recepcionista se ha equivocado

b Practica la conversación de la Sección a con tu compañero/a.

11 ¿Qué ha pasado?/What has happened?

Empareja los problemas con sus soluciones.

Huésped

1 He dejado mis llaves en la habitación, y la puerta se ha cerrado.

2 He perdido mi equipaje. Lo he dejado en el tren.

3 He pedido el desayuno en la habitación, pero todavía no ha llegado.

4 ¡Me han robado! ¡Mi bolso ha desaparecido!

5 Quisiera una habitación para esta noche.

Recepcionista

a Lo siento, pero el hotel está completo. Aquí hay una lista de hoteles. Puede llamar desde aquí para hacer una reserva, si quiere.

b Tengo su bolso aquí, señora. Se lo ha dejado en el restaurante.

c Llamaré a la estación, a la oficina de objetos perdidos.

d Llamaré al portero. Él le abrirá la puerta.

e La camarera se lo llevará en seguida.

12 Deme una solución

With a partner, think of solutions to the problems below. Then take turns to be the receptionist and the guest with a problem.

a I have lost my wallet, and can't pay my bill.

b The maid hasn't cleaned my room.

to wash up	**fregar los platos**
to clean	**limpiar**
the police	**la policía**

13 Responsabilidades

Empareja los trabajos con sus responsabilidades.

1 Mozo/a de cuadra	**a** Servir a los clientes
	b Planear actividades
2 Animador/a en un campamento de verano	**c** Limpiar las cuadras
	d Limpiar las mesas
	e Limpiar la cocina
3 Camarero/a	**f** Dar de comer a los caballos
	g Fregar los platos
4 Servicio doméstico	**h** Solucionar problemas
	i Ser responsable de la seguridad

14 ¡Qué trabajo!/What a job!

a Read Juana's letter and fill in the first part of the table below.

> Trabajar en una cuadra es duro, pero a mí, me encanta. Empiezas muy temprano por la mañana – y esto puede ser un problema si las cuadras están muy lejos de la casa. Pero estás fuera todo el día, al aire libre, y puedes montar a caballo.

EMPLEO	VENTAJAS	DESVENTAJAS
Moza de cuadra (Juana)	Me encanta. Estás fuera todo el día, ... Puedes montar ...	Es ... Empiezas ... Las cuadras pueden estar ...
Camarero (Mike)		
Animador (Julio)		
Servicio doméstico (Dolores)		

b Three people discuss the relative merits of their holiday jobs. **Rellena la tabla.**

El trabajo es muy duro.
Conoces a mucha gente.
Te dan la comida gratis.
Me gusta el ambiente.
No me gustan mis colegas.

No ganas mucho dinero.
Me llevo muy bien con mis colegas/el encargado/los niños.

 ## 15 ¿Te gusta tu trabajo?

Tell your partner what it is you like about your work or studies. For example:

A **¿Te gusta tu trabajo?**
B **Sí, porque es muy interesante.**
OR
No, porque es aburrido.

¡Extra!

16 ¿Cuánto ganas?/How much do you earn?

Existen nueve comunidades* en las que el salario que se cobra es superior a la media nacional – que es aproximadamente 1.710 € al mes. No obstante, entre los sueldos de los madrileños – los más elevados – y los de los murcianos – los más bajos – existe una diferencia de 712 €.

*Spain is divided into 17 **comunidades autónomas.**

a Underline the phrases in the text that mean the same as the ones below.

  i   in which the salary earned

  ii is above the national average

  iii However,

  iv the wages of people from Madrid

  v   the highest … the lowest

  vi those of the people from Murcia

(Adapted from INE, 2° trimestre de 1999; Q*uo* Núm 51)

b Escucha y rellena el cuadro.

SALARIO MENSUAL MEDIO POR TRABAJADOR	€ (aprox)
MADRID	2.090
PAÍS VASCO	
CATALUÑA	
CASTILLA Y LEÓN	
BALEARES	
ANDALUCÍA	
GALICIA	
MURCIA	1.378

17 Los seis perfiles más buscados/The six most sought-after characteristics

These are the six sorts of worker most sought after by Spanish employers. Match the type of worker to her/his characteristics and to the sort of job which would suit her/him best.

1 INDEPENDIENTE

2 ORGANIZADO

3 CON CAPACIDAD DE ESCUCHA

4 'MANITAS'

5 CREATIVO

6 PERSUASIVO

a Paciente, flexible, escucha con interés al cliente.

b Imaginativo, crítico, vanguardista, analítico, observador.

c Con gran habilidad manual; le interesan las nuevas tecnologías.

d Persona ordenada, metódica, con buena memoria.

e Persona extrovertida, sociable y perspicaz.

f Prefiere trabajar en solitario; analítico y observador con buena memoria, dedicación y constancia.

i Labores de electricidad, electrónica, mecánica.

ii Enfermería, psicología, ventanillas de reclamaciones, recursos humanos.

iii Marketing, publicidad; las bellas artes y la cultura; el cine.

iv Investigación, trabajos científicos, documentación.

v Trabajos de apoyo, como secretarias.

vi Labores comerciales y políticas; expertos en comunicación y turismo; abogados.

Gramática

- **The perfect tense**

  This is usually used as it is in English: I *have gone/seen/done, etc.*

  - **Form**

    Take the appropriate form of the verb **haber** in the present and add the past participle:

    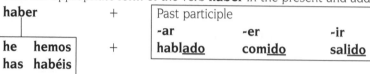

haber		+	Past participle		
			-ar	**-er**	**-ir**
he	**hemos**	+	**habl<u>ado</u>**	**com<u>ido</u>**	**sal<u>ido</u>**
has	**habéis**				
ha	**han**				

he hablado	I have spoken	**hemos trabajado**	we have worked
has comido	you have eaten	**habéis bebido**	you have drunk
ha salido	s/he/it has left	**han pedido**	they have ordered/asked for
	you have left		you have ordered/asked for

  - **Reflexives**

    The reflexive pronoun always comes first:

    me he levantado   I have got up

  - **Direct object pronouns**

    Direct object pronouns come before the verb:

    Lo he visto   I have seen it

  - **Irregular**

    There is a small group of frequently used verbs which have irregular past participles:

hacer	to do/make	**hecho**	done/made	**he hecho**	I have done/made
volver	to return	**vuelto**	returned	**has vuelto**	you have returned
escribir	to write	**escrito**	written	**ha escrito**	s/he has written
ver	to see	**visto**	seen	**hemos visto**	we have seen
decir	to say	**dicho**	said	**habéis dicho**	you have said
abrir	to open	**abierto**	opened	**han abierto**	they have opened

- **Writing letters and postcards**

  - **Formal**

Address of recipient	Your address
	Date

    Estimado/a señor/a (Name):
    He visto el anuncio y quisiera
    solicitar el puesto de …
    Le saluda atentamente
    (your name)

  - **Informal**

Your address
Date

    Querido/a (Name):
    ¿Qué tal? Hemos llegado a
    Puerto Rico y …
    Un abrazo (muy fuerte) de
    (your name)

Ejercicios de gramática

1 Put the correct form of the verb **haber** into the spaces.

a ¿Dónde _has_ ido? (tú)

b _Ho_ estado en Chile. (yo)

c _Haís_ vuelto muy tarde.(vosotros)

d _Hemos_ terminado. (nosotros)

e ¿ _Han_ llegado ya? (ellos)

f El tren _ha_ salido.

2 Change the verb in brackets to the past participle.

a He (ser) _____sido_____ animador en un campamento.

b Hemos (ver) _____ el anuncio.

c Han (decir) _____ que hay televisión.

d ¿No has (escribir) _____ la carta todavía?

e Alfonso ha (hacer) _____ su trabajo.

f ¿Habéis (coger) _____ el tren?

3 Complete this table.

PERFECT	PRESENT	FUTURE
he trabajado	trabajo	trabajaré
		llegaré
_____	vuelvo	_____
he salido	_____	_____

4 Change the verbs in brackets.

a (Terminar, yo) **He terminado** este ejercicio pero no (empezar, yo) _____ el otro.

b Ana y Bea (llegar) _____ pero Julio no (venir) _____.

c (Ganar, nosotros) _____ la lotería, pero no (comprar, nosotros) _____ una casa.

d ¿(Ver, vosotros) _____ esta película? (Tener, ella) _____ mucho éxito.

5 Translate this e-mail into English.

> Querido Jesús:
>
> ¿Has visto el anuncio de ayudante en una academia de idiomas?
> Quiero solicitar el puesto y he llamado a la academia para pedir
> más detalles. Ya he preparado mi currículum y mi profesor me
> ha escrito una referencia. ¿Has decidido si quieres trabajar en
> Francia en julio? Escribe o llámame pronto,
>
> María José

Vocabulario

1

¿Dígame?	Hello? (On phone)
actualmente	at the moment
anuncio (m)	advertisement
buena presencia (f)	good appearance
campamento (m) de verano	summer camp
diríjanse	apply
encargado/a	manager
mozo/a de cuadra	stable lad/girl
se necesita	required
niño/a	child
ponerse en contacto con	to contact
puesto (m)	post
solicitar	to apply for
venga	come (formal)

3

ayudante (m/f)	assistant
buenos modales (m pl)	good manners
carrera (f)	(degree) course
durante	during
equitación (f)	riding
escuela (f)	school
idioma (m)	language
independiente	independent
inteligente	intelligent
referencia (f)	reference
responsable	responsible
tiempo parcial	part time
trabajador/a	hard-working

4

tienda (f)	shop
ultramarinos (m pl)	groceries

6

informática (f)	Information Technology
licenciatura (f)	degree
técnico/a	technician

8

adquirir	to acquire
campo (m)	field
de ningún modo	no way
empresa (f)	firm
equipo (m)	team
estar dispuesto/a a	to be willing to
exigir	to demand
fama (f)	reputation
listo/a	keen, clever, ready
nada	nothing
por lo menos	at least

saber	to know (how to)
solo/a	alone
suficiente	enough

9

balcón (m)	balcony
doble	double
ducha (f)	shower
Estimado/a	Dear (formal letters)
habitación (f)	room
individual	single
Le saluda atentamente	Yours faithfully
media pensión (f)	half board
pensión completa (f)	full board
reserva (f)	reservation

10

dueño/a	owner
equivocarse	to make a mistake
recibir	to receive

11

completo/a	full
dejar	to leave (behind)
desaparecido	disappeared
en seguida	right away
equipaje (m)	luggage
huésped (m)	guest
llevar	to bring
objetos perdidos (m pl)	lost property
perder	to lose
robar	to rob (someone)
todavía	still, yet

13

animador/a	activities organiser, play leader
caballo (m)	horse
cuadra (f)	stall, stable
dar de comer a	to feed
mesa (f)	table
planear	to plan
seguridad (f)	security
servir	to serve
solucionar	to solve

14

al aire libre	outdoors
ambiente (m)	atmosphere
colega (m/f)	colleague
comida (f)	food, meals

For more vocabulary turn to the Appendix on p.182.

Práctica en parejas

1 Ring your partner to tell her/him about a job you have seen advertised. Your partner speaks first.

¿ _____ ?

Say 'Hello, it's (your name)'.

¿ _____ ?

Reply saying 'I have seen an advertisement in the paper for a job in a bar'.

¿ _____ ?

Say 'I have rung the bar and I have spoken to the manager'.

¿ _____ ?

Say 'I have an interview tomorrow at seven'.

¡ _____ !

2 a Your partner is interviewing you for a job as a teaching assistant (**ayudante**) in a school. Either talk about your own work experience, or say you have done the jobs below. Be prepared to answer questions like the ones in Section 8.

Worked as an au pair (**chica/o au pair**) in Spain June, July and August 2004
Worked as a part time lifeguard (**socorrista**) at a swimming pool 2002 – 2003

b Now you are interviewing your partner for a job as a shop assistant (**dependiente/a**) in a clothes shop. Ask her/his age and if s/he has any experience. Then ask two or three questions like the ones in Section 8.

3 a You are the receptionist of the Hotel Mayor and your partner is a client who wants to know about the hotel's facilities. Answer her/his questions. For example:
B **¿Hay baño en las habitaciones?**   A **Sí, todas las habitaciones tienen baño.**
B **¿Está cerca el hotel de la playa?**   A **No, no está cerca de la playa.**

	🛁	🚿	🗖	☎	🍷	🍽	🛏	🏊
El Hotel Mayor	✓	✓	✓	✓	✓		✓	
El Hotel Colón								

b Your partner is now the receptionist of the Hotel Colón, and you are the client wanting to know about the hotel's facilities.

Práctica en parejas

1 Your partner has rung to tell you about a job s/he has seen advertised. You speak first. Answer the phone (**¿Sí, dígame?**)

_____

Ask 'How are you?'

_____

Ask 'Have you rung the bar?'

_____

Ask 'What did he say?' (i.e. What has he said?)

_____

Say 'Good luck!' (**¡Suerte!**).

2 a You are interviewing your partner for a job as a teaching assistant (**ayudante**) in a school. Ask her/his age and if s/he has any experience. Then ask two or three questions like the ones in Section 8.

   b Your partner is interviewing you for a job as a shop assistant (**dependiente/a**) in a clothes shop. Either talk about your own work experience, or say you have done the jobs below. Be prepared to answer questions like the ones in Section 8.

     Worked part time in a supermarket 2004 – 2005
     Worked part time as an usher/ette (**acomodador/a**) in a cinema 2003 – 2004

3 a Your partner is the receptionist of the Hotel Mayor and you are a client who wants to know about the hotel's facilities. Ask questions and complete the table.
     For example: **¿Hay baño en las habitaciones?**
                 ¿Está cerca el hotel de la playa?

	🛁	🚿	⬜	☎	🍷	🍽	🛏	⛱
El Hotel Mayor								
El Hotel Colón		✓	✓		✓			✓

   b You are now the receptionist of the Hotel Colón, and your partner is the client wanting to know about the hotel's facilities. Answer her/his questions.

¿Dónde estuviste ayer?

In this unit you will learn how to talk about events in your life, what you did yesterday and during visits abroad. You will also develop your understanding of newspaper reports.

1 ¿Dónde estuviste ayer?/Where were you yesterday?

La madre de Miguel quiere saber dónde estuvo ayer. Completa las respuestas.

La madre de Miguel	Miguel
Hola, hijo. Te llamé ayer – ¿dónde estuviste?	Por la mañana estuve _____ .
¿Y por la tarde?	Fui a _____ .
¿Trabajaste mucho?	Sí, trabajé _____ .
¿Saliste por la noche?	No, no salí. Pasé toda la noche
	_____ .
¿Cuándo te acostaste?	Me acosté a _____ .
Trabajas demasiado, hijo.	
Hay que descansar un poquito.	Sí, mamá.

2 ¿Qué hiciste anoche?/What did you do last night?

Bea, la novia de Miguel, también quiere saber qué hizo anoche. Empareja las preguntas con sus respuestas.

Bea	Miguel
1 ¿Qué hiciste anoche?	**a** No oí el teléfono.
2 ¿Toda la noche?	**b** Nada. Me quedé en casa.
3 ¿Adónde fuiste?	**c** Volví a medianoche.
4 ¿Cuándo volviste?	**d** Fui al bar con Ricardo.
5 Pero te llamé a las doce y media …	**e** Toda la noche no. Salí un rato.

gramática

The preterite tense

Regular:					
	-ar	**llamé**	I phoned	**llamaste**	you phoned
	-er	**volví**	I returned	**volviste**	you returned
	-ir	**salí**	I went out	**saliste**	you went out
Irregular:		**estuve**	I was	**estuviste**	you were
		hice	I did	**hiciste**	you did
		fui	I went	**fuiste**	you went

With reflexive verbs the reflexive pronoun goes first: **me acosté** etc.

3 A practicar

Practica las dos conversaciones que Miguel tuvo con su madre y con su novia.

4 Ayer

Haz cinco preguntas a tu compañero/a sobre el día de ayer. Por ejemplo:

A ¿Qué hiciste ayer por la mañana?

B Por la mañana estuve en la biblioteca.

A ¿Adónde fuiste ayer por la tarde / anoche?

B Por la tarde fui a clase. Anoche salí con mis amigos, etc

ayer por la mañana	yesterday morning
ayer por la tarde	yesterday afternoon/evening
anoche	last night

5 La semana pasada

Haz preguntas a otro/a compañero/a sobre la semana pasada. Por ejemplo:

A ¿Qué hiciste el lunes pasado?

B El lunes fui al cine.

(A escribe *cine* a lado de LUNES en la tabla)

LUNES	
MARTES	
MIÉRCOLES	
JUEVES	
VIERNES	
SÁBADO	
DOMINGO	

the day before yesterday	**anteayer**
last Monday	**el lunes pasado**
last weekend	**el fin de semana pasado**
last week	**la semana pasada**

6 Y Miguel – ¿dónde estuvo anoche?

a Marca la respuesta que creas correcta.

Estuvo en casa estudiando.

Estuvo en el bar con Ricardo.

Estuvo en el bar con una amiga.

Estuvo en un restaurante trabajando para ganar dinero.

Estuvo en un casino jugando al black-jack.

Estuvo _____ (¿Qué opinas tú?)

b Escucha la conversación entre Miguel y Ricardo para conocer la verdad.

7 La historia de la vida de Miguel

a Ordena cronológicamente.

_____ Viajó durante un año por América: estuvo en Chile, Argentina y Paraguay.

__1__ Nació el 10 de octubre de 1979 en Granada.

_____ Volvió a España y fue a la Universidad de Granada donde actualmente estudia Cultura Latinoamericana.

_____ Aprobó el bachillerato en junio de 1997.

_____ Trabajó en bares y cafés tocando la guitarra.

_____ Fue al Colegio Ave María hasta 1997.

> **gramática**
>
> The preterite tense: 'he', 'she' and 'you' (formal)
>
> | Regular | | | Irregular | |
> |---|---|---|---|---|
> | **-ar** | **trabajó** | s/he/you worked | **estuvo** | s/he was/you were |
> | **-er** | **nació** | s/he was/you were born | **hizo** | s/he/you did |
> | **-ir** | **salió** | s/he/you went out | **fue** | s/he/you went |

b Test your partner's memory. Give five facts about Miguel's life, some true and some false in one small detail. Your partner has to say '**Verdadero**' or '**Falso**'. For example:

A **Miguel viajó durante dos años por América.**
B **Falso. Viajó durante un año por América.**

8 La historia de mi vida

Write a potted history of your life, including three things you did before going to college or university. For example:

Nací en … . Aprobé el bachillerato en … . Antes de ir a la universidad fui de vacaciones a Italia. También pasé dos meses en Canadá, donde trabajé como camarero/a en un bar… .

9 ¿Quién es?

In a group of four, put all the life stories on the table, face down. Each person selects one and reads it out. The others have to ask questions to find out whose life it is. For example:

¿Cuándo nació?
¿Qué hizo después de aprobar el bachillerato?
¿Trabajó/Viajó/Fue de vacaciones antes de ir a la universidad?

10 Lo pasé fenomenal/I had a great time

a Read this part of the presentation Carla gave on her return from an exchange visit.

> **El semestre pasado hice una visita de intercambio a una universidad española. La visita duró tres meses y lo pasé fenomenal.**
> **Cuando llegué a la universidad, fui directo a la oficina de Relaciones Internacionales, y la secretaria me dio la dirección de una casa. Al día siguiente volví a la universidad y una profesora me ayudó a organizar mi horario. Me sorprendió mucho el número de estudiantes en las clases – unos 70 u 80 –, pero pronto me acostumbré a llegar temprano a clase para poder coger sitio.**

b Con tu compañero/a, practica las preguntas y contéstalas.

i ¿Cuánto tiempo duró la visita de Carla?

ii ¿Cómo lo pasó?

iii ¿Qué le dio la secretaria?

iv ¿Quién le ayudó a organizar su horario?

gramática

(me/te/le) dio	**¿Cómo lo pasaste/pasó?** How did it go? (for you/her/him)?
s/he gave (me/you/him or her)	
(me/te/le) ayudó	**¿Cómo lo pasaron?** How did it go (for them)?
s/he helped (me/you/him or her)	

11 ¿Cómo lo pasaron?

a Estos estudiantes también hicieron un intercambio. Marca las casillas correctas.

Lo pasó bien ☺		Lo pasó mal ☹
☐	Fernando	☐
☐	Maribel	☐
☐	Itziar	☐
☐	Enrique	☑

b Empareja cada estudiante con la razón mencionada.
Match the name to the reason.

Fernando	**i**	No le gustó la profesora del intercambio.
Maribel	**ii**	Tardó seis semanas en encontrar alojamiento.
Itziar	**iii**	Alquiló un coche y viajó mucho por las afueras de la ciudad.
Enrique	**iv**	Pronto hizo muchos amigos.

12 Experiencias de intercambio

a Test your memory. **¿Quién lo dijo?**

i – Aprendí mucho, sí, pero no en la universidad. No fui muchas veces a clase …

ii – Un estudiante argentino me ayudó, y la primera noche me quedé en su casa.

iii – Hice muchos amigos, muy pronto …

iv – Pero la mañana siguiente traté de buscar una casa – sin éxito.

v – Me quedé en una residencia para estudiantes, que era muy cara.

vi – Y cuando traté de verla para pedir más trabajo, no estaba.

vii – Después de seis semanas encontré un piso en el centro …, y me mudé allí …

b Haz preguntas sobre los estudiantes de la Sección a. Por ejemplo:

A **¿Quién tardó seis semanas en encontrar alojamiento?**

B **Enrique.**

A **¿Dónde se quedó la primera noche?**

B **Se quedó … etc.**

> **¿Qué le pasó a X?**
> What happened to X?

13 ¿Qué le pasó a Fernando?

a Fernando had a disastrous evening. **Descubre lo que pasó. Ordena las frases cronológicamente.**

___**1**___ Cogió la llave de la casa en la agencia inmobiliaria.

_____ Fue al bar de enfrente para esperar a la dueña de la casa.

_____ La dueña volvió a la casa a las doce.

_____ Llegó a casa a las seis.

_____ La dueña no estaba.

_____ Ella abrió la puerta.

_____ En ese momento, Fernando vomitó en la escalera.

_____ Perdió la llave de la casa en el autobús.

_____ Empezó a beber cerveza y tequila, y pronto se emborrachó.

b Haz preguntas sobre Fernando. Por ejemplo:

Tú	Tu compañero/a
¿Dónde perdió la llave?	**Perdió la llave …**

¿A qué hora …?
¿Adónde …?
¿Qué …?
¿Cuándo …?

Palacio Cincuentenario, Barcelona

14 Asalto en la calle

Escucha la entrevista entre el detective y el testigo. Rellena los huecos en el artículo.

What happened?
¿Qué pasó?
¿Qué ocurrió?

Asalto en la calle

Ayer por (a) *la tarde* en la calle Jiménez (b) ...... jóvenes de unos (c) ...... ó ...... años amenazaron a una mujer con una navaja y le robaron el bolso. El asalto tuvo lugar a las (d) ...... y duró unos (e) ...... segundos. Los asaltantes se escaparon corriendo por la calle Bogotá.

15 Atraco en el banco

With a partner take on the roles of detective and witness to the bank robbery described below. For example:

Detective	Testigo
¿Cuándo ocurrió el atraco?	*Ocurrió ayer por la mañana.*
¿A qué hora …?	_____
¿Qué …?	_____
¿Cómo …?	_____

Atraco en el banco

Ayer por la mañana hubo un atraco en el Banco Bilbao Vizcaya en la calle Aragón. Tres jóvenes de unos 18 o 19 años entraron en el banco a las diez, y gritaron «¡Manos arriba!». Amenazaron a los empleados con una pistola y salieron corriendo con 10.000 €. Se escaparon en un Seat rojo.

gramática

The preterite tense

Regular			Irregular	
-ar	**asaltaron**	they attacked	**hicieron**	they did
-er	**volvieron**	they returned		
-ir	**salieron**	they left		

¡Extra!

16 Manifestación en Madrid

a Lee el artículo.

Manifestación en Madrid

6.000 estudiantes se manifestaron ayer en Madrid contra la privatización de la Universidad. Colectivos estudiantiles organizaron la protesta, que terminó con una fuerte carga policial.

---

b Contesta a las preguntas en español.

  i ¿Cuántos estudiantes asistieron a la manifestación?

  ii ¿Por qué se manifestaron los estudiantes?

  iii ¿Quién organizó la protesta?

  iv ¿Cómo terminó la manifestación?

  v ¿Quién resultó herido leve?

  vi ¿Quién fue detenido?

estudiantil	student (adj)
el enfrentamiento	confrontation
herido (leve)	(slightly) injured
detenido	arrested

c Replace the misprints in italics in the rest of the article by substituting the words given.

Colectivos *infantiles* de la *derecha* alternativa convocaron *hoy* en *las afueras* de Madrid a 6.000 *ancianos* para expresar su *aprobación para* la posible *colectivización* de la Universidad. La manifestación *empezó* con enfrentamientos entre un grupo de estudiantes y la policía. Tras la carga, un *policía* resultó herido *grave*. No hubo detenidos.

---

ayer	estudiantiles	privatización	leve	protesta	el centro
contra	izquierda	jóvenes	terminó	manifestante	

Gramática

● **The preterite tense**

For expressing something which happened at a particular time or for a defined period of time in the past: It *opened* at 12; They *stayed* for two hours, etc.

Regular

-ar		**-er**		**-ir**	
llamé	I phoned	**volví**	I returned	**salí**	I left
llamaste	you phoned	**volviste**	you returned	**saliste**	you left
llamó	s/he phoned	**volvió**	s/he returned	**salió**	s/he left
	you phoned		you returned		you left
llamamos	we phoned	**volvimos**	we returned	**salimos**	we left
llamasteis	you phoned	**volvisteis**	you returned	**salisteis**	you left
llamaron	they phoned	**volvieron**	they returned	**salieron**	they left
	you phoned		you returned		you left

Irregular

estar:	to be	**hacer:**	to do	**dar:**	to give
estuve	I was	**hice**	I did	**di**	I gave
estuviste	you were	**hiciste**	you did	**diste**	you gave
estuvo	s/he was	**hizo**	s/he did	**dio**	s/he gave
	you were		you did		you gave
estuvimos	we were	**hicimos**	we did	**dimos**	we gave
estuvisteis	you were	**hicisteis**	you did	**disteis**	you gave
estuvieron	they were	**hicieron**	they did	**dieron**	they gave
	you were		you did		you gave

● **Ser** and **ir** have the same form in the preterite:

fui	I went	*or*	I was
fuiste	you went		you were
fue	s/he went		s/he was
	you went		you were
fuimos	we went		we were
fuisteis	you went		you were
fueron	they went		they were
	you went		you were

haber: hubo there was

tener: tuve (like **estuve**)

seguir: seguí, seguiste, etc
but **siguió** and **siguieron**

pedir: pedí, pediste, etc
but **pidió** and **pidieron**

● **Indirect object pronouns**

me ayudó	s/he helped *me*
te dio	s/he gave *you*
le dijo	s/he told *him* or *her*

● **Reflexive pronouns**

me levanté	I got up
te levantaste	you got up
se levantó, etc	s/he got up

Ejercicios de gramática

1 Replace the infinitives in brackets with the appropriate part of the verb.

Ayer por la mañana (a) (ir) **fui** a clase. Por la tarde (b) (trabajar) _____ en la biblioteca y (c) (volver) _____ a casa a las ocho. (d) (Cenar) _____ con mis amigos y después (e) (ver) _____ un poco la tele. (f) (Acostarse) _____ las once y media.

2 A friend has just come back from an exchange visit in Zaragoza. Fill in the gaps in the questions with the correct forms of the verbs below.

estar	pasar	quedarse	llegar	durar	ir

a ¿Adónde **fuiste**?

b ¿Cuánto tiempo _____ en Zaragoza?

c ¿Cómo lo _____ ?

d ¿Dónde _____ ?

e ¿Cuándo _____ aquí?

f ¿Cuánto tiempo _____ el viaje?

3 Write about the people you met on your exchange visit.
Change the verbs in brackets.

a En la oficina de Relaciones Internacionales, me (dar) **dieron** la dirección de una casa.

b Me (gustar) _____ todos mis profesores excepto una.

c Unos 70 u 80 estudiantes (asistir) _____ a cada clase.

d Los estudiantes españoles me (ayudar) _____ mucho.

e El primer día dos chicas me (invitar) _____ a cenar.

4 Read the article and write down the questions a detective would ask a witness.
Ask questions beginning with:

a ¿Cuándo **ocurrió el atraco**?

b ¿Dónde …?

c ¿Qué …?

d ¿Cuánto tiempo …?

e ¿Adónde …?

f ¿Cómo …?

> Ayer a las 11:10 de la mañana hubo un atraco en el supermercado en la calle Orfeo. Tres hombres de edades comprendidas entre los 22 y 30 años entraron gritando en el supermercado por la puerta principal y amenazaron a los empleados y clientes con una pistola. Estuvieron en el supermercado unos cinco minutos exigiendo dinero de las cajas y se escaparon con 2.500 € en una furgoneta azul.

Vocabulario

1

ayer	yesterday
descansar	to rest
hay que	it's necessary
pasar	to spend
un poquito (m)	a little bit

2

anoche	last night
oír	to hear
un rato (m)	for a while

6

con	with
opinar	to think
para	in order to

7

actualmente	at present
aprobar	to pass
bachillerato (m)	exam similar in level to A levels
historia (f)	story
nacer	to be born
tocar	to play (an instrument)

8

antes de	before

9

después de	after

10

acostumbrarse	to get used to
dar	to give
intercambio (m)	exchange
poder	to be able
pronto	soon
siguiente	following
sorprender	to surprise
temprano	early

11

alojamiento (m)	accommodation
alquilar	to hire
encontrar	to find
tardar	to take

12

buscar	to look for
éxito (m)	success
mudarse	to move house
sin	without
tratar de	to try to
veces (f pl)	times

13

abrir	to open
coger	to collect
dueño/a	landlord/lady
emborracharse	to get drunk
empezar	to start
escalera (f)	stairs
esperar	to wait for
llave (f)	key
perder	to lose
vomitar	to be sick

14

amenazar	to threaten
artículo (m)	article
asaltante (m/f)	assailant
asalto (m)	assault
bolso (m)	bag
correr	to run
escaparse	to escape
jóven (m)	young
mujer (f)	woman
navaja (f)	penknife
ocurrir	to happen
pasar	to happen
robar	to rob
testigo (m/f)	witness
tener lugar	to take place

15

atraco (m)	robbery
gritar	to shout
¡Manos arriba!	Hands up!
pistola (f)	gun

16

anciano/a	elderly person
aprobación (f)	approval
fuerte	strong
grave	serious
manifestación (f)	demonstration

Práctica en parejas

1 Find out what your partner did yesterday. Ask the questions below. For example:

A **¿Ayer por la mañana estuviste en clase o en la cama?**

B **Estuve en clase.**

¿Ayer por la mañana estuviste	en clase / en la cama?
¿Por la tarde fuiste	a la biblioteca / a casa de tus amigos?
¿Pasaste la noche	estudiando / en el casino con tus amigos?
¿Volviste a casa	a medianoche / a las dos de la madrugada?
¿Te acostaste	a las doce y media / a las dos y media?

2 Take it in turns with your partner to find out about each other's holidays. Ask about the following:

– Where s/he went
– How long s/he stayed
– Who s/he went with

– Where s/he stayed
– When s/he came back
– If s/he had a good time

Ask questions beginning with:

¿Adónde ...?   **¿Dónde ...?**

¿Cuánto tiempo ...?   **¿Cuándo ...?**

¿Con quién ...?   **¿Lo ...?**

3 Complete Carla's diary by asking questions about what she did, where there is a blank in the diary. For example:

A **¿Qué hizo Carla el lunes por la mañana?** B **Fue a clase.**

A **¿Salió por la noche?**   B **Sí** or **No**, etc

	LUNES	MARTES	MIÉRCOLES
Mañana	_____	Me levanté tarde y me perdí la primera clase.	_____
Tarde	Hablé con Miguel en la librería.	_____	Vi a Miguel en la cantina.
Noche	_____	Esperé toda la noche, pero Miguel no llamó.	_____

Práctica en parejas

1 Find out what your partner did yesterday. Ask the questions below. For example:

A **¿Ayer por la mañana hiciste tu trabajo o hiciste la compra?**

B **Hice la compra.**

¿Ayer por la mañana hiciste	tu trabajo / la compra?
¿Por la tarde jugaste	al fútbol / al tenis?
¿Pasaste la noche	durmiendo / en el bar con tus amigos?
¿Te quedaste en casa	para estudiar / para ver la tele?
¿Llamaste por teléfono	a tus padres / a tu amigo /a?

2 Take it in turns with your partner to find out about each other's holidays. Ask about the following:

– Where s/he went	– Where s/he stayed
– How long s/he stayed	– When s/he came back
– Who s/he went with	– If s/he had a good time

Ask questions beginning with:

¿Adónde …?	**¿Dónde …?**
¿Cuánto tiempo …?	**¿Cuándo …?**
¿Con quién …?	**¿Lo …?**

3 Complete Carla's diary by asking questions about what she did, where there is a space in the diary. For example:

B **¿Qué hizo Carla el lunes por la tarde?**   A **Fue a clase.**

B **¿Fue a clase el martes por la mañana?**   A **Sí** or **No**, etc

	LUNES	MARTES	MIÉRCOLES
Mañana	Fui a clase.	_____	Pasé la mañana en la biblioteca.
Tarde	_____	Fui al gimnasio.	_____
Noche	Salí con Miguel. Volví muy tarde a casa.	_____	Invité a Jorge a cenar. Hice una paella. Lo pasamos muy bien – ¡sin Miguel!

10 Repaso

In this unit you will consolidate and practise what you have learnt up to now, while also revising your vocabulary in familiar topic areas.

1 a Rellena los huecos en el formulario.

Nombre _____	
Apellidos _____	
Dirección Calle Colón, nº ____	
Nacionalidad _____	
Fecha de nacimiento _____	
Lugar de nacimiento _____	
Profesión _____	Elena Ariza González

b Ask your partner questions like the ones on the recording, and take down his or her details.

c Ask and answer at least five questions each, taking turns to be Elena. For example:
A **¿Cuántas personas hay en tu familia?** B (Elena) **Somos …**

> Me llamo Elena. Vivo con mi familia en una casa muy grande en las afueras de Madrid. Somos cinco: mis padres, mi hermana Pino, mi hermano Nacho y yo. Nati, la novia de Nacho, vive bastante cerca con sus padres. Nacho y Nati quieren alquilar un piso en el centro, pero cuesta mucho y en este momento están ahorrando para poder pagar el alquiler.
>
> Voy cada día a la universidad, que está en el centro. Voy en moto, porque es más fácil aparcar. Estudio matemáticas y ciencias. Me gusta bastante pero tengo que trabajar mucho. Salgo los fines de semana con mis amigos y normalmente vamos a algún bar o al cine.

2 Write five sentences about yourself, your family, your house, your job and what you like doing, on a piece of paper. In a group of four, put all the papers on the table, face down. Each person picks one of the papers at random and the others ask questions to find out who wrote it. For example:

¿De dónde es?   **¿Cuántos hermanos tiene?**   **¿Qué estudia?** etc

3 Habla con tu compañero/a sobre lo que te gusta y lo que no te gusta.
Rellena la tabla. Por ejemplo:

A ¿Te gusta hacer puenting?

B **Sí, me encanta.** (A writes ✓✓ under B.)

✓✓ me encanta(n)
✓ me gusta(n)
✗ no me gusta(n)
✗✗ no me gusta(n)
nada

	A	B
Hacer puenting		
La música pop		
Las revistas de motos		
Los libros de ciencia ficción		
Las películas románticas		

 4 a Escucha a Inés invitando a Belén a ir al cine.
b Invita a tu compañero/a a ver la película.

LA MALA EDUCACIÓN

Pedro Almodóvar
Icaria Cineplex
10:00
Entradas 10 €

 5 Using the menu on page 32, practise ordering a meal in a restaurant. In a group of three, take on the following roles:

A is the waiter/waitress
B is a vegetarian
C doesn't like fish, chicken or olives

To remind you:
¿Qué quiere tomar?   Quiero/Quisiera …
¿Quiere …?   Para mí/ti/él/ella …
¿Para beber?   ¿Hay …?
No hay …   La cuenta, por favor.

6 Tell your partner what the people are doing in the photo. For example:
Un hombre y una mujer están hablando.

7 a Bea va de compras. ¿Qué compra? Rellena los huecos en la tabla.

	Prenda	Talla	Color	Problema	Precio
i	una falda	....	....	demasiado pequeña	....
		....	....		–
		....	....		....
		....	–		....
ii	unos zapatos	....	....		....
		....	–		–

b Corrige los errores. Correct the inaccuracies in *italics* in Bea's account of her shopping trip.

He ido a todos los grandes almacenes y ahora estoy en el Corte Inglés. El *primer vestido* que me he probado aquí era demasiado *grande*, y pedí *uno* más *pequeño* a la dependienta. Me ha traído *otro*, pero no me gusta el color. He visto *muchos vestidos* pero por fin me he quedado con *éste*, que me ha costado *25 €*. Pero no he podido encontrar *unas botas* del mismo color.

8 a Contesta al email de Jorge.

```
Hola, ¿qué tal?

La semana que viene tengo que ir a una conferencia muy cerca
de donde tú vives. ¿Puedo quedarme contigo? Voy a llegar el
lunes 16 a las 20:10. ¿Vas a venir a la estación a recogerme?
Si no, cogeré un taxi. Al final de la conferencia voy a tener
algunos días libres — ¿qué vamos a hacer? Y tu hermana tan
guapa — ¿va a estar en casa? Espero que sí.

Hasta muy pronto.

Un abrazo:

Jorge
```

b Jorge is getting ready to leave. Taking on the role of his friend, make sure he hasn't forgotten anything. For example:

A **¿Has cogido tus gafas de sol?**   B **Sí, he cogido mis gafas de sol.**
A **¿Has arreglado tu cuarto?**   B **No, no he arreglado mi cuarto todavía.**

coger las gafas de sol ✔   hacer la maleta
arreglar el cuarto   planchar la camisa ✔
lavar los pantalones ✔   comprar el billete ✔

todavía   yet

9 ¿Dónde tienen lugar estas conversaciones? Escucha y pon el número de la conversación al lado del sitio correcto.

a En el aeropuerto _____

b En la oficina de alquiler de coches _____

c En la RENFE _____

d En la estación de autobuses _____

10 En el aeropuerto

«Señores pasajeros del vuelo Iberia 1706 con destino a Nueva York por favor diríjanse inmediatamente a la puerta 8».

VUELO	DESTINO	SALIDA	PUERTA	OBSERVACIONES
IB1706	NUEVA YORK	16:25	8	ÚLTIMA LLAMADA
IB1918	LISBOA	16:55	2	CONTROL DE PASAPORTES
IB2020	GRECIA	17:05	3	RETRASO DE 1 HORA
IB1519	MÉXICO	17:15	4	

a Escribe las preguntas.

¿A qué hora sale el vuelo? Sale a las cuatro y veinticinco.

¿ _____ ? Iberia 1706.

¿ _____ ? De la puerta número 8.

¿ _____ ? No, no hay retraso.

b Haz preguntas a tu compañero/a sobre los otros vuelos.

11 Ordena la conversación y practícala con tu compañero/a.

Jorge

1 Quisiera reservar un billete de ida y vuelta a Sevilla.

2 ¿Hay uno más temprano?

3 ¿Y para volver?

4 ¿Hay que hacer transbordo?

5 El viernes 28 de marzo.

6 ¿A qué hora sale?

7 No fumador. ¿Cuánto es?

8 El miércoles 2 de abril.

Empleado

a ¿Cuándo quiere viajar?

b Sí, el Rápido que sale a las 16:40.

c A la vuelta sale de Sevilla a las 13:10.

d No, es directo.

e ¿Y su fecha de regreso?

f El Talgo sale a las 20:25 horas.

g 30 €

h ¿Fumador o no fumador?

12 Jorge está hablando con una joven en el tren. Escucha y contesta a las preguntas. Completa las respuestas.

a Iré a _____Estados Unidos._____ .

b Trabajaré en _____ .

c Viajaré un poco por _____ .

d Me quedaré en _____

e y luego iré a _____ .

f Volveré en _____ .

13 Haz preguntas a tu compañero/a sobre sus planes para los vacaciones.

¿Adónde irás?   ¿Con quién irás?
¿Cuándo saldrás?   ¿Qué harás?
¿Dónde te quedarás? ¿Cuándo volverás?

14 ¿Quién es el misterioso viajero? Contesta a las preguntas en inglés.

> Los pasajeros del vuelo 3662 de Delta Airlines ocupan sus asientos. La mayoría son hombres de negocios norteamericanos. Todos ignoran al joven alto del traje gris, camisa blanca y corbata verde que ocupa el asiento 1B. Sobre las rodillas tiene un ordenador portátil. ¿Quién es? Parece un ejecutivo, un banquero quizás. No. Es el heredero al trono de un país mediano de la vieja Europa. Se llama Felipe y un día reinará.
>
> Ha crecido con la democracia. Cuando Franco murió, él tenía sólo siete años. Comenzó su educación en Madrid y la terminó con un Master en Relaciones Internacionales que recibió en 1995 por la Universidad de Georgetown, en Washington. En la primavera del 2004, y después de un año de relaciones formales, Don Felipe de Borbón, a sus 37 años, contrae matrimonio con la antes periodista Doña Letizia Ortiz. El Príncipe se convierte así en el segundo Borbón que se casa con una mujer española. El primero fue Alfonso XII, que contrajo matrimonio con María de las Mercedes de Orleans.

a Describe the appearance of the person in this passage.

b What is his or her job?

c What major events in Spanish history took place when s/he was 7 and 37?

d How many of the Borbóns have married Spanish women? Whom did they marry?

88 15 Imagine your partner is a famous person and you are sitting next to her/him on a plane. Agree who s/he is going to be and ask five questions about his or her life. For example:

A **¿Dónde naciste?**   B (As Eva Perón) **Nací en Argentina.**

A **¿Estás casada?**   B **Sí, con el presidente de Argentina.**

A **¿Trabajaste antes de casarte?**   B **Sí, trabajé en algunos bares …**

A **¿Siempre has sido rica?**   B **No. He sido muy pobre.**

A **¿Te gusta ser famosa?**   B **Sí, me encanta.**

88 16 **Marca las cosas que tu compañero/a ha hecho. Por ejemplo:**

A **¿Has hablado con alguna persona famosa?**

B **No, no he hablado con ninguna persona famosa.**

¿Has …

hablado con alguna persona famosa?   ☐

ido alguna vez a un casino?   ☐

viajado en helicóptero?   ☐

robado algo de un supermercado?   ☐

besado al novio / a la novia de un/a amigo/a?   ☐

comido paella?   ☐

alguna vez	ever (anytime)
nunca or **jamás**	never
No he hablado nunca	I have never spoken

17 a Rellena los huecos.

Nací en (i) _____ en Teruel. Me casé en (ii) _____ y mis hijos nacieron en (iii) _____ y (iv) _____ . Mis padres murieron en (v) _____ durante la guerra civil, y el resto de la familia fuimos a América en (vi) _____ . Volvimos a España en (vii) _____ .

88 b Haz preguntas a tu compañero/a sobre su vida. Por ejemplo:

A **¿Cuándo/Dónde naciste?**   B **Nací en …**

¿Cuándo aprobaste el bachillerato?

¿Viajaste/Trabajaste antes de ir a la universidad?

¿Qué estudias actualmente?

¿Trabajas para pagar el curso?

¿Qué harás después de la universidad?

¡Extra!

 18 **Contesta a las preguntas en inglés.**

Los amantes de Teruel

Un joven de 22 años llamado Juan Martínez de Marcilla, se enamoró de Isabel Segura, hija de Pedro Segura, un hombre muy rico. Pidió su mano, pero el padre dijo que no, porque él no era rico. Así que Juan se fue a la guerra, y luchando contra los moros ganó mucho dinero. Después de cinco años volvió, rico, para casarse con Isabel. Pero el día en que Juan llegó a Teruel, Isabel estaba celebrando su boda con otro hombre, y cuando ella se negó a darle un beso (porque estaba casada), él se murió. Un poco más tarde ella murió también, y los dos fueron enterrados juntos en un sepulcro en 1217.

a Why didn't Isabel's father want her to marry Juan?

b What did Juan do when he was away?

c When did he come back?

d What was Isabel doing when he arrived?

e Why wouldn't she kiss him?

f Where were they buried?

19 **a** Study this chronology of Spanish history for a minute. Your partner will then read out each event, changing some details. Say whether it is '**Verdadero**' or '**Falso**', without looking at the text. For example:

A **España entró en la Comunidad Europea en 1987.**

B **Falso. España entró en la Comunidad Europea en 1986.**

1492 Cristobal Colón descubrió America.
1588 La Armada Invencible fue vencida por los ingleses.
1936 Comenzó la Guerra Civil española.
1939 La guerra terminó y empezó la dictadura del General Franco.
1975 Franco murió y la democracia fue establecida en España.
1986 España entró en la Comunidad Europea.

 b Test your partner by asking questions.
For example:

A **¿Cuándo comenzó la Guerra Civil?**

B **Comenzó en …**

A **¿Qué pasó/ocurrió en 1975?**

B **…**

Ejercicios de gramática

1 Complete this conversation by putting the right verbs in the spaces.

Magdalena

Hola. ¿Cómo (a) __te llamas__ ?
(d) _____ Magdalena.
No, (f) _____ en Castellón.
(h) _____ en un banco.

Martirio

(b) _____ Martirio. ¿Quién (c) _____ ?
¿(e) _____ en Alicante?
¿A qué te (g) _____ ?

2 Write what Carlitos does at these times every day.

a (Levantarse, 08:00)

Carlitos se levanta a las ocho de la mañana.

b (Salir de casa, 09:00)

c (Llegar a la universidad, 09:15)

d (Comer en la cantina, 13:00)

e (Volver a casa, 18:00)

f (Ir al bar con sus amigos, 22:00)

g (Acostarse, 24:00)

3 Write these numbers in words.

a 41

b 67

c 104

d 552

e 1778

f 9981

4 What are these people doing at the moment?

a (Ana, eating chips)

Ana está comiendo patatas fritas.

b (Gloria, leaving the house)

c (We, working hard)

d (You, arriving at the airport)

e (Vicente and Pepa, buying clothes)

f (I, speaking on the phone)

5 a How would you ask someone if s/he likes the following?
  i Las verduras
  ¿Te gustan las verduras?
  ii Beber cerveza
  iii Los animales

5 b How would you say the following in Spanish?
  i I like the film.
  Me gusta la película.
  ii I love Cuban music.
  iii I don't like football.
  iv I like it a lot.
  v I don't like it at all.

Ejercicios de gramática

6 Write what these people are going to do by using the appropriate form of **ir a** before the verb in brackets.

a Manolito (jugar) **va a jugar** al baloncesto. **d** Nosotros (ir) _____ al cine.

b Yo (estudiar) _____ esta noche. **e** ¿Cuándo (tú, venir) _____ a mi casa?

c Ellos (ver) _____ al profesor mañana. **f** (Vosotros, comer) _____ muy pronto.

7 Give directions to these places using the right form of the verbs.

> doblar   coger   seguir   ir   estar

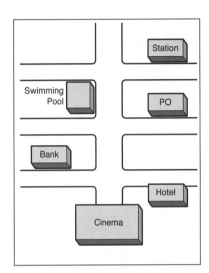

a from the cinema to the swimming pool
   Ve todo recto. La piscina está a la izquierda.

b from the cinema to the hotel

c from the cinema to the bank

d from the cinema to the post office

e from the cinema to the station

8 Write down these people's future plans.

María irá de vacaciones en junio.

a María	ir de vacaciones en junio.
b Nosotros	volver a América.
c Elías	casarse en junio.
d Yo	poder salir a las seis.
e Tú	acostarse a las doce.
f Ana y Bea	trabajar en Francia en agosto.
g Vosotros	tener que ahorrar dinero.

9 The people in Section 8 have now done what they were planning to do. Change the verbs to the perfect tense.

María ha ido de vacaciones.

10 Change this paragraph so that it describes what the writer did yesterday.

Cada día me levanto a las seis. Preparo el desayuno y salgo a las siete y media. Voy al trabajo en coche y llego a las ocho y cuarto. Al mediodía como en un bar enfrente de la oficina. Vuelvo a casa a las ocho y ceno a las nueve y media. Me acuesto a las once o las doce.

Ayer me levanté a las seis. ...

Juegos de palabras/WORD GAMES

1 In the course of this book you have covered the topics listed here. Write down ten words related to each theme.

> La familia   La casa   La rutina   Los estudios   La comida   El tiempo libre
> De compras   La ciudad   De viajes   De vacaciones   El trabajo   Los intercambios
> Las noticias   La historia

2 Put the following words into one of the categories in Section 1 above.

> entrevista   cita   billete   entrada   dinero   sueldo   chalet   piso

3 Gender wars

Call out a word with a feminine gender. Your partner must immediately call out a related word of the opposite gender within the same topic area.

For example: A   **casa** (f)   B   **jardín** (m)
                       A   **leche** (f)   B   **azúcar** (m)

4 Choose three words from one of the topic areas. Your partner has to use them all in one sentence. For example:

A **objetos perdidos   andén   salir** (partner can use any form of the verb)
B **Los objetos perdidos han salido del andén número 10.**

Your partner must now give you four words to combine in a sentence.
Continue, increasing the number of words each time.

5 When you see **-dad** at the end of a Spanish word, it often corresponds to *-ty* in English. For example: **socie<u>dad</u>** means *socie<u>ty</u>*. Can you guess the meanings of the words below? Can you think of any others?

> sociedad   unidad   capacidad   prioridad   facilidad   dificultad   normalidad
> uniformidad   necesidad   totalidad

6 All these words have the same five-letter ending. What is it, and what ending does it correspond to in English?

> rápida …   lenta …   general …   normal …   afortunada …   desafortunada …
> fácil …   difícil …

Práctica en parejas

1 Think of a person in your class. Your partner has to find out who you have in mind by asking no more than five questions like the ones below. You may answer only **Sí** or **No** or **No sé** ('I don't know').

¿Es francés o francesa?   ¿Es de Amsterdam?

¿Estudia geología?   ¿Tiene 25 años?

¿Tiene una casa grande?   ¿Le gustan los animales?

2 Ask questions to fill in the blanks in Elena's diary below. Then give your partner the information s/he asks for. For example:

A **¿Qué hace Elena el lunes por la tarde?**

B **Tiene la tarde libre.** (A writes *libre* in the diary)

	Por la mañana	**Por la tarde**
lunes	*clase de español*	
martes		
miércoles	*biblioteca*	
jueves		*gimnasio*
viernes	*libre*	*yoga*

3 Ask your partner how far these places are from Tarragona in time and fill in the table. For example:

A **¿A cuántas horas / cuántos minutos está Altafulla de Tarragona?**

B **Está a veinte minutos.**

	hrs/mins		hrs/mins
Altafulla	*20 mins*	Benidorm	_____
Calella	_____	Sitges	_____
Reus	_____	La Pineda	_____

Benidorm	**Reus**	**La Pineda**	**Tarragona**	**Altafulla**	**Sitges**	**Calella**
396km	8km	4km	0	20km	67km	172km

Práctica en parejas

1 Think of a person in your class. Your partner has to find out who you have in mind by asking no more than five questions like the ones below. You may answer only **Sí** or **No** or **No sé** ('I don't know').

¿Es francés o francesa?	¿Es de Amsterdam?
¿Estudia geología?	¿Tiene 25 años?
¿Tiene una casa grande?	¿Le gustan los animales?

2 Ask questions to fill in the blanks in Elena's diary below. Then give your partner the information s/he asks for. For example:

B **¿Qué hace Elena el lunes por la mañana?**
A **Tiene clase de español.** (B writes **clase de español** in the diary)

	Por la mañana	Por la tarde
lunes		libre
martes	laboratorio	piscina
miércoles		compras
jueves	clase de informática	
viernes		

3 Ask your partner how far these places are from Tarragona in distance and fill in the table. For example:

B **¿A qué distancia está Altafulla de Tarragona?**
A **Está a 20 kilómetros.**

	km			km
Altafulla	_20_	Benidorm	_____
Calella	_____	Sitges	_____
Reus	_____	La Pineda	_____

Benidorm	Reus	La Pineda	Tarragona	Altafulla	Sitges	Calella
5 hrs	10 mins	5 mins	0	20 mins	50 mins	2 hrs

Más práctica
FURTHER PRACTICE

1 Tú y los demás

1 En la oficina de Incarna

Contesta a las preguntas en inglés.

a What is Jorge's job?
b What is Beatriz's job?
c Where is Jorge from?
d Where does he live?
e Who is Raúl Gomera?

2 ¿Quién es Carla?

Read the conversation and give four details in English about Carla.

– Carla, no eres de aquí, ¿verdad?*
– No. Soy de Puerto Rico, pero vivo aquí en Miami.
– ¿Dónde trabajas?
– Trabajo en la universidad.
– ¿Eres estudiante?
– No. Soy administradora, pero también aprendo italiano.

* Used to confirm something. In the case above it could be translated as '*are you?*'

3 Ahora hablo yo

Take part in a similar conversation to the one above. Speak after the prompts.

4 Un número más

Listen to the numbers and say the next number after the prompt. For example, when you hear **dos** on the recording, say **tres**.

5 Pregúntale a Miguel

What questions would you ask to get the following answers? Write them in Spanish.

a Me llamo Miguel.
b Vivo en Edimburgo.

c No, no soy escocés. Soy inglés.
d Soy estudiante de informática.

6 En una academia de idiomas en Oviedo

Contesta a las preguntas en español.

Ignacio

¿De dónde es?   Es de …
¿Cuántos años tiene?
¿Dónde vive?
¿Cuál es su profesión?

Amanda

¿Es de Bilbao?   Sí/No, es de …
¿Vive en Santander?
¿Tiene 24 años?
¿Es intérprete?

7 Quiero matricularme

You are Laurie Dimock, and you want to enrol on a Spanish course. **Completa esta carta para el director de la academia de idiomas con los detalles del recuadro.**

> Estimado señor:
> Quiero matricularme en un curso de español.
>
> Atentamente
>
> *Laurie Dimock*

Laurie Dimock
22
Welsh, from Bangor
lives in Mexico
hotel receptionist

8 Mi amigo por correspondencia

Contesta a la carta de Juanita en español.

> Querido/a ...
>
> Soy española, de Málaga, pero vivo en Barcelona. Tengo 21 años. Soy estudiante y estudio inglés y alemán. ¡Aprendo mucho aquí! ¿Y tú? ¿De dónde eres? ¿Vives en Barcelona? ¿Cuál es tu profesión? ¿Y cuántos años tienes?
> Escríbeme pronto.
>
> *Juanita*

9 Una agencia de contactos

You are working for a Spanish computer dating agency and are responsible for keying in the details of the following people in Spanish. Write a paragraph about each one.

a Nadia Gil García (female), 25, Spanish, from Madrid, lives in Valencia, history teacher.

b Daniel Martínez Báez (male), 24, Spanish, lives in Bilbao, researcher.

c Siobhán Harpur (female), 21, Irish, from Dublin, learning French, works in a hotel.

10 Crucigrama

Complete the number crossword.

2 La familia en casa

1 La familia de Josefa

Josefa is telling you about her family. Match the names to the ages of the people she mentions, and their relationship to her.

Nombre	Edad	Relación
Eugenia	46	padre
Paulina	35	madre
Alberto	65	marido
Miguel	28	hermana mayor
Esther	64	hermana menor
Leonardo	40	hermano mayor
José	10	hijo

2 Me llamo Charo

Me llamo Charo. Tengo 26 años y soy española, de Valencia. Estoy casada, con dos hijos de seis y cinco años. Trabajo en un banco y mi marido es mecánico. Mis padres están divorciados. Mi madre vive en Valencia y es funcionaria. Mi padre vive en el campo y es agricultor. Tengo una hermana mayor, de 28 años. Se llama Susana. Está separada. Tiene dos hijos pequeños, de dos y cuatro años. Su marido vive en Pamplona. Mi hermano menor, Felipe, es ingeniero. No está casado, pero tiene novia. Su novia trabaja en el aeropuerto.

a ¿Cuántos hijos tienen Charo y su marido?
b ¿A qué se dedica el marido de Charo?
c ¿Cuántos hijos tienen los padres de Charo, y cómo se llaman?
d ¿Quién está divorciado, y quién está separado?
e ¿Cómo se llama la hermana mayor de Charo?
f ¿Quién trabaja en el aeropuerto?

3 Mi familia

Answer Charo's questions about your family. Include as many details as possible about their ages, jobs, marital status, etc.

4 Otra familia

Write a description of a family. It could be your own or a famous one like the British or Spanish royal families.

5 ¿Dónde viven?

Rellena los huecos.

	Juan	Ángela
¿Centro o afueras de la ciudad?	afueras	_____
¿Casa/piso/chalet/habitación?	casa	_____
¿Grande o pequeño/a?	grande	_____
¿Número de dormitorios?	_____	2
¿Salón o salón-comedor?	_____	salón-comedor
¿Cocina grande o pequeña?	_____	pequeña
¿Número de cuartos de baño?	_____	1
¿Garaje o aparcamiento?	garaje	_____
¿Jardín?	2	_____
¿Balcón?	_____	_____

6 ¡Qué casa!

You are negotiating a house/flat exchange with a couple from Andalucía. Read the description they have sent you of the accommodation offered and answer the questions.

> La casa es muy grande y bastante vieja. Hay dos plantas. Arriba hay cinco dormitorios, tres con cama de matrimonio, y uno con dos camas individuales. El dormitorio pequeño tiene una cama individual y un sofá. Todos tienen balcón. Hay tres cuartos de baño, todos con ducha y lavabo y uno con bañera. Abajo, en la planta baja hay dos salones, uno grande y bastante tradicional y el otro pequeño, con sillones, sofás, alfombras, etc. También hay un comedor, y la cocina es muy moderna con cocina eléctrica, frigorífico y dos lavadoras automáticas. Hay dos garajes, unos jardines muy bonitos, una piscina y una pista de tenis.

a ¿Cómo es la casa?
b ¿Cuántos dormitorios grandes hay?
c ¿Qué hay en el dormitorio pequeño?
d ¿Dónde están los salones?
e ¿Cómo es la cocina?
f ¿Qué hay en los jardines?

7 Alquiler de verano

You want to rent your own house or flat out for the summer. Write an advertisement describing it, for inclusion in a Spanish newspaper.

3 La rutina

1 Isabel, una mujer ocupada

Rellena los huecos en la agenda de Isabel.

	Por la mañana	Por la tarde
LUNES	10:00 Juicio	_____ Cita con el Sr. Graznar
MARTES	_____ Sra Gómez	_____ Restaurante El Juez
MIÉRCOLES	Juicio todo el día	_____ _____
JUEVES	10:00 _____	_____ _____
VIERNES	_____ _____	_____ _____

2 La rutina de Manuel

Manuel is Isabel's husband. Reorganize the sentences in this letter describing his day so that it makes sense.

> Trabajo hasta las dos. Me levanto a las siete y desayuno a las siete y media. Como en un bar y vuelvo al trabajo a las cinco. Termino a las ocho y ceno con Isabel a las diez. Me acuesto a medianoche. Salgo a las ocho y voy a la oficina.

3 ¿Qué hacen?

Use the clues to find out what jobs Isabel's five friends have. **Rellena la tabla.**

	Andrés	**Bea**	**Carlos**	**Diana**	**Enrique**
Profesión					
Por la mañana	duerme				
Por la tarde					sale
Por la noche				trabaja	

El estudiante y el artista duermen por la mañana.
La recepcionista y la profesora trabajan todo el día.
Andrés y Bea salen por la noche.
Carlos y la profesora trabajan por la noche.
El artista pinta por la noche y sale por la tarde.
El médico visita a los pacientes por la mañana y vuelve a la clínica por la tarde.
Andrés estudia por la tarde.

4 ¿Qué está haciendo Isabel?

Back in Isabel's office, Señor Graznar is waiting to see her, but she is very busy.
Rellena los huecos.

15:55	**Sr Graznar**	Hola, buenas tardes. Tengo cita con Isabel a las cuatro.
	Secretaria	Hola, buenas tardes. Siéntese aquí. Isabel (a) _____ _____ con un cliente.
16:20	**Sr Graznar**	¿Está libre ahora?
	Secretaria	No. Ahora (b) _____ _____ por teléfono.
16:40	**Sr Graznar**	¿Qué (c) _____ _____ ahora Isabel?
	Secretaria	(d) _____ _____ un informe.
16:50	**Sr Graznar**	¿Sabe que (e) _____ _____ ?
	Secretaria	Sí, sabe que usted (f) _____ _____ .
17:10	**Sr Graznar**	¡Isabel (g) _____ _____ !
	Secretaria	Sí. Tiene otra cita a las cinco. Vuelva usted mañana.

> está   estoy   haciendo   esperando   hablando   saliendo
> escribiendo   conversando

---

5 En el restaurante

Isabel is in the restaurant with her client. Take on the role of the client and speak after the prompts.

4 El tiempo libre

1 ¿Qué les gusta leer?

What sorts of books and magazines do Eduardo, Carmen and Andrés like? **Marca la casilla correcta.**

		Verdadero	Falso
a	Carmen dice «A mí no me gusta leer.»	☐	☐
b	A Eduardo le encantan las novelas policíacas.	☐	☐
c	Andrés dice «No me gustan nada las revistas de motos.»	☐	☐
d	Carmen pregunta «¿A ti no te gustan los libros de ciencia ficción?»	☐	☐
e	A Eduardo le gustan bastante las revistas de moda.	☐	☐

2 Me encanta Barcelona

Querido Ramón:

... ¿Lo que me gusta en Barcelona? Pues todo. Hay muchos edificios muy interesantes desde el punto de vista arquitectónico - me gustan la casa de Gaudí y la Sagrada Familia, por ejemplo. También me encanta la calle que se llama Las Ramblas. Siempre hay teatro en la calle: me gustan los títeres y las estatuas humanas, y hay muchos pintores y artistas de todo tipo ...

Un abrazo a todos

Ángela

a ¿Cómo se llama el arquitecto que le gusta a Ángela?
b ¿Qué le gusta ver en Las Ramblas?

el edificio	building
los títeres	puppet shows
siempre	always
la calle	street

3 ¿Quieres ver una película?

Empareja la pelicula con su descripción.

1 *La vida es bella* (Benigni)

2 *Titanic* (Cameron)

3 *Arma Letal 4* (Donner)

4 *Evita* (Parker)

a llena de acción y con mucha violencia

b humor, imaginación, romanticismo y amargura en la Italia fascista

c una biografía de Eva Perón, con Madonna

d amor y muerte con Leonardo di Caprio

 4 No quiero salir contigo

Empareja las preguntas con su respuesta.

a Miguel, ¿quieres salir mañana?

b ¿Por qué?

c ¿Por la noche?

d ¿Puedes salir el martes?

e ¿Todo el día?

f Miguel, ¿no quieres salir conmigo?

g ¿Por qué?

Todo el día.

No, no quiero salir contigo.

Mañana no puedo.

Porque prefiero salir con Juana.

Por la noche.

Tengo que trabajar.

No. El martes tengo clase.

| **conmigo** with me | **contigo** with you |

 5 ¿Quieres salir esta noche?

A friend has rung to invite you out. Speak after the prompts.

 6 El diario

Susana is rather distracted and makes several mistakes in her diary. **Corrige el diario.**

LUNES	*MARTES*	*MIÉRCOLES*
De compras con Alicia a las 10:00	Gimnasio con Bea a las 4:30	Exposición de Arte con Alicia a las 12:00 en la entrada del museo
Cine con Carlos a las 10:30		

5 El dinero

Ámame o Mátame

¿Qué va a pasar en este último episodio? ¿Margarita se va a dar cuenta de que su novio y su mejor amiga son amantes? ¿Cómo pueden estar juntos para siempre Leonardo y Livia? ¿Y quién es el misterioso Salvador? Esta noche miles de espectadores van a saberlo todo …

1 Ámame o mátame

a Read the TV guide and say what sort of programme '**Ámame o Mátame**' is.

b In this episode the action revolves round three notes.

   i ¿Quién va a viajar a Estambul?

   ii ¿Quién va a París?

   iii ¿Quién va a estar en el Bar Jinete a las 10:00?

Una nota en la puerta del frigorífico. Viernes.

Querida Margarita: Tengo que viajar urgentemente a Estambul. Te voy a llamar desde el aeropuerto. Voy a volver el lunes. Hasta luego, Leonardo

Un e-mail recibido más tarde.

Querida Margarita:
No puedo salir contigo esta noche. Este fin de semana voy a París. Voy a comprar mucha ropa (me gusta la moda francesa). Vuelvo el lunes por la tarde.
Un abrazo
Livia

Una nota en el casillero de Margarita.

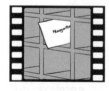

Querida Margarita:
Este fin de semana, tu novio no va a viajar a Estambul, y Livia no va a ir a París. Van a estar juntos en el Bar Jinete esta noche a las 10.
Salvador (camarero en el Bar Jinete)

c **¿Qué va a suceder? Usa tu imaginación y completa la historia. Por ejemplo:**

Margarita va a ir al Bar Jinete. Va a matar a Livia y a Leonardo y después va a comprar un yate y viajar por el mundo.

d ¿Qué pasa en el bar? Marca la casilla correcta.

	Verdadero	Falso
i Margarita llega al bar a las 9:00.	☐	☐
ii Pide un vaso de sangría.	☐	☐
iii Leonardo y Livia no están en el bar.	☐	☐
iv Margarita habla con Salvador.	☐	☐
v Margarita no va a salir con Salvador.	☐	☐

e Margarita y Salvador salen de compras. ¿Qué compran?

f Leonardo y Livia han ganado la lotería. ¿Cuánto van a dar a cada persona?

i La madre de Leonardo _____ €

ii El padre de Leonardo _____ €

iii La hermana de Leonardo _____ €

iv El hermano de Leonardo _____ €

v Los hermanos de Livia _____ €

vi Los padres de Livia _____ €

g Livia has changed her plans. Take her part in the conversation at a car showroom. Speak after the prompts.

rápido	fast	**aire acondicionado**	air conditioning
reproductor de CDs	CD player	**cierre centralizado**	central locking
altavoces	loudspeakers		

h Al día siguiente Leonardo recibe una carta de Livia. ¿Qué dice?

Queridísimo Leo:

Mañana voy a ir a Palm Springs con César, el vendedor de coches. Vamos a casarnos en Las Vegas.

Hasta luego; un abrazo

Livia

6 En la ciudad

1 El plano de la ciudad

a Coloca los edificios en el plano.

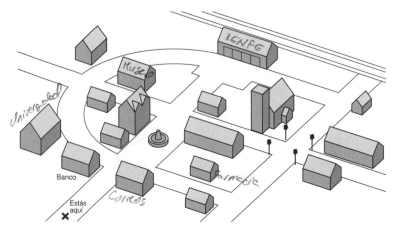

b Give the locations of the buildings on the map above, speaking in the pauses. You will hear the correct answer after each pause on the recording.

2 ¿Dónde están?

Place the buildings on the plan by putting **A**, **B**, **C** etc where you think they go.

La academia **A** está en la esquina derecha.
El banco **B** está entre la academia y el cine **C**.
El cine está enfrente del polideportivo **D**.
El polideportivo está al lado de la estación **E** en la esquina.
La farmacia **F** está entre la estación y la galería de arte **G**.
El hospital **H** está entre el polideportivo y la iglesia **I**.
La iglesia **I** está a mano izquierda.

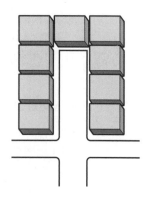

3 ¿A qué distancia?

How far away are these places in your own town from each other?
Escribe tres frases. Por ejemplo:

La comisaría está a 10 minutos andando del parque.

a Police Station/Park
b Hospital/Sports Centre
c Bank/Shopping Centre
d Cinema/University

4 Ve por la calle Ferrán

a Using the map below, give the directions requested, from the Arco Youth Hostel (**albergue**).

Speak after the prompts.

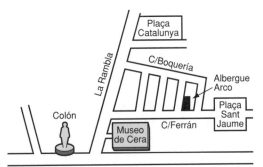

Plaça Catalunya

C/Boquería

La Rambla

Albergue Arco

Colón

Plaça Sant Jaume

Museo de Cera

C/Ferrán

> **Al salir del edificio**
> On leaving the building

b Using the map above, write directions to the **Albergue Arco** from the following places:

i The Plaça Sant Jaume
ii The Plaça Catalunya
iii The Wax Museum (**el museo de cera**)

5 El consultorio de Tía María

Match the questions to the answers on this problem page.

Querida Tía María ...

1 Todos los días son iguales. Voy a la universidad por la mañana, salgo con mis amigos por la tarde, bebo demasiado y fumo sesenta cigarrillos al día. Me aburro. ¿Qué puedo hacer?

2 Mi novia bebe y fuma y no hace ejercicio. Tampoco va a la universidad. Me preocupo por ella. ¿Cómo puedo ayudarla?

3 Mi novio nunca quiere pagar la cuenta cuando estamos en un restaurante. ¡Pero yo no soy rica, y no puedo pagarlo todo! ¿Qué puedo hacer?

4 Trabajo en un bar para pagar mi curso, pero no me gusta el trabajo, y no tengo tiempo para estudiar. ¿Qué puedo hacer?

Tía María dice ...

a Busca otro trabajo.
b Busca otro novio.
c Habla con ella. Pregúntale por qué bebe y fuma tanto y no quiere estudiar.
d Es muy fácil. Busca otros amigos, deja de beber y de fumar y practica un deporte de riesgo como el puenting.

7 En el futuro

1 El horóscopo

Rellena los huecos con las palabras del recuadro.

a Acuario   Conocerás a la _____ de tus sueños.
b Piscis   Los _____ te aportarán buena fortuna.
c Aries   Tu _____ te traicionará.
d Tauro   Ganarás mucho _____ .
e Géminis   Viajarás a un país _____ .
f Cáncer   Tendrás un nuevo _____ .

empleo
amante
dinero
extranjero
números 5 y 10
persona

2 En el año 2020

Write down three of your own predictions for the year 2020.
For example:
Tendré un buen trabajo y ganaré mucho dinero.
Viviré en una granja en el sur de Francia con dos caballos y un perro.
Hablaré cinco idiomas y seré un intérprete importante para la ONU … etc

3 En el aeropuerto

Señor Alberti wants to change his flight. **Escribe los detalles.**

	FECHA	VUELO	DESTINO	SALIDA	LLEGADA
Change from:					
Change to:					

4 En la sala de embarque

¿Qué hará Susana en sus vacaciones? Marca la casilla correcta.

	Verdadero	Falso
a «Iré a los Estados Unidos.»	☐	☐
b «Trabajaré en Colombia en el verano.»	☐	☐
c «Después viajaré un poco por América.»	☐	☐
d «Me quedaré en Macedonia.»	☐	☐
e «Luego iré a casarme con un amigo en Miami.»	☐	☐
f «Iré en octubre.»	☐	☐

5 ¡Buen viaje!

Write an answer to this e-mail from Claudio. Tell him you can't come with him because you have to work. Tell him about one other thing you expect to do this weekend, and say you will see him next week.

```
¡Hola!

Este fin de semana voy a salir al campo - ¿quieres venir?

Iré con unos amigos y vamos a acampar, pero la primera noche nos quedaremos en
un hostal barato. Iremos en bicicleta, porque es más agradable y menos caro que
ir en coche. Es más saludable también. Volveremos el domingo, por la noche.

Espero que puedas venir. De todas formas, te veré la semana que viene. ¡Qué
pases un buen fin de semana!

Hasta luego,

Claudio
```

6 En mis vacaciones

Answer your friend's questions about what you'll do in the holidays.

7 El problema del tráfico

Which of the following points of view best reflects your own views on the traffic problem?

a Hay demasiado tráfico y produce mucha contaminación. Ir en bicicleta o en autobús es mucho más ecológico. Para solucionar el problema de la contaminación, hay que mejorar el transporte público y prohibir los coches en la ciudad.

b No tenemos ningún problema con la contaminación y el calentamiento global. Cada persona tiene derecho a viajar como quiera. Hay que construir más carreteras y bajar el precio de la gasolina.

8 Las predicciones de Vostradamus

a Vostradamus is the lesser known brother of the famous Nostradamus. He also made predictions about the future, but they were less successful. Rewrite what he got wrong.

En el siglo XXI los seres humanos volarán por el aire en barcos, y cruzarán el mar en bicicletas. Viajarán por tierra en submarinos. Cada día irán al trabajo a caballo. Será posible viajar alrededor del mundo en menos de un minuto.

b Write down two or three predictions of your own for 22nd century modes of transport.

En el siglo XXII los seres humanos ...

8 Trabajo de verano

1 Solicitando trabajo

You have seen an advert for an assistant (**un ayudante**) at a language school. Ring the school to apply for the job. Speak after the prompts.

2 ¿Cómo es el trabajador más buscado?

Dinámico, comunicativo, seguro de sí mismo, resolutivo, con conocimientos de informática y dominio de, al menos, un segundo idioma. Así es el trabajador que piden actualmente las empresas. Y es que, hoy en día, la actitud hacia el trabajo es tanto o más importante que la formación.

Fuente: *Quo Núm 37 (adapted)*

a Which of the six most sought after qualities above do you have?

b What is as important as training nowadays?

3 Las cualidades más valoradas

a If you were an employer, which of the qualities below would you look for in a prospective employee? Rank them in order of importance.

i	Facilidad para trabajar en equipo	**vii**	Deseo de aprender
ii	Adaptación a la cultura de la empresa	**viii**	Capacidad de trabajo
iii	Tolerancia al fracaso	**ix**	Flexibilidad
iv	Vida personal equilibrada	**x**	Iniciativa
v	Capacidad de comunicación	**xi**	Resolución
vi	Confianza personal		

b Listen to the employer talking about some of the above qualities and tick the ones he mentions.

4 La solicitud de trabajo

Rellena esta solicitud para el puesto vacante en la academia de idiomas.

NOMBRE	APELLIDOS
DOMICILIO ACTUAL	
EDAD	ESTADO CIVIL
EDUCACIÓN (CON FECHAS)	
EXPERIENCIA PROFESIONAL (CON FECHAS)	

5 ¿Quién puede ayudarme?

You are working in a hotel. Who will you call to sort out the guests' problems? Match the problem to the person who can help.

No se preocupe, señor/a. Llamaré …

1 El ascensor no funciona.
2 El wáter está atascado.
3 No hay papel higiénico en el baño.
4 No puedo cerrar la ventana.
5 ¡Me han robado!

a al fontanero.
b al ingeniero.
c al portero.
d a la policía.
e al servicio de habitaciones.

6 Cómo quejarse en el trabajo

There are always several ways of voicing a complaint. Choose the better option.

a 1 La fotocopiadora no funciona y no he podido hacer el trabajo.
  2 Voy a llamar al técnico, a ver si puede reparar la fotocopiadora.
b 1 Antonio y yo tenemos el mismo trabajo, pero él cobra más que yo.
  2 Yo trabajo mucho más que Javi (que es muy vago) pero él cobra más que yo.
c 1 Esta semana he trabajado 15 horas, pero me has pagado sólo 12.
  2 ¿Por qué me has pagado sólo 12 horas cuando he trabajado 15?
d 1 No voy a hacer todas estas horas extras. Busca a otra persona.
  2 No quiero hacer las horas extras, pero las haré.
  3 No puedo hacer todas las horas extras pero haré dos o tres para ayudarte.

7 Todo sobre mi trabajo

a Rewrite the letter shown on the right, with everything as a negative experience.

For example:

He empezado el trabajo y no me gusta nada.

b Describe your holiday job in a letter to a friend. Mention the following:
  – the hours you work
  – your duties
  – the advantages and disadvantages of the job
  – whether you like it or not, and why.

> Querida Lucía
>
> He empezado el trabajo y me gusta mucho. Empiezo muy temprano por la mañana y termino tarde, pero el trabajo es interesante y variado. Me llevo muy bien con mis colegas y mis jefes, y me gusta conocer a los clientes. No pagan muy bien pero ha sido una experiencia muy buena y he podido practicar el español.
>
> ¿Qué tal tu trabajo?
>
> Escríbeme pronto.
>
> Un abrazo de
>
> Lucinda

aburrido boring
siempre igual always the same

¿Dónde estuviste ayer?

1 ¿Qué tal las vacaciones?

Ordena las frases.

> Tomé el sol, me bañé en el mar
> Volví a la playa por la tarde,
> Pasé toda la mañana en la playa.
> Y al mediodía fui a comer a un restaurante.
> Y pasé el resto de la semana en la cama.
> Sin embargo, al día siguiente cogí una insolación,
> Y salí a una discoteca por la noche.
> Llegué a Mojácar a las siete de la mañana
> Y fui directo al apartamento.

2 ¡Qué desastre!

¿Mariví, Nicolás o Manolo?

Escucha y coloca el nombre en el espacio.

¿Quién –

a olvidó su bolso en el taxi? _Mariví_

b dejó sus llaves en la habitación? _____

c se puso enfermo después de comer gambas? _____

d perdió el avión y el tren? _____

e llegó tarde al espectáculo? _____

f vomitó en la cama? _____

3 Has estado de vacaciones

Escucha y contesta a las preguntas sobre tus vacaciones.

4 Mándame una postal

Write a postcard to a Spanish friend from your holiday in Spain. Include the following information:

a Say you arrived yesterday evening at 7.30 and you went straight to your apartment.

b Say you had a meal in a restaurant and spent the rest of the evening in a bar.

c This morning you went to the beach and had lunch in a café.

d You returned to the beach in the afternoon and swam in the sea.

e Now you are in your apartment, about to go out.

5 Cuestionario europeo

¿Qué sabes de la Unión Europea?

1 ¿En 1946 quién propuso la creación de los Estados Unidos de Europa?
  A El norteamericano Woodrow Wilson
  B El británico Winston Churchill
  C El alemán Karl Marx

2 ¿El tratado de Roma se firmó en qué año?
  A 1967
  B 1977
  C 1957

3 ¿Cuál es el país que tiene menos habitantes en la Unión Europea?
  A Malta
  B España
  C Bélgica

4 ¿Quién no volvió a las negociaciones de Luxemburgo en 1966?
  A Konrad Adenauer
  B Harold Wilson
  C Charles de Gaulle

5 ¿Dónde está el Tribunal Europeo de Justicia?
  A Maastricht
  B Luxemburgo
  C La Haya

6 ¿Cuántos miembros hay en el Parlamento Europeo?
  A 500
  B 732
  C 824

Respuestas:
1B 2C 3A
4C (thus provoking the 'Crisis of the empty Chair')
5C 6B

Repaso

 1 Jóvenes dependientes

Rank the reasons given why young Spanish people prefer to live at home, according to which you think are the most and least common. See if you were right by looking at the Answers and fill in the percentages.

España es uno de los países de la Unión Europea donde mayor porcentaje de jóvenes menores de 24 años vive con sus padres, según la Comisión Europea. ¿Por qué tardan tanto en independizarse?

	%
La vivienda es cara.	____
Prefieren las comodidades sin responsabilidades.	____
Los padres no son muy estrictos.	____
Los jóvenes se casan más tarde.	____
No tienen posibilidades de independizarse antes.	____
Los padres necesitan la ayuda económica de los hijos.	____
Quieren tener una situación estable antes de vivir solos.	____

[Adapted from *Quo* No 47, source: 'Young Europeans', European Commission 1997.]

 2 La independencia cuesta cara

¿Cuáles son los gastos mensuales de alquilar un piso en España? Escucha y rellena los espacios.

GASTOS MENSUALES

Alquiler	____ €			
Luz	____ €	Gas (sin calefacción): natural	____ €	
Agua	____ €	Butano	____ €	
Teléfono	____ €	Calefacción (de gas natural)	____ €	
Comunidad de vecinos:		sin servicios (ascensor, calefacción)	____ €	
		con servicios	____ €	

El alquiler varía desde ____ € a ____ €. Es más caro en Cataluña, el País Vasco y Madrid y menos caro en Huelva, Cáceres y Huesca. Además, en España cuando alquilas un piso tienes que pagar el primer mes de alquiler y también una fianza de ____ € a ____ €.

[Adapted from *Quo* No 47, several sources.]

3 Dos personajes históricos

Dolores Ibarruri
Hija y esposa de mineros, la dirigente comunista nació en 1895 en Bilbao. Participó en la lucha obrera desde muy joven, mostrando una gran capacidad oratoria. Salió de España durante la guerra civil y continuó su actividad política en el exilio. Volvió en 1977.

Montezuma
Nació en 1480 y fue gobernante del imperio Azteca en México. Cuando llegó Hernán Cortés en 1519, creyó que era el dios Quetzalcoatl. Cortés lo tomó como rehén. Cuando los aztecas se sublevaron en 1520, Montezuma intentó apaciguarlos, pero murió apedreado.

Contesta a las preguntas en inglés.

a Where was the Aztec empire?
b Where was the communist leader born?
c Who was politically active from a young age?
d Who fought on the side of the workers?
e Who was a great speaker?
f Who thought Cortés was a god?
g Who was taken hostage?
h Who was exiled from Spain?
i Who tried to calm the Aztec revolt?
j Who was stoned to death?

4 ¿Qué sabes de la historia española?

1 ¿Cuántos años duró la ocupación romana en España?
   A 200 años
   B 400 años
   C 600 años

2 ¿Cuántos años duró la ocupación árabe en España?
   A 400 años
   B 600 años
   C 800 años

3 ¿Qué pasó en 1492?
   A Los moros fueron vencidos en Granada.
   B Los judíos fueron expulsados de España.
   C Cristóbal Colón viajó a las Américas.

4 ¿Qué pasó en 1808?
   A Napoleón invadió España.
   B Los británicos tomaron Gibraltar.
   C Se abolió la Inquisición

Clave
1 B 3 A, B & C
2 C 4 A

GUIDE TO GRAMMATICAL TERMS

Language learners often feel unsure about grammatical terms. The following list gives some simple definitions. Examples are underlined; terms used which are defined elsewhere in the list are given in bold. Examples are drawn from English: reference is made to Spanish only when something distinctive about that language needs to be noted. This Guide is concerned only with the meanings of grammatical terms: there is a Spanish Grammar Summary beginning on page 146.

Adjective   A word used to describe a **noun** ("an <u>interesting</u> woman"; "the curry is <u>hot</u>"). See also **demonstrative adjective**, **possessive adjective**.

Adverb   A word which describes the action of a **verb** ("She sings <u>beautifully</u>", "He cooks <u>well</u>") or modifies (= gives further information about) an adjective ("It's a <u>really</u> expensive car") or another adverb ("She sings <u>really</u> well").

Agree   In English, **adjectives** don't change their form but in Spanish they have to agree with the noun they are describing in **gender** and **number**: if the noun is feminine, the adjective must be in the feminine form, if the noun is plural, so is the adjective.

Article   <u>The</u> (called the definite article), <u>a</u> or <u>an</u> (the indefinite article).

Auxiliary verb   A **verb** combining with another verb to form a **compound tense**. ("She <u>has</u> gone" = auxiliary verb "to have" here used to form the Perfect tense by combining with the **past participle** of the verb "to go".)

Comparative   Form of an **adjective** ("That room is <u>bigger</u> than this one"; "They've bought a <u>more expensive</u> car") or **adverb** ("She sings <u>more beautifully</u> than I do") expressing a greater degree.

Compound tense   A **tense** formed by combining an **auxiliary verb** with another verb. For example the future tense ("He <u>will see</u> you next week" – auxiliary verb "will" combined with the **infinitive** "see"), the perfect tense ("We <u>have</u> already <u>seen</u> him" – auxiliary verb "Have" combined with the **past participle** "seen").

Conjunction   A word which joins parts of a sentence ("He was tired <u>and</u> he wanted to go home"; "They arrived early <u>because</u> they wanted a good place").

Demonstrative adjective   These "point out" **nouns** (<u>this</u> chair/<u>these</u> chairs; <u>that</u> house/<u>those</u> houses).

Direct object   The word which directly undergoes the action of the verb. In the sentence "She sent her mother a present", what she sent was a present, so that is the direct object. She didn't send her mother! See also **indirect object**.

Gender   In Spanish, all **nouns** have a grammatical **gender**, masculine or feminine, and **adjectives** have to **agree**.

Imperative   Verb form used in giving commands and instructions ("<u>Turn</u> left now!").

Indirect object   A secondary **object**. In the sentence "She sent her mother a present", the **direct object**, the thing which is sent, is the present. It was sent to her mother, the indirect object.

Intransitive verb   Verb that doesn't take a **direct object**, e.g. "to arrive" ("She <u>arrived</u> at one o'clock").

Infinitive   The basic form of a **verb** ("<u>to sing</u>"; "<u>to write</u>").

Irregular verb   **Verb** that varies from the standard pattern.

Noun   Word denoting a person ("<u>student</u>"), thing ("<u>book</u>") or abstract idea ("<u>happiness</u>").

Number   Whether a word is **singular** or **plural**.

Object   The **noun** or **pronoun** which undergoes the action of the verb. "We bought a <u>house</u>"; "I saw <u>him</u>."

Object pronoun   **Pronoun** used when it's the **object** of the **verb**. <u>Me, you, him, her, it, us, them</u>.

Past participle   Part of the **verb** which combines with an **auxiliary verb** to form the Perfect tense ("they have <u>arrived</u>"; "I have <u>seen</u>").

Plural   More than one: the plural of "man" is "<u>men</u>".

Possessive adjective   e.g. "<u>my</u> house", "<u>your</u> friend", "<u>his</u> car" etc.

Preposition   e.g. "<u>on</u> the table"," <u>under</u> the chair", "<u>to</u> the station", "<u>for</u> the teacher" etc.

Pronoun   Word taking the place of a **noun**. "Peter saw the waitress" becomes "<u>He</u> saw <u>her</u>."

Reflexive verb   In Spanish, a **verb** formed with an extra pronoun (called a reflexive pronoun). E.g. llamar<u>se</u> (to be called, literally "to call oneself"): <u>me</u> llamo Carlos (I'm called/my name is Carlos, literally "I call myself Carlos"); <u>se</u> llama Ana (she's called Ana).

Regular verb   **Verb** that follows a standard pattern.

Relative pronoun   **Pronoun** used to refer back to a noun earlier in the sentence. e.g. "The man <u>who</u> lives there is very old"; "The book <u>which</u> he chose …"; "The woman/film <u>that</u> he saw…".

Singular   One rather than many: the singular of "bananas" is "<u>banana</u>".

Subject   Who or what carries out the action of the **verb**. "A <u>student</u> sent me this email."; "<u>We</u> are travelling next week."; "The <u>letter</u> arrived yesterday".

Subject pronoun   **Pronoun** used when it's the **subject** of the **verb**: <u>I, you, he, she, it, we, they</u>.

Transitive verb   **Verb** which takes a direct object, unlike an **intransitive verb**, which doesn't e.g. "to catch" ("She <u>caught</u> a train").

Tense   Form taken by a **verb** to show when the action takes place. e.g. Present tense: "They <u>live</u> in New York"; Past tense: "They <u>lived</u> in New York"; Future tense: "They <u>will live</u> in New York" etc.

Verb   Word indicating an action ("They <u>ate</u> their dinner") or state ("The book <u>lay</u> on the table"). Different **tenses** are used to show when something happened.
See also **auxiliary verb**, **intransitive verb**, **irregular verb**, **reflexive verb**, **regular verb**, **transitive verb**.

GRAMMAR SUMMARY

The alphabet

There used to be 30 letters in the Spanish alphabet, and in some old dictionaries you will find the four 'extra' ones – **ch**, **ll**, **ñ**, and **rr** – listed in separate sections. Thus **chico** will be found under **ch**, not **c**. However, now the only 'extra' letter is **ñ** – so in new dictionaries **chico** is found under **c** and **llegar** is found under **l**.

There are five **vowels** in Spanish, as in English. They are **a**, **e**, **i**, **o** and **u**, and they only have one sound each. All the other letters are called **consonants**.

El alfabeto									
A	B	C	D	E	F	G	H	I	J
K	L	M	N	Ñ	O	P	Q	R	S
T	U	V	W	X	Y	Z			

Nouns and articles

A noun is the grammatical term for a thing, person, place, animal, event or idea. All nouns have a gender in Spanish. That is, they are either masculine or feminine. Masculine nouns frequently end in **-o** and feminine ones in **-a**:

    un pis<u>o</u> (masculine)   a flat   **una cas<u>a</u>** (feminine)   a house

As in English, they also have a number, singular or plural:

    <u>un</u> piso (singular)   <u>a</u> flat   **<u>unos</u> pisos** (plural)   <u>some</u> flats
    <u>una</u> casa   <u>a</u> house   **<u>unas</u> casas**   <u>some</u> houses

In Spanish articles have the same number and gender as the noun. Thus **el**, **la**, **los** and **las** all mean 'the'; **un** and **una** both mean 'a'; **unos** and **unas** mean 'some':

Gender   Number

                    singular   plural

masculine	**<u>el</u> libro**	<u>the</u> book	**<u>los</u> libros**	<u>the</u> books
feminine	**<u>la</u> novel<u>a</u>**	<u>the</u> novel	**<u>las</u> novel<u>as</u>**	<u>the</u> novels
masculine	**<u>un</u> colegi<u>o</u>**	<u>a</u> college	**<u>unos</u> colegios**	<u>some</u> colleges
feminine	**<u>una</u> escuel<u>a</u>**	<u>a</u> school	**<u>unas</u> escuel<u>as</u>**	<u>some</u> schools

Some nouns end in other letters, so the only way you can tell what gender they are is by looking at the article. Thus **<u>la</u> calle** is feminine; **<u>el</u> restaurante** is masculine. Others may end in **-a** and be masculine, or end in **-o** and be feminine: **<u>la</u> mano** is feminine; **<u>el</u> día** is masculine.

Adjectives

Adjectives describe nouns and they have to 'agree' in number and gender with the nouns they are describing. Most adjectives go after the noun in Spanish.
Many Spanish adjectives end in **-o**, like **moderno**:

	masculine	feminine
singular	**un** pis**o** modern**o** a modern flat	**una** cas**a** modern**a** a modern house
plural	**unos** pis**os** modern**os** some modern flats	**unas** cas**as** modern**as** some modern houses

Other adjectives end in **-e**, like **grande**. These have only two forms – singular and plural:

	masculine	feminine
singular	**un** pis**o** grande a big flat	**una** cas**a** grande a big house
plural	**unos** pis**os** grande**s** some big flats	**unas** cas**as** grande**s** some big houses

Adjectives such as **popular**, which end in a consonant, often have only two forms. To form the plural, **-es** is added:

	masculine	feminine
singular	**un libro popular** a popular book	**una novela popular** a popular novel
plural	**unos libros popular_es_** some popular books	**unas novelas popular_es_** some popular novels

Possessive adjectives

You can use possessive adjectives to indicate who owns the noun. **Mi** (my), **tu** (your) and **su** (his, her, their, your*) have only two forms, singular and plural:

One thing owned		More than one thing owned	
mi coche	my car	**mis coches**	my cars
tu coche	your car	**tus coches**	your cars
su coche	his car, her car, their car, your* car	**sus coches**	his cars, her cars their cars, your* cars

*formal

Nuestro (our) and **vuestro** (your) have four forms:

One thing owned		More than one thing owned	
nuestro libro	our book	**nuestros libros**	our books
nuestra novela	our novel	**nuestras novelas**	our novels

Demonstrative adjectives

These are used to specify a particular object or person, and they have four forms:

	masculine		feminine	
singular	**este libro**	<u>this</u> book	**esta novela**	<u>this</u> novel
plural	**estos libros**	<u>these</u> books	**estas novelas**	<u>these</u> novels

Comparative of adjectives

El coche es <u>más</u> caro <u>que</u> la bici.	The car is <u>more</u> expensive <u>than</u> the bike.
La bici es <u>menos</u> cara <u>que</u> el coche.	The bike is <u>less</u> expensive <u>than</u> the car.
El tren es <u>tan</u> caro <u>como</u> el coche.	The train is <u>as</u> expensive <u>as</u> the car.

¿Cuánto?

When **¿Cuánto?** is used as an adjective (when it comes before a noun), it has four forms:

¿Cuán<u>to</u> tiem<u>po</u> tienes?	How much time do you have?
¿Cuán<u>ta</u> so<u>pa</u> quieres?	How much soup do you want?
¿Cuán<u>tos</u> herman<u>os</u> tienes?	How many brothers do you have?
¿Cuán<u>tas</u> herman<u>as</u> tienes?	How many sisters do you have?

But when you are asking the price of something, **¿Cuánto?** doesn't change:

¿Cuánto es la falda?	How much is the skirt?
¿Cuánto son los zapatos?	How much are the shoes?

Questions

To ask a question you can use a verb. Note that verbs can be both questions and statements:

Vive en Málaga.	He lives in Málaga.
¿Vive en Málaga?	Does he live in Málaga?

You can also use question words and verbs:

¿<u>Quién</u> eres?	Who are you?
¿<u>Cómo</u> estás?	How are you?
¿<u>Dónde</u> vives?	Where do you live?
¿<u>Qué</u> haces?	What do you do?
¿<u>Adónde</u> vas?	Where do you go (to)?
¿<u>Cuál</u> es?	Which is it?
¿<u>Cuándo</u> empieza?	When does it start?

Pronouns

A pronoun can be used in place of a noun, often to avoid repetition:

John went to the supermarket where John bought some wine.

John went to the supermarket where <u>he</u> bought some wine.

'He' is a pronoun.

Subject pronouns

Singular		**Plural**	
yo	I	**nosotros**	we (all male or male and female)
tú	you	**nosotras**	we (all female)
él/ella	he/she	**vosotros**	you (all male or male and female)
usted*	you	**vosotras**	you (all female)
		ellos/ellas	they (male/female)
		ustedes*	you

*Also written **Vd./Vds.**

You

There are five words for 'you' in Spanish. The one you use depends on whether you are being formal or friendly, how many people you are talking to and what sex they are:

Informal

tú	for when you are addressing one person
vosotros*	for when you are addressing more than one person, and they are all male, or male and female
vosotras*	for when you are addressing more than one person, and they are all female

Formal

usted	for when you are addressing one person
ustedes	for when you are addressing more than one person

*In Spain only. In Latin America different forms are used.

Tú and **vosotros** are generally used when speaking to people you know by their first names – young people, members of your family, neighbours, teachers. **Usted** and **ustedes** are for people you would normally address by their title, (Mr or Mrs, Dr, Professor), or to whom you wish to show particular respect. If you are a young person you will be addressed as **tú** in almost all situations, including in shops and most interviews. To use **usted**, even to a friend's parents (if they are youngish), can be seen as being standoffish. However, to use **tú** can be seen as being rude, so it is best to start with **usted** when addressing someone you don't know well who is of retirement age or older. They will let you know if they want you to use **tú**.

Subject pronouns are often omitted in Spanish, because in most cases the verb endings make it clear who is performing the action:

Viv<u>o</u> en Ecuador	can only mean	<u>I</u> live in Ecuador.
Tien<u>es</u> dos hermanas	can only mean	<u>You</u> have two sisters.

But

Viv<u>e</u> en Ecuador	can mean	<u>He</u> or <u>She</u> lives in Ecuador.
	or	<u>You</u> live in Ecuador (formal).

Thus the subject pronoun can be used to avoid misunderstandings, or for emphasis:

Juan y María fueron a la playa. <u>Él</u> se bañó y <u>ella</u> tomó el sol.

Juan and María went to the beach. <u>He</u> bathed in the sea and <u>she</u> sunbathed.

Object pronouns

The object of a verb can be described as the 'recipient' of the action.

She sees the boy.	'The boy' is the object.
She sees him.	'Him' is the object pronoun, often used to avoid repetition.
She gives the book to the boy.	'The book' is the direct object and 'the boy' is the indirect object.
She gives it to him.	'It' is the direct object pronoun and 'him' is the indirect object pronoun in this sentence.

In this course you have seen these object pronouns:

me	**te**	**le, lo**	**la**	**los, las**
(to) me	(to) you	(to) him/it	(to) her/it	(to) them

di<u>me</u> la verdad	tell <u>me</u> the truth	**<u>lo</u> he visto**	I have seen <u>it</u>

Verbs

A verb can indicate the action, mental or physical, in a sentence. Verbs are often used to say someone <u>does</u> (has done, did, will do etc) something. They are also used to express a condition or state: he <u>is</u>, she <u>seems</u>, and so on.

All Spanish verbs belong to one of three groups, depending on whether the infinitives end in **-ar**, **-er** or **-ir**: **estudi<u>ar</u>** (to study), **aprend<u>er</u>** (to learn), **viv<u>ir</u>** (to live). The form of the verb changes according to <u>who</u> or <u>what</u> is the subject (often the person doing the action) and <u>when</u> the action is being performed (in the past, present or future). Most of the verbs within each of the three groups are regular, that is their endings change in the same way, but there are many irregular verbs.

Present tense

Verbs in the present form are often used to express generalities and to describe habitual actions: It *rains* in Spain; He *goes* to work; She *gets* up at seven (every day).

	-AR		**-ER**		**-IR**	
subject pronoun	**estudi<u>ar</u>**	to study	**aprend<u>er</u>**	to learn	**viv<u>ir</u>**	to live
yo	**estudi<u>o</u>**	I study	**aprend<u>o</u>**	I learn	**viv<u>o</u>**	I live
tú	**estudi<u>as</u>**	you study	**aprend<u>es</u>**	you learn	**viv<u>es</u>**	you live
él, ella, usted	**estudi<u>a</u>**	s/he studies you study	**aprend<u>e</u>**	s/he learns you learn	**viv<u>e</u>**	s/he lives you live
nosotros/as	**estudi<u>amos</u>**	we study	**aprend<u>emos</u>**	we learn	**viv<u>imos</u>**	we live
vosotros/as	**estudi<u>áis</u>**	you study	**aprend<u>éis</u>**	you learn	**viv<u>ís</u>**	you live
ellos, ellas ustedes	**estudi<u>an</u>**	they study you study	**aprend<u>en</u>**	they learn you learn	**viv<u>en</u>**	they live you live

Two irregular verbs in the present

ser	to be			**ir**	to go		
soy	I am	**somos**	we are	**voy**	I go	**vamos**	we go
eres	you are	**sois**	you are	**vas**	you go	**vais**	you go
es	s/he is	**son**	they are	**va**	s/he goes	**van**	they go
	you are		you are		you go		you go

Some verbs are irregular in the **yo** (I) form of the present:

estar (to be) **estoy** (I am)
hacer (to do) **hago** (I do)

Verb tables can be found in most dictionaries.

Ser and estar

Ser and **estar** both mean 'to be', but they work in different ways. **Ser** is often used when you want to express something that never changes, while **estar** is for temporary states or conditions. Study their different uses.

Ser is always used in the following situations:

– with an adjective for describing unchanging traits or characteristics:
  Soy alta y morena.   I am (and always will be) tall and dark.

– with a noun for identifying someone or something:
  Es una casa.   It is a house.

– to express nationality and origin:
  Soy de Nigeria; soy nigeriana.   I am from Nigeria; I am Nigerian.

– to show possession:
  Es mi coche. Es el coche de Juan.   It is my car. It's Juan's car.

– for telling the time:
  Es la una; son las dos.   It's one o'clock; it's two o'clock.

Estar is always used in the following situations:

– to express location:
  Está a la izquierda.   It's on the left.

– to discuss health:
  ¿Cómo estás? Estoy bien.   How are you? I am well.

– with an adjective for describing a (usually temporary) state or condition:
  Estoy cansado.   I am tired.

Note that in Spanish other verbs are sometimes used where 'to be' is used in English:

Tener (to have)	**Tengo 20 años.**	<u>I am</u> 20 years old.
Haber (to have)	**Hay un libro en la mesa.**	<u>There is</u> a book on the table.
	Hay dos libros en la mesa.	<u>There are</u> two books on the table.

Reflexive verbs

Reflexive verbs have the normal **-ar**, **-er** or **-ir** endings, but also have a reflexive pronoun to indicate that the person is doing something <u>to</u>, <u>by</u> or <u>for</u> him/herself. These are **me** (myself), **te** (yourself), **se** (himself/herself/yourself), **nos** (ourselves), **os** (yourselves), and **se** (themselves/yourselves):

llamar<u>se</u>   to be called (literally to call oneself)

<u>me</u> llam<u>o</u>	I am called (I call myself)	**<u>nos</u> llam<u>amos</u>**	we are called
<u>te</u> llam<u>as</u>	you are called	**<u>os</u> llam<u>áis</u>**	you are called
<u>se</u> llam<u>a</u>	s/he is called; you are called	**<u>se</u> llam<u>an</u>**	they/you are called

Root-changing verbs

The root of a verb is the part before the **-ar**, **-er** or **-ir** ending. Root-changing verbs have the normal endings, but a vowel in the root of the verb also changes in most of the verb forms in the present. They do <u>not</u> change in the **nosotros** and **vosotros** forms. These changes are:

e to **ie** (qu<u>e</u>rer, t<u>e</u>ner, v<u>e</u>nir, s<u>e</u>ntarse)   **e** to **i** (d<u>e</u>cir, p<u>e</u>dir)

o to **ue** (p<u>o</u>der, alm<u>o</u>rzar, ac<u>o</u>starse)   **u** to **ue** (j<u>u</u>gar – the only verb in this group)

querer	to want	**poder**	to be able to	**pedir**	to ask for
qu<u>ie</u>ro	I want	**p<u>ue</u>do**	I can	**p<u>i</u>do**	I ask for
qu<u>ie</u>res	you want	**p<u>ue</u>des**	you can	**p<u>i</u>des**	you ask for
qu<u>ie</u>re	s/he wants	**p<u>ue</u>de**	s/he can	**p<u>i</u>de**	s/he asks for
	you want		you can		
queremos	we want	**podemos**	we can	**pedimos**	we ask for
queréis	you want	**podéis**	you can	**pedís**	you ask for
qu<u>ie</u>ren	they/you want	**p<u>ue</u>den**	they/you can	**p<u>i</u>den**	they/you ask for

Tener, **venir** and **decir** are root-changing verbs which are also irregular in the **yo** form: **tengo** (I have); **vengo** (I come); **digo** (I say). Some verbs are reflexive and root-changing: **s<u>e</u>ntarse** (to sit down): **<u>me</u> s<u>ie</u>nto** etc; **ac<u>o</u>starse** (to go to bed): **<u>me</u> ac<u>ue</u>sto** etc

Present continuous

The present continuous is used to describe an action that is in progress at a particular moment: What <u>are</u> you do<u>ing</u>? I <u>am</u> writ<u>ing</u> a letter. It is formed with part of **estar** and the present participle or gerund (say<u>ing</u>, do<u>ing</u>):

estar + present participle   present participle

estoy lleg<u>ando</u>	I <u>am</u> arriv<u>ing</u>	**-ar** verbs:	
estás beb<u>iendo</u>	you <u>are</u> drink<u>ing</u>	**llegar:**	**lleg<u>ando</u>**
está sal<u>iendo</u>	s/he <u>is</u> leav<u>ing</u>	**-er** verbs:	
	you <u>are</u> leav<u>ing</u>	**beber:**	**beb<u>iendo</u>**
estamos habl<u>ando</u>	we <u>are</u> speak<u>ing</u>	**-ir** verbs:	
estáis com<u>iendo</u>	you <u>are</u> eat<u>ing</u>	**salir:**	**sal<u>iendo</u>**
están escrib<u>iendo</u>	they <u>are</u> writ<u>ing</u>		
	you <u>are</u> writ<u>ing</u>		

Talking about the future

There are three ways of expressing the future in Spanish. They are often interchangeable.

1 Present tense – for scheduled events:
El tren <u>sale</u> a las 3. The train leaves at 3.

2 'Going to' (**Ir a** + infinitive) – for plans and intentions:
<u>Voy a salir</u> a las 3.   I'm going to leave at 3.

3 Future tense – for predictions and intentions:
Sald<u>ré</u> a las 3.   I'll leave at 3.

Present tense

The present is used as in English for scheduled events: 'The shop opens at 6'; 'The plane arrives at 8', and so on. See above for the verb forms.

Going to …

Use part of the verb **ir** (*to go*) + **a** + infinitive to say what you are <u>going</u> to do:

voy a ver	I'm going to see	**vamos a llegar**	we're going to arrive
vas a salir	you're going to leave	**vais a viajar**	you're going to travel
va a volver	s/he's going to return	**van a venir**	they're going to come

With a reflexive verb the pronoun often goes on the end:
voy a quedar<u>me</u> I'm going to stay; **vas a levantar<u>te</u>** you're going to get up, etc

Future tense

Add the endings **-é, -ás, -á, -emos, -éis, -án** to the infinitive:

llegaré	I will arrive	**llegaremos**	we will arrive
llegarás	you will arrive	**llegaréis**	you will arrive
llegará	s/he/you will arrive	**llegarán**	they/you will arrive

Irregular verbs have the same endings, but the root of the verb changes:

salir	to leave:	**sald<u>ré</u>, saldrás**	I//you you will leave, etc
tener	to have:	**tend<u>ré</u>, tendrás**	I//you you will leave, etc
poder	to be able to:	**podré, podrás**	I/you will be able to, etc
venir	to come:	**vendré, vendrás**	I/you will come, etc
hacer	to do:	**haré, harás**	I/you will do, etc
decir	to say:	**diré, dirás**	I/you will say, etc

Reflexive verbs have the pronouns at the beginning except in the infinitive:

quedarse	to stay		
me quedaré	I will stay	**nos quedaremos**	we will stay
te quedarás	you will stay	**os quedaréis**	you will stay
se quedará	s/he/you will stay	**se quedarán**	they/you will stay

Talking about the past

In this book you have looked at two ways of talking about something in the past.

1 The Perfect is usually used as in English: I have gone/seen/done, etc.
2 The Preterite or simple past: I went/I saw/I did, etc.

Perfect tense

To form the perfect you take the appropriate form of the verb **haber** (to have) and add the past participle of the main verb. To form the past participle of **-ar** verbs add **-ado** to the root. For **-er** and **-ir** verbs add **-ido**:

haber		+	past participle		
			-ar	-er	-ir
he	hemos	+	habl**ado**	com**ido**	sal**ido**
has	habéis				
ha	han				

-ar	**hablar**	to speak	**he hablado**	I have spoken
-er	**comer**	to eat	**has comido**	you have eaten
-ir	**salir**	to leave	**ha salido**	s/he has left/you have left

Reflexive verbs

The reflexive pronoun always comes first: **me he levantado** I (have) got up

Direct object pronouns

Direct object pronouns always come before the verb: **lo he visto** I (have) seen it

Irregular past participles

There is a small group of verbs which have irregular past participles. Here are some of them:

hacer	to do	**hecho**	done	**he hecho**	I have done
volver	to return	**vuelto**	returned	**has vuelto**	you have returned
escribir	to write	**escrito**	written	**ha escrito**	s/he has written
ver	to see	**visto**	seen	**hemos visto**	we have seen
decir	to say	**dicho**	said	**habéis dicho**	you have said
poner	to put	**puesto**	put	**han puesto**	they have put

Preterite tense

For expressing something which happened at a particular time or for a defined period of time in the past: 'It opened at 12'; 'They stayed for two hours', etc. Add the endings below to the root.

-ar		**-er**		**-ir**	
llamé	I phoned	**volví**	I returned	**salí**	I left
llamaste	you phoned	**volviste**	you returned	**saliste**	you left
llamó	s/he/you phoned	**volvió**	s/he/you returned	**salió**	s/he left
llamamos	we phoned	**volvimos**	we returned	**salimos**	we left
llamasteis	you phoned	**volvisteis**	you returned	**salisteis**	you left
llamaron	they/you phoned	**volvieron**	they/you returned	**salieron**	they left

Irregular verbs

estar		**hacer**		**dar**	
estuve	I was	**hice**	I did	**di**	I gave
estuviste	you were	**hiciste**	you did	**diste**	you gave
estuvo	etc	**hizo**	etc	**dio**	etc
estuvimos		**hicimos**		**dimos**	
estuvisteis		**hicisteis**		**disteis**	
estuvieron		**hicieron**		**dieron**	

Ser and **ir** have the same form in the preterite:

fui	I went	*or*	I was	**haber**:		**hubo** there was
fuiste	you went		you were	**tener**:		**tuve** (like **es<u>tuve</u>**)
fue	s/he went		s/he was	**seguir**:		**seguí, seguiste**, etc
	you went		you were		*but*	**s<u>i</u>guió** and **s<u>i</u>guieron**
fuimos	we went		we were	**pedir**:		**pedí, pediste**, etc
fuisteis	you went		you were		*but*	**p<u>i</u>dió** and **p<u>i</u>dieron**
fueron	they went		they were			
	you went		you were			

Direct object pronouns come before the verb

<u>**me**</u> **ayudó**	s/he helped <u>me</u>
<u>**te**</u> **dio**	s/he gave <u>you</u>
<u>**le**</u> **dijo**	s/he told <u>him</u> or <u>her</u>

Reflexive verbs

<u>**me**</u> **levanté**
<u>**te**</u> **levantaste**
<u>**se**</u> **levantó**, etc

Imperative

The imperative is used to give instructions, directions and orders. In most cases you can also use the simple present tense. See page 70.

The imperative forms below are only used when addressing a person or people informally. To give formal instructions the subjunctive forms are used. These are not presented in this book.

	Talking to one person		**Talking to two or more**
dob<u>l</u>ar	**dob<u>l</u>a**	turn	**dob<u>l</u>ad**
co<u>ger</u>	**co<u>ge</u>**	catch/take	**co<u>ged</u>**
sub<u>ir</u>	**sub<u>e</u>**	go up	**sub<u>id</u>**

With root-changing verbs the vowel changes only when talking to one person.

s<u>e</u>guir	**s<u>i</u>gue**	continue	**seguid**

Some verbs are irregular in the singular form, i.e. when talking to one person.

sal<u>ir</u>	**sal**	leave	**salid**
ir	**ve**	go	**id**

With reflexive verbs the reflexive pronoun is attached to the verb and the **d** in the plural forms is omitted.

levantarse	**levántate**	get up	**levantaos**
sentarse	**siéntate**	sit down	**sentaos**

Prepositions

Prepositions show the relationships between other words in a sentence, for example 'in', 'on', 'to', 'from', etc. They are often used differently in Spanish, so at first it is best to learn them in context.

Mode of transport
To say 'by' train, car, bike, use **en**:   **en tren, coche, bicicleta**, etc
To say 'on' foot, use **a**:   **a pie**

To describe where something is:

a la izquierda/derecha	on the left/right
al lado del cine	next to the cinema
al final de la calle	at the end of the street
en la esquina	on the corner
enfrente del bar	opposite the bar
cerca/lejos de aquí	near to/far from here
entre el bar y el café	between the bar and the café

Some prepositions have more than one equivalent in English:

a	can mean 'to' or 'at':	**Voy al centro.**	I go to the centre.
		Voy a las tres.	I go at 3 o'clock.
de	can mean 'from' or 'of':	**Soy de Cádiz.**	I am from Cádiz.
		Un libro de arte.	'A book of art'. (an art book)

The personal 'a'
When the direct object of the verb is human, you must use **a**: **Voy a ver a Juan.**

Gustar

Gustar means 'to please', and it is used to express likes and dislikes.
To say you like one thing:

(a mí*) me gusta	**(a ti*) te gusta**	**(a él/ella/usted*) le gusta**
I like it (it pleases me)	you like it	he/she likes it; you like it

***A mí, ti, él, ella, usted** etc are often used for emphasis, to express a contrast or to eliminate any possible misunderstanding. They mean to me/you/him/her/you, etc.

To say you like more than one thing:

me gustan	**te gustan**	**le gustan**
I like them	you like them	he/she likes them; you like them

To express dislike use **no**:

   no me gusta   I don't like it   **no te gustan**   you don't like them

VOCABULARY

Please note:
1 Several of the words here have different meanings. The ones given here are only the ones needed in this book, and you should take care when using them in other contexts. If you are in doubt, refer to a dictionary.
2 Genders of nouns are given here, but you will need to refer to a dictionary to find out if a particular word is an adjective, preposition, verb, etc.

A

a	to; by
a menos que	unless
a pie	on foot
abajo	downstairs
abogado/a	lawyer
abrazo (m)	embrace
un abrazo de (in letters)	Love from
abrigo (m)	coat
abril	April
abrir	to open
absolutamente	absolutely
abuelo/a	grandparent
aburrido/a	boring/bored
acabar	to finish
acabar de	to have just
academia (f)	academy
aceptar	to accept
aceituna (f)	olive
ácido/a	acid
acomodador/a	usher/ette
acompañar	to go with
acostarse	to go to bed
acostumbrarse	to get used to
actividad (f)	activity
actriz/actor	actor
actual	now, present
actualmente	at the moment
acuerdo, de	all right; agreed
adiós	good bye
administrador/a	administrator
¿Adónde?	To where?
adorar	to adore
adquirir	to acquire
aéreo/a	air (adj)
aerobic (m)	aerobics
aeropuerto (m)	airport
afueras (f pl)	outskirts
agencia (f) inmobiliaria	estate agent's
agosto	August
agua (f)	water
ahorrar	to save

aire (m); al aire libre	air; outdoors
alcanzar	to reach
alcohol (m)	alcohol
alemán/ana	German
Alemania	Germany
alfombra (f)	rug
algo	something
alimentar	to fuel, to feed
allí	there
almacén (m)	department store
almorzar	to have lunch
almuerzo (m)	lunch
alojamiento (m)	housing, lodging
alquilar	to rent, hire
alquiler (m)	hire, rental
alternativa (f)	alternative
alto/a	high
ama (f) de casa	housewife
amante (m/f)	lover
amarillo/a	yellow
ambiental	environmental
ambiente (m)	atmosphere, environment
amenazar	to threaten
amigo/a	friend
analítico/a	analytical
anciano/a	old person
andar	to walk
andén (m)	(railway) platform
animador/a	activities organiser, play leader
año (m)	year
anoche	last night
anteayer	the day before yesterday
antes	former(ly)
antes de	before
anuncio (m)	advertisement
apagar	to turn off
aparcamiento (m)	car park
aparcar	to park
apellido (m)	surname

Vocabulary

apoyo (m) — support
aprender — to learn
aprobación (f) — approval
aprobar — to pass (an exam)
aproximadamente — approximately
aquí — here
árbol (m) — tree
árbol genealógico — family tree
argentino/a — Argentinian
Armada (f) — Armada
armario (m) — cupboard, wardrobe
arreglar — to fix
arriba — upstairs
arte (m) — art
artículo (m) — item, article
artista (m/f) — artist
asado/a — roast
asaltante (m/f) — assailant
asaltar — to assault
asalto (m) — assault
ascensor (m) — the lift
así que — so
asiento (m) — seat
asignatura (f) — subject
asistir — to be present
Atenas — Athens
atraco (m) — robbery
atractivo/a — attractive
auditorio (m) — auditorium
aumentar — to increase
autobús (m) — bus
automóvil (m) — automobile
avión (m) — aeroplane
ayer — yesterday
ayudante (m/f) — assistant
ayudar — to help
ayuntamiento (m) — town hall
azar (m) — chance
azúcar (m) — sugar
azul — blue
azulejo (m) — tile

B

bachillerato (m) — Final High School qualification (like A level or Highers)
bailar — to dance
bajar — to put down
bajarse — to get off
bajo — down, below
bajo/a — low, short
balcón (m) — balcony
banco (m) — bank

bañera (f) — bath
baño (m) — bathroom
banquero (m) — banker
barato/a — cheap
bastante — quite, rather
basura (f) — rubbish
batalla (f) — battle
beber — to drink
bebida (f) — drink
bellas artes (f pl) — Fine Arts
besar — to kiss
beso (m) — a kiss
biblioteca (f) — library
bici(cleta) (f) — bicycle
¡Bienvenido! — Welcome!
billete (m) — ticket
blanco/a — white
bocadillo (m) — sandwich
boda (f) — wedding
bolso (m) — handbag
bombero (m) — fireman
bonito/a — pretty
bota (f) — boot
brazo (m) — arm
buceo (m) — scuba diving
bueno/a — good
buscar — to look for
buzón de voz (m) — voice mail

C

caballo (m) — horse
cada — each
café (m) — coffee; café
caja (f) — box, crate
caja (f) de ahorros — savings bank
calamares (m pl) — squid
calentamiento (m) — warming
calle (f) — street
cama (f) — bed
camarero/a — waiter/ress
cambiar — to change
cambio (m) — change
camisa (f) — shirt
campamento (m) — camp
campo (m) — ground, the country(side), field
canal (m) — canal, channel
cantina (f) — canteen
capacidad (f) — capacity, ability
carga (f) — charge
carne (f) — meat
caro/a — expensive
carrera (f) — (degree) course, career

carta (f)	letter	comedor (m)	dining room
cartera (f)	wallet	comer	to eat
casa (f)	house	comercial	commercial
casado/a	married	comercializar	to put on the
casarse	to get married		market
casino (m)	casino	comida (f)	meal; food
catedral (f)	cathedral	comisaría (f)	police station
cava (m)	sparkling wine	¿Cómo?	How?
celebrar	to celebrate	cómodo/a	comfortable
célula (f)	cell	compañero/a	classmate;
cena (f)	dinner		companion; mate
cenar	to have dinner	compañía (f)	company
centro (m)	centre	completar	to complete
centro comercial	shopping centre	completo/a	full; completed
cerca (de)	near (to)	componente (m)	component
cereal (m)	cereal	compra (f)	shopping
cerrar	to close	comprar	to buy
cerveza (f)	beer	compras, de	shopping
chalet (m)	house	comunicación (f)	communication
champiñón (m)	mushroom	comunidad (f)	autonomous
chaqueta (f)	jacket	autónoma	community
charlar	to chat	Comunidad (f)	European
cheque (m)	cheque	Europea	Community
chino/a	Chinese man/woman	con	with
ciclismo (m)	cycling	concierto (m)	concert
ciencia (f)	science	concluir	to conclude;
ciencia ficción (f)	science fiction		finish
científico/a	scientific, scientist	concurso (m)	competition
cifra (f)	figure	conducir	to drive, driving
cine (m)	cinema	conductor/a	driver
círculo (m)	circle	conferencia (f)	lecture, conference
cita (f)	appointment	conocer	to (get to) know
ciudad (f)	city; town	conseguir	to get (a job)
claro	sure, of course	constancia (f)	perseverance
clase (f)	class, lecture	consumismo (m)	consumerism
clásico/a	classical	consumo (m)	consumption
cliente/a	customer	contado, al	in cash
clima (m)	climate	contaminación (f)	pollution
cobrar	to earn	contaminar	to pollute
coche (m)	car	contemporáneo/a	contemporary
cocina (f)	cooker; kitchen	contestar	to answer
cocinero/a	cook	conmigo/tigo	with me/you
coger	to take, to catch	contra	against
colectivización (f)	collectivisation	contraer	to contract, enter into
colectivo (m)	collective	conveniente	convenient
colega (m/f)	colleague	conversación (f)	conversation
colegio (m)	school	convocar	to call (together)
collar (m)	necklace	copa (f)	drink; glass
colocar	to put	corbata (f)	tie
colombiano/a	Colombian	correcto/a	correct
color (m)	colour	corregir	to mark; correct
combustible (m)	fuel	Correos (m)	post office
comedia (f)	comedy	correr	to run

Vocabulary

costar	to cost	despacho (m)	office
creativo/a	creative	después de	after
crecer	to grow	destino (m)	destination
crédito (m)	credit	desventaja (f)	disadvantage
creer	to believe	detener	to arrest
crítico/a	critical	día (m)	day
cruce (m)	crossroads	diciembre	December
cuadra (f)	stable(s)	dictadura (f)	dictatorship
cuadro (m)	chart; picture	¿Dígame?	Hello? (on the phone)
¿Cuál?	Which?	diferencia (f)	difference
cualquier	any	difícil	difficult
¿Cuánto/a/s?	How much/many?	dificultad (f)	difficulty
cuarto (m)	room; quarter	dinero (m)	money
cuarto (m) de baño	bathroom	dirección (f)	address
cuarto/a	fourth	director/a	director
cubano/a	Cuban	dirigirse	to apply to
cuenta (f)	bill	discoteca (f)	disco
culebrón (m)	soap opera	diseñador/a	designer
cultura (f)	culture	diseño (m)	design
currículum (m)	c.v.	disponer de	to have available
curso (m)	course	dispuesto/a	prepared; willing
		divorciado/a	divorced
D		doblar	to turn
danés/esa	Dane; Danish	doble	double
daño (m)	harm	documentación (f)	documentation
dar	to give	documental (m)	documentary
dar de comer a	to feed	doméstico/a	domestic
dar miedo	to frighten	domicilio (m)	dwelling; residence
dar paseos	to go for walks	dominar	to dominate
de	of/from	domingo	Sunday
debajo de	beneath; under	¿Dónde?	Where?
decidir	to decide	dormir	to sleep
decir	to say/tell	dormitorio (m)	bedroom
dedicación (f)	dedication	drama (m)	drama; play
dejar de	to stop	drama (m) psicológico	psychological play
delante de	in front of	ducha (f)	shower
demasiado	too	dueño/a	owner; landlord/lady
demasiado/a	too much	durante	during
democracia (f)	democracy	durar	to last; take
departamento (m)	department	duro/a	hard
dependiente/a	shop assistant	DVD (m)	DVD
deporte (m)	sport		
deportivo/a	sports (adj)	**E**	
depósito (m)	tank	ecológico/a	ecological, environmentally friendly
derecha (f)	right		
Derecho (m)	Law		
desaparecer	to disappear	economía (f)	economy; economics
desayunar	to have breakfast	edad (f)	age
desayuno (m)	breakfast	edificio (m)	building
descansar	to rest	Edimburgo	Edinburgh
descubrir	to discover	educar	to educate; bring up
descuento (m)	discount	efectivo, en	in cash
desde	from	efecto, en	in fact

ejecutivo/a	executive	establecer	to establish
ejercitar	to exercise	estación (f)	station
él	he; him	estadio (m)	stadium
el/la/los/las	the	estantería (f)	shelves
elección (f)	election; choice	estar	to be
electricidad (f)	electricity	estéreo (m)	stereo
electrónico/a	electronic	Estimado/a	Dear (formal letters)
elevado/a	high	esto/a/s	this; these
ella	she; her	estrella (f)	star
emborracharse	to get drunk	estrés (m)	stress
emisión (f)	emission	estudiante (m/f)	student
empezar	to start	estudiantil	student (adj)
empleado/a	employee	estudiar	to study
empresa (f)	firm	estudio (m)	study
empresariales (f pl)	business (studies)	estupendo	great
en	in, on, by	evadirse	to escape
en seguida	straight away	evitar	to avoid
enamorarse	to fall in love	exámen (m)	exam
encantar	to delight	exigir	to demand
encargado/a	manager	existir	to exist
encontrar	to find; meet	éxito (m)	success
encuesta (f)	survey	experiencia (f)	experience
enero	January	exposición (f)	exhibition
enfermería (f)	nursing	exterior, al	outside
enfermero/a	nurse	extranjero/a	foreign; foreigner
enfermo/a	ill	extrovertido/a	extroverted
enfrentamiento (m)	confrontation		
enfrente de	opposite	**F**	
ensalada (f)	salad	fácil	easy
enterrado/a	buried	facilidad (f)	facility; ease
entrada (f)	entrance; ticket	facultad (f)	faculty
entrar	to enter	falda (f)	skirt
entre	between	falso/a	false; untrue
entrevista (f)	interview	faltar	to lack; be needed
entusiasmo (m)	enthusiasm	fama (f)	reputation
equipaje (m)	luggage	familia (f)	family
equipo (m)	team	famoso/a	famous
equitación (f)	riding	farmacia (f)	chemist's
equivocarse	to make a mistake	febrero	February
error (m)	mistake	fecha (f)	date
escalera (f)	stairs	fenomenal	great
escaparse	to escape	festival (m)	festival
escocés/escocesa	Scot; Scottish	fiesta (f)	party
escondite (m)	hiding place	fila (f)	row
escribir	to write	filosofía (f)	philosophy
escuchar	to listen	fin (m)	end
escuela (f)	school	final (m)	end
escultura (f)	sculpture	firmar	to sign
espacio (m)	gap; space	física (f)	physics
español/a	Spaniard; Spanish	flamenco (m)	flamenco
espejo (m)	mirror	flan (m)	crème caramel
esperar	to wait	flexible	flexible
esquina (f)	corner	florero (m)	flower vase

Vocabulary

footing (m) — jogging
forma (f) — way
formulario (m) — form
fortalecer — to strengthen
francés/francesa — French
Francia — France
frase (f) — sentence
frecuencia (f) — frequency
frecuente — frequent
fregar los platos — to wash up
frigorífico (m) — fridge
fruta (f) — fruit
fuente (f) — fountain
fuera — outside
fuerte — strong
fuerza (f) — strength
fumador/a — smoking (adj.)
fumar — to smoke
funcionario/a — civil servant
furgoneta (f) — van
fútbol (m) — football

G

gafas (f pl) de sol — sunglasses
galería (f) — gallery
galés/galesa — Welsh
galleta (f) — biscuit
ganar — to earn
garaje (m) — garage
gasolina (f) — petrol
gasolinera (f) — petrol station
gastar — to spend
gazpacho (m) — cold soup
gente (f) — people
geografía (f) — geography
gimnasio (m) — gymnasium
global — global
grabar — to record
grande — big
gratis — free
grave — serious
griego/a — Greek
gris — grey
gritar — to shout
grupo (m) — group
guapo/a — handsome; good-looking; pretty
guerra (f) — war
gustar a — to please

H

habilidad (f) — skill
habitación (f) — room

hablar — to speak
hacer — to do
hacer ejercicio/ gimnasia — to work out
hacer transbordo — to change (trains)
hacia — towards
hasta — until
hasta luego — see you soon
hay — there is/are
hay que — you have to, it's necessary to
helado (m) — ice cream
helicóptero (m) — helicopter
heredero (m) — heir
herido/a — injured
hermano/a — brother/sister
hijo/a — son/daughter
hijos (m pl) — children
hola — hello
holandés/holandesa — Dutch
hombre (m) — man
hora (f) — hour; time
horario (m) — timetable
hospital (m) — hospital
hostal (m) — guesthouse
hotel (m) — hotel
hoy — today
huésped (m) — guest

I

ida, de — single (ticket)
ida y vuelta, de — return (ticket)
idioma (m) — language
iglesia (f) — church
ignorar — to be unaware of; not to know
ilusión (f) — hope
imagen (f) — picture; image
imaginativo/a — imaginative
impuesto (m) — tax
incendio (m) — fire
incómodo/a — uncomfortable
inconveniente — inconvenient
independencia (f) — independence
independiente — independent
indicar — to indicate
indio/a — Indian
individual — single (room)
infantil — childish; for/of children
informática (f) — Information Technology
informe (m) — report

infrarrojo	infra red
ingeniería (f)	engineering
ingeniero/a	engineer
Inglaterra	England
inglés/inglesa	English
iniciativa (f)	initiative
inmediatamente	immediately
inmunológico/a	immunising, immune
indoro (m)	toilet
instalar	to instal
inteligente	intelligent
intercambio (m)	exchange
interés (m)	interest
interesado/a	interested
interesante	interesting
internacional	international
invencible	invincible
investigación (f)	investigation
investigador/a	researcher
ir	to go
ir de compras	to go shopping
ir de vacaciones	to go on holiday
Irlanda	Ireland
irlandés/irlandesa	Irish
italiano/a	Italian
izquierda (f)	left

J

jamás	never
jamón (m)	ham
japonés/japonesa	Japanese
jardín (m)	garden
jardinero/a	gardener
jerez (m)	sherry
joven	young
jubilado/a	retired
juego (m)	game
juego de azar	game of chance
jueves	Thursday
jugar	to play
julio	July
junio	June
juntar	to match; join
juntos/as	together

L

labor (f)	labour; work
laboratorio (m)	laboratory
lado; al lado de	side; next to
lámpara (f)	lamp
lavabo (m)	basin
lavadora (f)	washing machine
lavar	to wash

lavarse el pelo	to wash one's hair
Le saluda atentamente	Yours faithfully
leche (f)	milk
leer	to read
lejos (de)	far (from)
lengua (f)	language
lenguado (m)	sole
lento/a	slow
letra (f)	letter (as in A, B, C)
levantar	to lift
levantarse	to get up, to stand up
leve	slight
libre	free
librería (f)	bookshop
libro (m)	book
licenciatura (f)	degree
limonada (f)	lemonade
limpiar	to clean
lista (f)	list
listo/a	keen, clever, ready
literatura (f)	literature
llamada (f)	call
llamarse	to be called
llave (f)	key
llegada (f)	arrival
llegar	to arrive
lleno/a	full
llevar	to bring
llevarse bien	to get on well
lluvia (f)	rain
lo que	what; that which
Lo siento	I'm sorry
lotería (f)	lottery
luchar	to fight; struggle
luego	then
lugar (m)	place
lujo (m)	luxury
luna (f)	moon
lunes	Monday

M

madre (f)	mother
madrileño/a	person from Madrid
madrugada (f)	early morning; dawn
mal	bad; badly
maleta (f)	suitcase
mañana (f)	morning; tomorrow
manifestación (f)	demonstration
manifestante (m/f)	demonstrator
manitas (m/f)	handyman/woman (colloquial)
mano (f)	hand

Vocabulary

¡Manos arriba!	Hands up!	monstruo (m)	monster
mantequilla (f)	butter	monte (m)	mountain
manual	manual	montar a caballo	to ride (horse)
marido	husband	morado/a	purple
marketing (m)	marketing	morir	to die
martes	Tuesday	moro/a	Moor
marzo	March	moto(cicleta) (f)	motorbike
más	more; else	motor (m)	engine
más … que	more … than	moverse	to move
matemáticas (f pl)	mathematics	mozo/a de cuadra	stable lad/girl
materialista	materialistic	mucho/a/s	a lot; many
matricularse	to enrol, to register	mueble (m)	(item of) furniture
matrimonio (m)	married couple; marriage	muebles (m pl)	furniture
		mujer (f)	wife; woman
mayo	May	multa (f)	fine
mayor	older	mundo (m)	world
mayoría (f)	majority	murciano/a	person from Murcia
me	(to) me; myself	museo (m)	museum
mecánico/a	mechanic	música (f)	music
media (f)	average, half	músico/a	musician
mediano/a	medium	muy	very
medianoche	midnight		
medias (f pl)	tights	**N**	
médico/a	doctor	nacer	to be born
mediodía (m)	midday	nacimiento (m)	birth
mejor	better	nacional	national
memoria (f)	memory	nacionalidad (f)	nationality
menor	younger	Naciones (f pl) Unidas	United Nations
menos	less, except	nada	not at all/nothing
mensual	monthly	naranja (f)	orange
menú (m)	menu	natación (f)	swimming
mermelada (f)	jam	navaja (f)	pocket knife
mes (m)	month	necesidad (f)	necessity
mesa (f)	table	necesitar	to need
mesita (f) de noche	bedside table	negar	to deny
metálico, en	in cash	negocio (m)	business
metódico/a	methodical	negro/a	black
metro (m)	underground	nieto/a	grandchild
mezquita (f)	mosque	niño/a	child
mi/s	my	no	not; no
miedo (m)	fear	noche (f)	night
miércoles	Wednesday	nombre (m)	name
mil (m)	(one) thousand	normalidad (f)	normality
minuto (m)	minute	normalmente	normally
mirar	to look; watch	norteamericano/a	American
misterioso/a	mysterious	nosotros/as	we; us
moda (f), de	fashionable	noticias (f pl)	news
modales (m pl)	manners	novela (f)	novel
modelo (m/f)	model	novelista (m/f)	novelist
moderno/a	modern	noviembre	November
modo, de ningún modo	way; no way	novio/a	boy/girlfriend
momento (m)	moment	Nueva Zelanda	New Zealand
monedero (m)	purse	nuevo/a	new

número (m)	number
nunca	never

O

o	or
objetos (m pl) perdidos	lost property
obra (f) de arte	work (of art)
observación (f)	remark
observador/a	observant
obstante, no	however
octubre	October
ocupar	to occupy
ocurrir	to happen
oferta (f)	offer
oficina (f)	office
ópera (f)	opera
opinar	to think
ordenado/a	tidy
ordenador (m)	computer
organizado/a	organized
orquesta (f)	orchestra
otro/a	other; another

P

paciente	patient
padre (m)	father
padres (m pl)	parents
paella (f)	paella
pagar	to pay for
pago (m)	payment
pan (m)	bread
pan (m) tostado	toast
pantalones (m pl)	trousers
para	(in order) to; for
parada (f)	bus stop
parar(se)	to stop
parecer	to seem
pared (f)	wall
pareja (f)	couple; partner
parque (m)	park
pasado/a	last
pasado mañana	the day after tomorrow
pasajero (m)	passenger
pasaporte (m)	passport
pasar	to spend (time), to come in, to happen
pasillo (m)	corridor
patatas (f pl) fritas	chips or crisps
patinaje (m)	skating
pedal (m)	pedal
pedir	to ask for; order
película (f)	film
pensar	to think

pensión (f) (media/completa)	half/full board
peor	worse
pequeño/a	small
perder	to lose
perdone	excuse me
perfil (m)	profile; background
periódico (m)	newspaper
periodista (m/f)	journalist
permiso (m)	licence
permitir	to allow
pero	but
persona (f)	person
perspicaz	perceptive
persuasivo/a	persuasive
pescado (m)	fish
petrolero/a	(of) petrol
pie (m)	foot
pierna (f)	leg
piloto (m)	pilot
pintar	to paint
pintor/a	painter
pintura (f)	painting
piragüismo (m)	canoeing
piscina (f)	swimming pool
piso (m)	flat, floor
pistola (f)	gun
planchar	to iron
planear	to plan
planetario (m)	planetarium
plano (m)	plan, map
planta (f)	floor; plant
planta (f) baja	ground floor
playa (f)	beach
plaza (f)	square
plomo (m)	lead
pobre	poor
poco (m)	(a) little, a bit, few
poder	to be able to
polaco/a	Polish
polar	polar
policía (m/f)	police officer
policíaco/a	police, detective (adj)
policial	police (adj)
polideportivo (m)	sports centre
política (f)	politics
pollo (m)	chicken
pollo (m) asado	roast chicken
Polonia	Poland
poner (una película)	to put on a film
ponerse	to become
por	in; during; through; by; along
por favor	please

Vocabulary

por fin — finally
por lo menos — at least
por lo tanto — therefore
porcentaje (m) — percentage
¿Por qué? — Why?
porque — because
portátil — portable
portero/a — porter
posible — possible
postre (m) — dessert
precio (m) — price
preferir — to prefer
pregunta (f) — question
prenda (f) — garment
preparar — to prepare
presencia (f) — appearance
presentarse — to introduce oneself
primero/a — first
primo/a — cousin
prioridad (f) — priority
prisa; no hay prisa — there's no hurry
privatización (f) — privatisation
probar — to try; prove
problema (m) — problem
procedencia (f) — from
producir — to produce
profesión (f) — profession; job
profesional — professional
profesor/a — teacher
programa (m) — programme
pronto — soon
protesta (f) — protest
psicología (f) — psychology
psicológico/a — psychological
publicidad (f) — publicity
público/a — public
puenting (m) — bungee-jumping
puerta (f) — door, gate
puesto (m) — post
puro (m) — cigar

Q

que — who, which, than
¿Qué? — What?
quedarse — to stay
querer — to want
querido/a — dear
¿Qué tal? — How are you?
¿Quién? — Who?
química (f) — chemistry
quinto/a — fifth
quisiera — I would like
quizás — perhaps

R

radio (f) — radio
rápido/a — fast
rato (m) — while
realidad (f) — reality
recepción (f) — reception
recepcionista (m/f) — receptionist
recibir — to receive
recoger — to collect
recurso (m) — resource
reducir — to reduce
referencia (f) — reference
refresco (m) — soft drink
regalo (m) — present
regional — regional
reinar — to reign
relación (f) — relation
relax (m) — relaxation
rellenar — fill in
remo (m) — oar
RENFE (f) — train station; national rail network (Spain)
repetir — to repeat
requerir — to require
reserva (f) — reservation
reservar — to book
residencia (f) — residence
responder — reply
responsable — responsible
respuesta (f) — answer
restaurante (m) — restaurant
resultar — to become; get
retrasado/a — delayed
retraso (m) — delay
reunión (f) — meeting
rico/a — rich
robar — to rob someone
rock (m) duro — hard rock
rodilla (f) — knee
rojo/a — red
romántico/a — romantic
ropa (f) — clothes

S

sábado — Saturday
saber — to know (how to)
sala (f) — large room
salario (m) — salary
salida (f) — departure
salir — to go out
salón (m) — sitting room
salsa (f) — sauce (dance)
saludable — healthy

saludar	to greet	solitario/a	solitary
saludo (m)	greeting	sólo	only
salvo	except	solo/a	alone
sano/a	healthy	soltero/a/s	single person/people
satélite (m)	satellite	solucionar	to solve
se(p)tiembre	September	sonrisa (f)	smile
secretario/a	secretary	sopa (f)	soup
sector (m)	sector	sorprender	to surprise
seguida, en	right away	su	his; her; their; your
seguir	to continue	subir	to go up; to rise
segunda mano, de	second hand	subirse	to get on/in
segundo (m)	second (time)	subrayar	to underline
segundo/a	second	sudamericano/a	South American
seguridad (f)	security	sueldo (m)	wage
seguro (m)	insurance	suelo (m)	floor
selva (f)	rainforest	sueño (m)	dream
semáforo (m)	traffic light	¡Suerte!	Good luck!
semana (f)	week	suficiente	sufficient; enough
semana que viene, la	next week	súper	super; 4 star petrol
semestre (m)	semester	superior	superior; above
seminario (m)	seminar	supermercado (m)	supermarket
señalar	to indicate; to tick	supersónico/a	supersonic
sencillo	single (ticket)		
senegalés/senegalesa	Senegalese	**T**	
sentarse	to sit down	talla (f)	size
señor	Mr; Sir	también	also
señora	Mrs; Madam	tampoco	neither
separado/a	separated	tan … como	as … as
sepulcro (m)	tomb; sepulchre	tanto/a	so much
ser	to be	tapa (f)	snack; appetiser
serie (f) policíaca	detective series	tardar	to take; to last; to be late
servicio (m)	service		
servicios (m pl)	toilets	tarde (f)	afternoon; evening
servir	to be used, to serve	tarde	late
si	if; whether	tarjeta (f)	card
sí	yes	tarjeta (f) de crédito	credit card
siempre	always	te	(to) you; yourself
siesta (f)	siesta	teatro (m)	theatre
siglo (m)	century	técnico/a	technician
siguiente	following	tecnología (f)	technology
silla (f)	chair	tele(visión) (f)	TV
sillón (m)	armchair	teléfono (m)	telephone
sin	without	telescopio (m)	telescope
sintético/a	synthetic	televisor (m)	TV set
sistema (m)	system	temprano	early
sitio (m)	place	tender	to tend
sobre todo	above all	tener	to have
sobrino/a	nephew/niece	tener lugar	to take place
sociedad (f)	society	tener que	to have to
sociología (f)	sociology	tenis (m)	tennis
sofá (m)	settee	tequila (m)	tequila
soldado (m/f)	soldier	tercero/a	third
solicitar	to apply for	terminar	to finish

Vocabulary

testigo (m/f) — witness
tiempo (m) — time
tiempo (m) parcial — part time
tienda (f) — shop
tirar — to throw out
tocador (m) — dressing table
tocar — to play (an instrument), to touch
todavía — still, yet
todo/a — all; every
todo recto — straight on
tomar — to have/to take
tomar el sol — to sunbathe
tonelada (f) — ton
tónica (f) — tonic
tortilla (f) — omelette
totalidad (f) — totality
trabajador/a — worker; hard-working
trabajar — to work
trabajo (m) — work
tradicional — traditional
traducción (f) — translation
traer — to bring
tráfico (m) — traffic
traje (m) — suit
transporte (m) — transport
tras — after
trasladarse — to move house
tratar de — to try to
trémulo/a — tremulous; trembling
tren (m) — train
trono (m) — throne
tropical — tropical
tu — your
tú — you
tú mismo — yourself
turco/a — Turkish
turismo (m) — tourism

U
último/a — last
ultramarinos (m pl) — groceries
un/a — a
únicamente — only
unidad (f) — unit
uniformidad (f) — uniformity
Unión Europea (f) — European Union
universidad (f) — university
unos/as — some
urbanización (f) — housing estate
usted/es — you
utilizar — to use

V
vacaciones (f pl) — holiday
vale — OK
valer — to be worth
valor (m) — value
vanguardista (m) — forward looking
vegetariano/a — vegetarian
vehículo (m) — vehicle
velocidad (f) — speed
vencer — to conquer; to beat
venezolano/a — Venezuelan
venir — to come
ventana (f) — window
ventanilla de reclamación — customer services
ver — to see/watch
verano (m) — summer
verdad (f) — truth
verdadero/a — true
verde — green
verdura (f) — greens
verificar — to check
versión (f) — version
vestido (m) — dress
vez/veces (f) — time/times
viajar — to travel
viajero (m) — traveller
vida (f) — life
vídeo (f) — video
viejo/a — old
viernes — Friday
vino (m) — wine
violento/a — violent
violeta — violet
visual — visual
vitrina (f) — glass case
vivir — to live
volver — to return
vomitar — to be sick
vosotros/as — you
vuelo (m) — flight
vuelta (f) — return

W
wáter (m) — toilet

Y
y — and
yate (m) — yacht
yo — I

Z
zapato (m) — shoe
zumo (m) — juice

ANSWERS

Unit 1

5 1 d **2** e **3** b **4** a **5** c

7 **a** ¿Quién eres?/¿Cómo te llamas?
b ¿Dónde vives? **c** ¿Eres de Sevilla?
d ¿Eres español? **e** ¿Eres policía? **f** ¿Eres bombero?

9 **b** **i** Estudio derecho en la universidad.
ii Aprendo italiano en la universidad de Roma. **iii** María estudia literatura y arte.
iv ¿Qué idiomas aprende Ana en su curso?
v Yo estudio empresariales con francés.

13 **a** Federico, 52 años **b** Manuel, 49 años
c Alberto, 20 años **d** Jacinta 65 años.

¡Extra!

16 Segoshi Tanizaki; *japonés; estudiante; política;*
Barcelona; Tokio.
Carla Bertolini; *italiana;* diseñadora; arte y diseño; Llobregat; *Milano.*
Peter; *inglés;* periodista; *español; Barcelona; Salisbury.*
Xavier Marchand; senegalés; ingeniero; *español; Barcelona;* Senegal.

17 **a** He lives in the town centre in a big house with 5 university students. **b** He works in a hotel. **c** She is studying English in Durham.
d She shares with two people. **e** They are Danish and Chinese. The Danish man studies philosophy and the Chinese woman works in the university office.

Ejercicios de gramática

1 **a** vivo; soy; escribo; trabajo; aprendo
b trabajas; eres; comes
c estudia; trabaja; vive; es

2 **a** ¿Cúantos años tienes?; ¿Cuál es tu profesión?; ¿Qué estudias?; ¿Dónde vives?
b ¿Cuántos años tiene?; ¿Cuál es su profesión?; ¿Qué estudia?; ¿Dónde vive?

3 **a** estudiante **b** mexicana **c** profesor
d francés **e** profesora **f** argentina

Unit 2

3 **a** Mi padre se llama Vicente. Mi madre se llama Victoria. Sí, tengo una hermana mayor y un hermano menor. Mi hermana tiene treinta años. Mi hermano estudia periodismo. No, pero mi hermana tiene dos hijos. Su hija se llama Raquel y su hijo se llama Luis.

4 **a**

b **i** Su hermana se llama Marta. **ii** Su hermano es médico. **iii** Su hijo es David. **iv** Su marido tiene 35 años. **v** Sus padres tienen 64 y 59 años.

5 Nombre: Nadia
Estado civil: *casada*
Profesión: *actriz*
Profesión del marido: ingeniero
Número de hijos: 0
Número de hijas: 2
Edad de los/las hijos/as: 6 y 2
Número de hermanos: 1
Número de hermanas: 1
Profesión de los/las hermanos/as: *profesor de inglés y dentista*
Profesión de los padres: jubilados

6 **a** 1 **b** 3 **c** 2 **d** 4

7 **a** grande **b** moderno **c** moderna **d** vieja
e pequeños

8 All the vocabulary needed is in the vocabulary section on page 22.

9 Conversación 1 No tiene tres dormitorios.
Tiene cuatro.
Conversación 2 No es muy vieja. Es bastante moderna. No tiene un dormitorio muy pequeño. Tiene un dormitorio muy grande.
No tiene garaje.

10 **a** Elisa is offered a very pretty flat in the centre of town with two bedrooms, a kitchen, a bathroom and a dining/sitting room.
b It's €1,000 a month.

11 1 e **2** a **3** f **4** b **5** c **6** d

13 Elisa has all the items except a sofa, lamps, pictures, a stereo and a telephone.

¡Extra!

14 Grandparents: Isabel (64), Juan (67); daughter: Juana (33), Jorge (45) her husband; sons: Carlos (11), Roberto (8).

15 **a** el salón **b** el dormitorio **c** el cuarto de baño **d** la cocina

20 All the vocabulary needed is in the vocabulary section on page 22.

Ejercicios de gramática

1 **a** No, Andrés es mi marido. **b** No, Lena y Laura son mis hijas. **c** No, Román y Juan son mis hermanos.

2 **a** mis **b** mi **c** mi **d** su **e** sus **f** tus **g** tu **h** tu **i** tus

3 **a** es **b** es **c** está **d** son **e** están **f** está

4 Se llaman Eulalia y Eugenia y <u>son</u> estudiantes. <u>Estudian</u> ciencias y <u>aprenden</u> mucho en la universidad. <u>Están</u> solteras pero <u>tienen</u> muchos amigos.

5 Tengo una casa grande y <u>bonita</u> con tres dormitorios <u>cómodos</u>. En el salón hay tres <u>pequeñas</u> ventanas, un sofá <u>viejo</u> y unos sillones <u>modernos</u>. La cocina también es <u>moderna</u> pero no muy <u>grande</u>.

Unit 3

1 **a** **i** 07:10 **ii** 16:15 **iii** 23:20 **iv** 07:55

   b **ii** 12.10 **iii** 15.45 **iv** 15.05 **v** 00.20 **vi** 09.40

2 **b** 07:45 Desayuno a las ocho menos cuarto. **c** 08:30 Salgo de casa a las ocho y media. **d** 08:45 Llego a la universidad a las nueve menos cuarto. **e** 09:00 Voy a clase a las nueve. **f** 14:00 Como en la cantina a las dos. **g** 20:00 Vuelvo a casa a las ocho. **h** 22:00 Ceno a las diez.

3 **a** **i** Me levanto a las 07:45. **ii** Desayuno a las 08:00. **iii** Salgo de casa a las 08:40. **iv** Voy a clase a las 09:00. **v** Como a las 13:30. **vi** Vuelvo a casa a las 19:00. **vii** Ceno a las 22:00.

4 **a** lunes: *clase de español*; *tenis*; *acostarme temprano*

martes: *laboratorio*; trabajar; acostarme temprano
miércoles: clase de informática; ir al gimnasio; ir al cine
jueves: *biblioteca*; *trabajar*; ir a la discoteca
viernes: libre; *libre*; cenar con amigos

   b **1**b **2**f **3**e **4**a **5**c **6**d

   c **ii** Hago ejercicio en el gimnasio *los miércoles por la tarde*. **iii** *Los martes por la mañana* tengo laboratorio. **iv** *Los jueves por la noche* voy a la discoteca. **v** *Los miércoles por la noche* voy al cine. **vi** Tengo clase de español *los lunes por la mañana*.

5 **a** *Ve la televisión* is the only correct answer.

   b **i** Se levanta a las diez. **ii** Empieza a trabajar a las cinco. **iii** Come en un bar. **iv** Termina de trabajar a las nueve. **v** Va (Vuelve) a casa. **vi** Vuelve a casa a las diez.

6 **a** **i** ama de casa **ii** portero **iii** secretaria **iv** médico

7 **a** Estoy leyendo un libro. **b** Estamos viendo la televisión. **c** Estamos escuchando música. **d** Estoy comiendo un sándwich. **e** Estoy escribiendo una carta. **f** Estoy haciendo la compra.

9 **b** El martes Carmen está comiendo. **c** El miércoles Carmen está estudiando. **d** El jueves Carmen está preparando la cena. **e** El viernes Carmen está escribiendo un informe. **f** El sábado Carmen está viendo la tele. **g** El domingo Carmen está desayunando.

10 See the **Vocabulario** Section on page 36.

12 **a** Pepe: **ii** ✗ **iii** ✗ **iv** ✗ **v** ✗
   Ana: **ii** ✓ **iii** ✓ **iv** ✓ **v** ✗

13 **a** Juana pide un vino tinto y una ración de calamares. **b** Lucía pide un jerez y aceitunas.

14 **a** gazpacho **b** lenguado **c** agua mineral **d** flan **e** helados **f** postre

¡Extra!

15 **a** **puede ser**, can be; **más sano**, more healthy; **relax**, relaxation; **fortalecen**, strengthen; **dormir**, to sleep; **todos los días**, every day; **ayuda**, helps; **el estrés**, stress.
   b todos los días 62%; dos o tres veces por semana 13%; una vez por semana 10%; con menos frecuencia 15%.

16 The stress of avoiding work.

Ejercicios de gramática

1 **a** vivo **b** estudio **c** aprendo **d** Voy
e como **f** trabajo **g** veo **h** salgo

2 **a** ¿…vives? Vivo… **b** ¿…te levantas? Me
levanto… **c** ¿…llegas…? Llego… **d** ¿…
comes…? …como… **e** ¿…terminas…?
Termino…

3 **a** ¿A qué hora te levantas? ¿A qué hora se
levanta (usted)? **b** ¿Dónde comes? ¿Dónde
come (usted)? **c** ¿A qué hora terminas? ¿A qué
hora termina (usted)? **d** ¿Sales mucho? ¿Sale
(usted) mucho?

4 Examples: Vosotros estáis saliendo de clase. Tú
estás escribiendo en el libro. Nosotros estamos
hablando con Javier. etc

5 Examples: X está escribiendo. X está hablando
con Y. X y Y están trabajando. etc

Unit 4

1 **a:** Me gusta tomar el sol. Me gusta dar paseos
por el campo. **b:** Me gusta ir al cine. Me gusta
salir con amigos. **c:** Me gusta ver la tele. Me
gusta jugar al fútbol.

2 **a i** No, no me gusta. **ii** No, no me gusta.
iii Sí, me gusta. **iv** Sí, me gusta. **v** Sí, me
gusta. **vi** Sí, me gusta.

3 **a** 1d 2e 3a 4c 5b

b i Sí, me gusta. **ii** No, no me gusta mucho.
iii Sí, me encanta. **iv** No, no me gusta
nada. **v** Sí, me gusta mucho.

d i F **ii** F **iii** F **iv** F **v** F

5 **a** Andrés: le gusta la tele; le gustan las
vacaciones; no le gusta el deporte; no le
gustan los coches.

Bea: le gusta ir de compras; le gustan los
coches; no le gusta el deporte; no le gustan las
clases.

Carlos: le gusta ir de compras; le gustan las
clases; no le gusta la tele; no le gustan las
vacaciones.

b i Bea **ii** Bea **iii** Bea

9 They don't go to any of the discos. They decide
instead to stay in and watch TV.

10 1d 2a 3c 4b

12 **a** Tengo que trabajar. **b** Tengo que estudiar.
c Tengo que preparar la cena.

14 **a** ¿Cuándo vais? **b** ¿Quién toca? **c** ¿A qué hora
empieza? **d** ¿Cuánto cuestan las entradas?

15 1d 2e 3a 4b 5c

¡Extra!

16 **a** los culebrones, los dramas psicológicos, las
series policíacas, las comedias **b** las entrevistas
con los famosos y los concursos **c** las noticias
en la tele, los documentales, las películas
violentas

17 **a** ✓ **b** ✗ **c** ✓

Ejercicios de gramática

1 **a** me gustan **b** te gustan **c** me gusta **d** te
gustan **e** me gustan **f** le gustan **g** le gustan

2 **a** Prefiero ir al teatro. **b** Quiero jugar al tenis.
c Tengo que estudiar. **d** Prefiero ver las
noticias.

3 **estamos** we are   **estáis** you are
queremos we want   **queréis** you want
preferimos we prefer **preferís** you prefer
tenemos we have   **tenéis** you have

4 **a** Quieres Prefiero **b** puede Tiene **c** vais
d queremos podemos tenemos

Unit 5

1 **a** He's going to buy a big house in the country,
a plane, a luxury yacht and lots of cars. He's not
going to save anything, he's going to spend all his
money, starting right now.

2 **b i** 101 **ii** 250 **iii** 545 **iv** 1995 **v** 3.886
vi 7.733.571

4 **a** en agosto **b** en septiembre **c** en octubre
d en noviembre **e** en diciembre **f** en enero
g en febrero **h** en marzo

5

NOMBRE	DESTINO	SALIDA	VUELTA
Señor Cid	Marruecos	10 de octubre	24 de octubre
Juana la Loca	Lisboa	5 de abril	1 de mayo
Pepe Botella	París	21 de mayo	nunca

7 **a i** Termina en junio. **ii** Van a ir a Sudamérica.
iii Van a ver a los/unos amigos de Juana.
iv Van a pasar tres meses viajando.
v Miguel va a reservar los billetes mañana.

b Example: Querida Juana: Este verano Julio y yo vamos a viajar por África. Primero vamos a ver a mis amigos en Tanzania. Luego ellos van a acompañarnos a Kenia. Vamos a pasar tres meses en total viajando por África. Julio va a reservar los billetes el miércoles. ¿Qué vais a hacer tú y Miguel estas Navidades? Un abrazo Lucía

9 Look in the **Vocabulario** Section, page 60.

10 **1** una falda; 42 **2** un traje; 44 **3** unos pantalones; 50

11 Look in the **Vocabulario** Section, page 60.

12 **a** roja **b** azul, verde **c** amarillos **d** moradas, grises

14 **a** Esta falda es demasiado grande. **b** Estos pantalones son demasiado pequeños. **c** Este abrigo es demasiado caro. **d** Estas botas son demasiado pequeñas.

16 **a** Mariví un florero 50 €; Luis una cartera 45 €; Raquel un collar 40 €; Alfonso una pintura 150 €

b **i** They are all too expensive. **ii** A dress for Carolina.

17 It comes to €900, and the problem is he doesn't have enough cash.

¡Extra!

19 **a** **i** €186 **ii** €117; **b** Because it's a way of escaping from reality.

20 **b** Miguel **c** Miguel **d** Juana **e** Juana **f** Miguel **g** Miguel

Ejercicios de gramática

1 **a** vas **b** Voy **c** vas **d** Voy **e** vais **f** Vamos **g** vais **h** va **i** van **j** vais **k** vamos

2 **b** jueves dieciséis de septiembre de 2007 **c** viernes veintidós de mayo de 1999 **d** sábado treinta de marzo de 2020 **e** domingo primero de enero de 2009

3 554 – quinientos cincuenta y cuatro; 6.689 – seis mil seiscientos ochenta y nueve; 17.777 – diecisiete mil setecientos setenta y siete; 43.167 – cuarenta y tres mil ciento sesenta y siete; 122.943 – ciento veintidós mil novecientos cuarenta y tres

4 **b** Estos … pequeños. **c** Estas … grandes. **d** Este … barato.

Unit 6

2 **a**

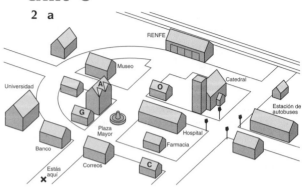

3 **a** car **b** bus **c** bicycle **d** foot **e** train **f** underground

4 **a** **ii** lejos; 30 **iii** cerca; 10 **iv** lejos; 15

5 **a** **ii** opposite **iii** between **iv** on the corner

6 **a** segunda; izquierda; en **b** tercera; derecha; enfrente de **c** al lado de; quinta; izquierda **d** entre; tercera; derecha

7 Dobla a la izquierda 2; Sigue todo recto 4; Ve todo recto 1; Coge la primera calle a la derecha 3; Dobla a la derecha 6; Coge la segunda calle a la izquierda 5

8 You should end up back at the station.

10 **a**

	número	súbete en	bájate en
i	19	centro comercial	Plaza Nueva
ii	12	Plaza Nueva	hospital
iii	15	Plaza Mayor	biblioteca

11 **a** House g

12 **a** **i** On the 1st floor on the right. **ii** Next to the toilets. **iii** On the second floor. Coming out of the lift you turn left and it's the third door on the right at the end of the corridor. **iv** Opposite the secretary's office, the third door on the left.

13 **a/b**

Pasa.	1 Come in.
Cierra la puerta.	2 Close the door.
Siéntate aquí.	3 Sit down here.
Rellena este formulario.	4 Fill in this form.
Escribe tu nombre.	5 Write your name.
Espera un momento.	6 Wait a minute.
Dame tu currículum.	7 Give me your CV.

¡Extra!

14 a To the cinema to see *Diarios de Motocicleta*.
b By bus. **c** It's at the Cine Rex, which is in the centre of town. He tells you to get the No 17 bus at the University and get off at the Plaza Mayor. **d** 20 minutes by bus, and 5 minutes on foot. **e** At 9.45, outside the cinema.

15 a At 11.00. **b** Bring something to eat or drink and your friends. **c** Underground. **d** On the second floor on the right.

Ejercicios de gramática

1 Mi casa está al lado de la iglesia, enfrente del parque. A la izquierda hay un hotel pequeño (*or* un pequeño hotel). Al final de la calle entre la piscina y el polideportivo hay un cine grande.

2 a ii súbete **iii** bájate **iv** ve **v** dobla **vi** sigue
b ii subíos **iii** bajaos **iv** id **v** doblad **vi** seguid

3 a i Pasa **ii** Cierra **iii** Espera **iv** Siéntate
v Rellena **vi** Escribe
b i Pasad **ii** Cerrad **iii** Esperad
iv Sentaos **v** Rellenad **vi** Escribid

4 The commands you make should be similar to the following:

Abre la ventana. Escucha música. Levántate de la cama. Coge el teléfono. Lee el libro. Bebe leche. Sal de la casa. Come verduras.

Unit 7

1 4 El año que viene hablaré español muy bien. 1 Mañana iré a clase. 3 El próximo verano viajaré a un país extranjero. 2 La semana que viene cenaré con amigos en un restaurante indio. 5 Dentro de 40 años seré abuelo/a.

2 a i el invierno que viene **ii** pasado mañana **iii** dentro de 5 años **iv** nunca **v** pronto

3 a i Llegará el martes. **ii** Se quedará en un hotel. **iii** Irá en coche. **iv** Volverá en dos semanas.

4 a i Sale a las dos menos cinco. **ii** Llega a las seis. **iii** Es Iberia 1919. **iv** Sale de la puerta número dos.

5 a At the hotel. **b** At the hotel. **c** He will call him from the hotel. **d** He suggests they go for a drink at 8 or 9 o'clock.

6 a ii ¿Cuánto es el seguro? **iii** ¿Tiene

gasolina? **iv** ¿Qué tipo de gasolina usa?
v ¿Acepta usted tarjetas de crédito?

7 Sevilla. Ida y vuelta. Segunda clase. No fumador. 13€. Sale a las 10:25. Llega a las 12:10. Es directo. Del andén número 15.

9 a Juana va a Barcelona. **b** Miguel va a Barcelona también. **c** Sale a las 10:12. **d** Sale del andén número 5.

11 b i Pasaremos unos días juntas. **ii** ¿Cuánto tiempo os quedaréis allí? **iii** Esta noche buscaré un hostal barato. **iv** ¡Eres un sol!
v Nunca olvidaré.

12 Está en la esquina, enfrente del banco. Vienen cada 20 minutos. Sí, para en el Parque Güell. Tarda unos 25 minutos.

13 a V **b** V **c** F **d** F **e** F

¡Extra!

15 a i, ii, iii, v, ix
b i, ii, v

16 1c 2e 3a 4b 5d

Ejercicios de gramática

1 a ¿A qué hora llega el tren? **b** ¿A qué hora sale el autobús? **c** ¿Cuánto tiempo dura el viaje?
d ¿A qué hora llega a París? **e** ¿De qué andén sale el tren? **f** ¿De qué puerta sale el vuelo?

2 a iré **b** Me levantaré **c** tendré **d** Saldré
e veré **f** Haré **g** escucharé **h** aprenderé
i buscaré

3 a iremos **b** Nos levantaremos **c** tendremos
d Saldremos **e** veremos **f** Haremos
g escucharemos **h** aprenderemos
i buscaremos

4 a irás **b** volverás **c** harás **d** empezarás

5 a iréis **b** volveréis **c** haréis **d** empezaréis

6 b menos … que **c** menos …que / tan … como **d** más … que **e** tan … como / más … que **f** menos … que

Unit 8

1 a Mike has worked in a bar and a restaurant in Scotland, but he has never worked in Spain. At the moment he is a student.
b i He visto su anuncio en el periódico.
ii Quisiera solicitar el puesto de … **iii** He trabajado en un bar … **iv** … pero no he

trabajado nunca en España. **v** ¿Qué hace actualmente? **vi** Venga mañana por la mañana …

2 Sí, he decidido … Sí, he llamado … Sí, he hablado … Sí, he escrito …

3 Juana **b** Mike **a** Julio **c**

6 Licenciatura en Empresariales *e Informática*; Barman 2001–2003; Camarero 2003– ahora; No es técnico

7 Dolores probably didn't get the job because she arrived late for the interview, her attitude was rather off-hand, she didn't bring her CV to the interview, she only wanted the job for the money, and she was negative about her course.

8 **1** a **2** b and c **3** a and c **4** b **5** a **6** c

9 a/b

NOMBRE	FECHAS	HABITACIÓN DOBLE / INDIVIDUAL	PENSIÓN MEDIA / COMPLETA	BALCÓN	BAÑO/ DUCHA
SERRAT	21 -25 junio	doble	completa X 2	sí	baño
PONS	15-17 mayo	individual	media	sí	ducha

10 **a** **2**c **3**d **4**b

11 **1**d **2**c **3**e **4**b **5**a

13 **1**c,f **2**b,h,i **3**a,d **4**e,g

14 a/b

EMPLEO	VENTAJAS	DESVENTAJAS
Moza de cuadra	Me encanta; estás fuera todo el día al aire libre; puedes montar a caballo.	Es duro; empiezas muy temprano; las cuadras pueden estar muy lejos de la casa.
Camarero	Conoces a mucha gente; me gusta el ambiente en el restaurante; me llevo bien con todos.	No ganas mucho dinero.
Animador	Me llevo muy bien con los niños; conoces a mucha gente.	No ganas mucho.
Servicio doméstico	Te dan la comida gratis.	El trabajo es muy duro; no me gustan mis colegas; no gano casi nada.

¡Extra!

16 **a** **i** en las que el salario que se cobra **ii** es superior a la media nacional **iii** No obstante **iv** los sueldos de los madrileños **v** los más elevados … los más bajos **vi** los de los murcianos

b

SALARIO MENSUAL MEDIO POR TRABAJADOR	€ (aprox)
MADRID	2.090
PAÍS VASCO	2.047
CATALUÑA	1.884
CASTILLA Y LEÓN	1.717
BALEARES	1.628
ANDALUCÍA	1.621
GALICIA	1.510
MURCIA	1.378

17 **1** f,iv **2** d,v **3** a,ii **4** c,i **5** e,iii **6** b,vi

Ejercicios de gramática

1 **b** He **c** Habéis **d** Hemos **e** Han **f** ha

2 **b** visto **c** dicho **d** escrito **e** hecho **f** cogido

3

he llegado	llego	llegaré
he vuelto	vuelvo	volveré
he salido	salgo	saldré

4 **a** he empezado **b** han llegado … ha venido **c** Hemos ganado … hemos comprado **d** Habéis visto … Ha tenido

5

Dear Jesús

Have you seen the advertisement for an assistant in a language school? I want to apply for the post and I have rung the college to ask for more details. I have already prepared my CV and my teacher has written me a reference. Have you decided if you would like to work in France in July? Write or ring me soon,

María José

Unit 9

1 Por la mañana estuve en la universidad. Fui a la biblioteca. Sí, trabajé todo el día. Pasé toda la noche estudiando. Me acosté a las once y media.

2 **1**b **2**e **3**d **4**c **5**a

6 **b** He was in a bar, playing his guitar with a country and western band.

7 **a 1** Nació el 10 de octubre … **2** Fue al Colegio Ave María … **3** Aprobó el bachillerato … **4** Viajó durante un año … **5** Trabajó en bares y cafés … **6** Volvió a España …

11 **a** Fernando and Itziar had a good time; Maribel and Enrique didn't.

b Fernando **iv** Maribel **i** Itziar **iii** Enrique **ii**

12 **a i** Itziar **ii** Enrique **iii** Fernando **iv** Enrique **v** Enrique **vi** Maribel **vii** Enrique

13 **a 1** Cogió la llave … **2** Perdió la llave de la casa en el autobús. **3** Llegó a casa a las seis. **4** La dueña no estaba. **5** Fue al bar de enfrente para esperar … **6** Empezó a beber … **7** La dueña volvió a la casa a las doce. **8** Ella abrió la puerta. **9** En ese momento Fernando vomitó en la escalera.

14 **b** dos **c** 17 ó 18 **d** tres y media **e** diez

¡Extra!

16 **b i** 6.000 **ii** Se manifestaron contra la privatización de la universidad. **iii** Colectivos estudiantiles organizaron la protesta. **iv** Terminó con una fuerte carga policial. **v** Un manifestante resultó herido leve. **vi** No hubo detenidos.

c Colectivos *estudiantiles* de la *izquierda* alternativa convocaron *ayer* en el *centro* de Madrid a 6.000 *jóvenes* para expresar su *protesta contra* la posible *privatización* de la Universidad. La manifestación *terminó* con enfrentamientos entre un grupo de estudiantes y la policía. Tras la carga, un *manifestante* resultó herido *leve*. No hubo detenidos.

Ejercicios de gramática

1 **b** trabajé **c** volví **d** Cené **e** vi **f** Me acosté

2 There are several possible answers.
b estuviste **c** pasaste **d** te quedaste **e** llegaste **f** duró

3 **b** gustaron **c** asistieron **d** ayudaron **e** invitaron

4 There are several possible questions.
b ¿Dónde tuvo lugar? **c** ¿Qué pasó?
d ¿Cuánto tiempo duró el atraco?
e ¿Adónde fueron? **f** ¿Cómo se escaparon?

Unit 10

1

Nombre	Elena
Apellidos	Ariza González
Dirección	Calle Colón, núm 26, 2°B, 28011 Madrid
Nacionalidad	Española
Fecha de nacimiento	28 de agosto de 1982
Lugar de nacimiento	Madrid
Profesión	Estudiante

7 **a**

	Prenda	Talla	Color	Problema	Precio
i	una falda	38	roja	Demasiado pequeña	€25
			negra/ amarilla	no le gustan	-
			azul	demasiado cara	€45
			verde	-	€27
ii	unos zapatos	37	todos grises	no los tienen en verde	€36

b He ido a todos los grandes almacenes y ahora estoy en el Corte Inglés. **La primera falda** que me he probado aquí era demasiado **pequeña**, y pedí **una** más **grande** a la dependienta. Me ha traído **otra**, pero no me gusta el color. He visto **muchas faldas** pero por fin me he quedado con **ésta**, que me ha costado **27 €**. Pero no he podido encontrar **unos zapatos** del mismo color.

8 Your answer should be something like this:

Querido Jorge:

Sí, puedes quedarte conmigo, e iré a la estación a recogerte. Al final de la conferencia saldremos al campo en el coche. Si quieres, acampemos. Y mi hermana, lo siento pero no va a estar en casa. Está viajando por Francia.
Hasta el lunes.

Un abrazo:

9 **a**2 **b**4 **c**1 **d**3

10 **a** ¿Cuál es el número del vuelo? ¿De qué puerta sale?

Answers

¿Hay retraso?

11 There are a few different possibilities.
1a **5**e **8**h **7**g **6**f **2**b **3**c **4**d

12 **b** Trabajaré en un campamento de verano.
c Viajaré un poco por América. **d** Me quedaré
en el campamento … **e** …y luego iré a casa de
mis amigos en Miami. **f** Volveré en octubre.

14 **a** He is tall, wearing a grey suit, a white shirt
and a green tie. He looks like an executive,
maybe a banker. **b** He is the heir to the throne
of Spain. **c** When he was 7, Franco died; when
he was 37, he got married. **d** Two; they married
María de las Mercedes de Orleans and Letizia
Ortiz.

17 **a** **i** 1906 **ii** 1927 **iii** 1928 **iv** 1931 **v** 1937
vi 1938 **vii** 1975

18 **a** He wasn't rich. **b** He fought the Moors and
earned a lot of money. **c** After five years.
d Getting married. **e** Because she was
married. **f** Together in a tomb.

Ejercicios de gramática

1 **b** Me llamo **c** eres **d** Soy (or Me llamo)
e Vives **f** vivo **g** dedicas **h** Trabajo

2 **b** Sale de casa a las nueve de la mañana.
c Llega a la universidad a las nueve y cuarto
de la mañana. **d** Come en la cantina a la una
de la tarde. **e** Vuelve a casa a las seis de la
tarde. **f** Va al bar con sus amigos a las diez
de la noche. **g** Se acuesta a las doce (or a
medianoche).

3 **a** cuarenta y uno **b** sesenta y siete
c ciento cuatro **d** quinientos cincuenta y
dos **e** mil setecientos setenta y ocho
f nueve mil novecientos ochenta y uno

4 **b** Gloria está saliendo de casa.
c (Nosotros) estamos trabajando mucho.
d (Tú) estás llegando al aeropuerto.
e Vicente y Pepa están comprando ropa.
f (Yo) estoy hablando por teléfono.

5 **a** **ii** ¿Te gusta beber cerveza? **iii** ¿Te gustan los
animales?
b **ii** Me encanta la música cubana. **iii** No me
gusta el fútbol. **iv** Me gusta mucho. **v** No me
gusta nada.

6 **b** voy a estudiar **c** van a ver **d** vamos a ir
e vas a venir **f** vais a comer

7 There are other possible answers.
b Dobla a la derecha. El hotel está a la
derecha. **c** Dobla a la izquierda. El banco está
a la derecha. **d** Coge la segunda calle a la
derecha. Correos está a la izquierda.
e Ve todo recto y coge la tercera calle a la
derecha. La estación está a la izquierda.

8 Your sentences should be similar to these
ones. **b** Nosotros volveremos a América.
c Eliás se casará en junio. **d** Yo podré salir a
las seis. **e** Tú te acostarás a las doce.
f Ana y Bea trabajarán en Francia en agosto.
g Vosotros tendréis que ahorrar el dinero.

9 Your sentences should be similar to these:
b Nosotros hemos vuelto de América.
c Eliás se ha casado. **d** Yo he podido salir.
e Tú te has acostado. **f** Ana y Bea han
trabajado en Francia. **g** Vosotros habéis tenido
que ahorrar el dinero.

10 Ayer me levanté a las seis. Preparé el desayuno
y salí a las siete y media. Fui al trabajo en
coche y llegué a las ocho y cuarto. Al mediodía
comí en un bar enfrente de la oficina. Volví a
casa a las ocho y cené a las nueve y media. Me
acosté a las once o las doce.

Juegos de palabras

5 Other words which end in **-ad**, and which you
have seen in this book, are: **nacionalidad,
universidad, ciudad, facultad.**

6 **-mente**. It corresponds to -ly in English and is
an adverb. Thus **rápida<u>mente</u>** means quickly,
etc.

Más práctica 1

1 **a** lawyer **b** secretary **c** Argentina **d** Madrid
e company director

2 She is not from here; she is from Puerto Rico;
she lives in Miami; she works in the university;
she is not a student; she is an administrator;
she is also learning Italian.

5 **a** ¿Cómo te llamas? / ¿Quién eres?
b ¿Dónde vives? **c** ¿Eres escocés? **d** ¿Cuál es
tu profesión?

6 Ignacio: Es de Perú. Tiene 21 años. Vive en
Oviedo. Es estudiante de medicina.
Amanda: Sí, es de Bilbao. No, vive en Oviedo.
No, tiene 25 años. No, es secretaria.

7 Estimado señor:
Quiero matricularme en un curso de español. Me llamo Laurie Dimock y tengo 22 años. Soy galés/galesa, de Bangor, pero vivo en México. Soy recepcionista en un hotel.
Atentamente Laurie Dimock

8 Example reply:
Querida Juanita:
Soy de (where you are from) y vivo en (where you live). Soy (your job) y tengo (your age) años. Soy (your nationality). Estudio (what you study).
Un abrazo de (your name)

9 **a** Nadia Gil García tiene 25 años. Es española, de Madrid, pero vive en Valencia. Es profesora de historia. **b** Daniel Martínez Báez tiene 24 años. Es español y vive en Bilbao. Es investigador. **c** Siobhán Harpur tiene 21 años. Es irlandesa, de Dublín. Aprende francés y trabaja en un hotel.

10

		S	E	I	S		C
	V	I			E		A
T	R	E	C	E			T
	I	T		O	C	H	O
Q	U	I	N	C	E		R
	T	E					C
D	I	E	C	I	N	U	E	V	E

Más práctica 2

1 Paulina, 28, hermana menor; Alberto, 46, marido; Miguel, 40, hermano mayor; Esther, 64, madre; Leonardo, 65, padre; José, 10, hijo.

2 **a** Tienen dos hijos. **b** Su marido es mecánico. **c** Tienen tres hijos. Se llaman Susana, Charo y Felipe. **d** Los padres de Charo están divorciados y su hermana, Susana, está separada. **e** Se llama Susana. **f** La novia de Felipe trabaja en el aeropuerto.

5 Juan: 5, salón, grande, 3, garaje, 2, no. Ángela: piso, centro, pequeño, aparcamiento, no, 3.

6 **a** Es muy grande y bastante vieja. **b** Hay 4 dormitorios grandes. **c** Hay una cama individual y un sofá. **d** Están en la planta baja. **e** Es muy moderna. **f** Hay una piscina y una pista de tenis.

Más práctica 3

1 lunes: 4:00 – cita con el Sr Graznar; martes: 10:00 – a la oficina Sra Gómez, 3:00 – restaurante El Juez; miércoles: juicio todo el día; jueves: 10:00 – juicio, 4:00 – casa del Sr Graznar; viernes: Trabaja en casa todo el día.

2 Me levanto a las siete y desayuno a las siete y media. Salgo a las ocho y voy a la oficina. Trabajo hasta las dos. Como en un bar y vuelvo al trabajo a las cinco. Termino a las ocho y ceno con Isabel a las diez. Me acuesto a medianoche.

3 Andrés: duerme, estudia, sale – estudiante; Bea: trabaja, trabaja, sale – recepcionista; Carlos: visita a los pacientes, vuelve a la clínica, trabaja – médico; Diana: trabaja, trabaja, trabaja – profesora; Enrique: duerme, sale, pinta – artista

4 **a** está conversando **b** está hablando **c** está haciendo **d** está escribiendo **e** estoy esperando **f** está esperando **g** está saliendo

Más práctica 4

1 **a** F **b** F **c** F **d** F **e** V

2 **a** Se llama Gaudí. **b** Le gusta ver los títeres y las estatuas humanas, los pintores y los artistas de todo tipo.

3 **1**b **2**d **3**a **4**c

4 **a** Mañana no puedo. **b** Tengo que trabajar. **c** Por la noche. **d** No. El martes tengo clase. **e** Todo el día. **f** No, no quiero salir contigo. **g** Porque prefiero salir con Juana.

6

lunes	martes	miércoles
De compras con Alicia a las 12:00	Gimnasio con Bea a las 4:30h	Exposición de Arte con Bea a las 12:00 en la entrada del museo
	Cine con Carlos 10:30	

Más práctica 5

1 **a** It's a soap opera.

b **i** Leonardo va a viajar a Estambul. **ii** Livia va a París. **iii** Leonardo y Livia van a estar en el Bar Jinete a las 10.

d **i** V; **ii** F (Pide un jerez seco); **iii** V; **iv** V; **v** F (Margarita va a salir con Salvador)

e Compran un traje nuevo para Salvador.

f i 1500 €; **ii** 1500 €; **iii** 2000 €; **iv** 1000 €; **v** 1400 €; **vi** 1200 €

h It says that tomorrow she is going to Palm Springs with César the car salesman, and that they are going to get married in Las Vegas.

Más práctica 6

1 a

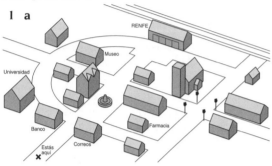

2

E	F	G
D		C
H		B
I		A

4 b Your directions should be similar to these:
i Desde la Plaça Sant Jaume ve por la calle Ferrán. Coge la segunda calle a la derecha y el albergue está a la derecha.
ii Desde la Plaça Catalunya ve por la Rambla. Coge la segunda calle a la izquierda. Es la calle Boquería. Coge la tercera calle a la derecha y el albergue está a la izquierda.
iii Desde el Museo de Cera dobla a la derecha. Coge la primera calle a la derecha. Es la calle Ferrán. Coge la tercera calle a izquierda y el albergue está a mano derecha.

5 1d 2c 3b 4a

Más práctica 7

1 a persona **b** números 5 y 10 **c** amante **d** dinero **e** extranjero **f** empleo

3

	FECHA	VUELO	DESTINO	SALIDA	LLEGADA
Change from	24 enero	Iberia 1607	Tenerife	15.40	–
Change to	21 enero	Iberia 1801	Tenerife	17.50	20.30

4 a V **b** F **c** V **d** F **e** F **f** F

5 Your answer could be something like this:

Querido Claudio:

Lo siento, pero no puedo ir contigo al campo, porque tengo que trabajar. Este fin de semana trabajaré el sábado todo el día, y el domingo voy a ver a mis padres. Te veré la semana que viene.

Un abrazo,

Your name

8 a There are a few possible variations to the changes made below:

En el siglo XXI los seres humanos volarán por el aire en aviones, y cruzarán el mar en barcos. Viajarán por tierra en coches. Cada día irán al trabajo en coche. Será posible viajar alrededor del mundo en una semana.

Más práctica 8

2 b Your attitude towards the job.

3 b He mentions the following: viii, vii, i, ix, iv, iii

5 1b 2a 3e 4c 5d

6 a2 **b**1 **c**1 **d**3

7

> Querida Lucía:
>
> He empezado el trabajo y no me gusta nada. Empiezo muy temprano y termino tarde, y el trabajo es aburrido y siempre igual. No me llevo muy bien con mis colegas y mis jefes y no me gusta conocer a los clientes. No pagan muy bien, no ha sido una experiencia muy buena y no he podido practicar el español.
>
> Escríbeme pronto
>
> Un abrazo de
>
> Juana

b Your letter might be something like this:

> Querido Jaime
>
> He empezado un trabajo de verano. Trabajo desde las ocho de la mañana hasta las dos y desde las cinco hasta las ocho de la tarde. Tengo que fregar los platos y limpiar la cocina. Me gusta porque me llevo muy bien con mis colegas y he podido practicar el español, pero no se paga muy bien.
>
> Un abrazo de
>
> Your name

Más práctica 9

1 **1** Llegué a Mojácar … **2** Pasé toda la mañana en la playa. **3** Tomé el sol, me bañé en el mar **4** y al mediodía fui a comer a un restaurante. **5** Volví a la playa por la tarde **6** y salí a una discoteca por la noche. **7** Sin embargo, al día siguiente cogí una insolación **8** y pasé el resto de la semana en la cama.

2 **b** Nicolás **c** Manolo **d** Mariví **e** Nicolás **f** Manolo

4 Your postcard should be similar to the following:

> Querida María:
>
> Llegué ayer por la tarde a las siete y media y fui directo al apartamento. Comí en un restaurante y pasé el resto de la noche en un bar. Esta mañana fui a la playa y comí en un café. Volví a la playa por la tarde y me bañé en el mar. Ahora estoy en el apartamento y voy a salir.
>
> Un abrazo
> *Your name*

Más práctica 10

1

	%
La vivienda es cara	28
Prefieren las comodidades sin responsabilidades	6
Los padres no son muy estrictos	30
Los jóvenes se casan más tarde	32
No tienen posibilidades de independizarse antes	80
Los padres necesitan la ayuda económica de los hijos	15
Quieren tener una situación estable antes de vivir solos	34

2

GASTOS MENSUALES	
Alquiler	500€–620€
Luz	30€
Agua	8€ o 9€
Teléfono	40€ o 45€
Gas (sin calefacción):	
natural	8€
Butano	8€
Calefacción (de gas natural)	50€
Comunidad de vecinos:	
sin servicios (ascensor, calefacción)	50€
con servicios	115€

El alquiler varía desde 580€ a 300€. Es más caro en Cataluña, el País Vasco y Madrid y menos caro en Huelva, Cáceres y Huesca. Además, en España cuando alquilas un piso tienes que pagar el primer mes de alquiler y también una fianza de 500€ a 620€.

3 **a** In Mexico **b** In Bilbao **c** Dolores Ibarruri **d** Dolores Ibarruri **e** Dolores Ibarruri **f** Montezuma **g** Montezuma **h** Dolores Ibarruri **i** Montezuma **j** Montezuma

APPENDIX: Additional vocabulary

Unit 1

10

carta (f)	letter
economía (f)	economics
funcionario/a	civil servant
psicología (f)	psychology
relaciones internacionales (f pl)	international relations
sociología (f)	sociology
venezolano/a	Venezuelan

11

número	number

For numbers 1–100 see page 6

12

¿Cuántos años tiene?	How old is s/he? / How old are you? (formal)
¿Cuántos años tienes?	How old are you?
Tengo …años.	I'm … years old.
Tiene … años.	S/he is … years old.

16

actual	current/present
domicilio (m)	address
estudios (m pl)	studies
formulario (m)	form
nacionalidad (f)	nationality
nombre (m)	name
permanente	permanent
rellenar	to fill in

17

Acabo de …	I've just …
aquí	here
casa (f)	house
centro (m)	centre
chino/a	Chinese
ciudad (f)	city/town
danés/danesa	Danish
filosofía (f)	philosophy
grande	big
hotel (m)	hotel
matricularse	to enrol, register
No está mal.	It's not bad.
Querido/a …	Dear …
oficina (f)	office
pagar	to pay for
también	also
trabajo	I work
un/a	a
Un abrazo …	Love from …

Unit 2

13 *continued*

teléfono (m)	telephone
ventana (f)	window

15

armario (m)	wardrobe/cupboard
bañera (f)	bath (tub)
cama (f)	bed
cocina (f)	cooker
ducha (f)	shower
espejo (m)	mirror
frigorífico (m)	fridge
inodoro (m)	toilet
lavabo (m)	basin
lavadora (f)	washing machine
pared (f)	wall
tocador (m)	dressing table

16

suelo (m)	floor

Unit 3

10 *continued*

pan (m)	bread
pescado (m)	fish
sopa (f)	soup
verduras (f pl)	vegetables
vino (m)	wine
zumo (m)	juice

11

almuerzo (m)	lunch
beber	to drink
desayuno (m)	breakfast
tomar	to have to eat or drink

12

azúcar (m)	sugar
hábitos alimentarios (m pl)	eating habits
vegetariano/a	vegetarian

13

aceituna (f)	olive
bar (m)	bar
bebida (f)	drink
calamares (m pl)	squid
champiñón (m)	mushroom
jamón (m)	ham
jerez (m)	sherry
patatas fritas (f pl)	chips/crisps

pedir	to ask for
refresco (m)	soft drink
sangría (f)	sangria
tapa (f)	snack
tortilla (f)	omelette
vino blanco/tinto (m)	white/red wine

14

cliente/a (m/f)	client/customer
cuenta (f)	bill
de postre	for dessert
de primer plato	for the first course
de segundo plato	for the second course
flan (m)	crème caramel
gazpacho (m)	gazpacho
helado (m)	ice cream
lenguado (m)	sole
menú del día (m)	set menu
paella (f)	paella
para beber	to drink
pollo asado (m)	roast chicken
restaurante (m)	restaurant
tortilla española (f)	Spanish omelette

15

ayudar	to help
estrés (m)	stress
nada	nothing
sano/a	healthy

16

demasiado/a	too much
director/a	director
enfermo/a	ill
hoy	today
pasar	to spend (time)

Unit 5

19 *continued*

ilusión (f)	hope
materialista	materialistic
nunca	never
¿Por qué?	Why?
porque	because
realidad (f)	reality
sociedad (f)	society
sueño (m)	dream
tanto	so much
tender (tiende)	to tend (tends)
valor (m)	value

20

antes de	before
dejar de …	to give up …
lista (f)	list
lo que	that which / what

nada (más)	nothing (else)
necesitar	to need
tirar	to throw out

21

alcohol (m)	alcohol
arreglar	to fix
de segunda mano	second-hand
fin de semana (m)	weekend
transporte público (m)	public transport
tú mismo	yourself
utilizar	to use
vehículo (m)	vehicle

Unit 7

15 *continued*

calentamiento (m)	warming
cambio (m)	change
clima (m)	climate
conductor/a	driver
consumo (m)	consumption
emisión (f)	emission
empleado/a	employee
incendio (m)	fire
lluvia (f)	rain
monte (m)	mountain
motor (m)	engine
recibir	to receive
selva (tropical) (f)	(rain) forest, jungle
solucionar	to solve

16

aéreo/a	air (adj)
alcanzar	to reach
alimentar	to fuel
batalla (f)	battle
célula (f)	cell
combustible (m)	fuel
comercializar	to put on the market
cualquier	any
de esta forma	in this way
disponer	to have
dominado/a	dominated
ejercitar	to exercise
empresa (f)	firm
fuerza (f)	strength
gasolinera (f)	petrol station
infrarrojo	infra red
moverse	to move
pocos/as	few
servir	to be used
siglo (m)	century
tonelada (f)	tonne (metric)
vitrina (f)	glass case

Unit 8

14 *continued*

conocer	to (get to) know
desvantaja (f)	disadvantage
duro/a	hard
esto	this
fuera	outside
gratis	free
llevarse bien con	to get on well with
montar a caballo	to ride
ventaja (f)	advantage

16

bajo/a	low
cobrar	to earn
comunidad (f) autónoma	autonomous community
elevado/a	high
madrileño/a	person from Madrid
media (f)	average
mensual	monthly
murciano/a	person from Murcia
no obstante	However
sueldo (m)	wage

17

constancia (f)	perseverance
enfermería (f)	nursing
habilidad (f)	skill
investigación (f)	research
manitas (m/f)	handyman/woman (colloquial)
ordenado/a	tidy
perfil (m)	profile, characteristic, background
perspicaz	perceptive
recursos humanos (m pl)	human resources
vanguardista (m/f)	forward looking
ventanilla (f) de reclamación	customer services

CD TRACK LIST

Two CDs are supplied with this book. They contain all the audio material to accompany the exercises in this book.

- Where there is an audio element for an exercise it is marked with a 🎧 icon.
- Every exercise has its own track which will help you locate the material very easily.
- All the audio for the **Más práctica** section is on CD2.
- Tutors who require digital licences for this audio material should visit http://www.palgrave.com/modernlanguages/license.asp#Digital.

Intro & 1 Tú y los demás

01 El lenguaje de la clase
02 El abecedario
03 Sección 1a
04 Sección 2: Carmen
05 Sección 2: Michael
06 Sección 5b
07 Sección 8a
08 Sección 9a
09 Sección 11
10 Sección 12
11 Sección 13
12 ¡Extra! Sección 16: 1
13 ¡Extra! Sección 16: 2
14 ¡Extra! Sección 16: 3
15 ¡Extra! Sección 16: 4

2 La familia en casa

16 Sección 1
17 Sección 2
18 Sección 3a
19 Sección 5
20 Sección 6: 1
21 Sección 6: 2
22 Sección 6: 3
23 Sección 6: 4
24 Sección 7
25 Sección 9: 1
26 Sección 9: 2

27 Sección 10
28 Sección 13
29 ¡Extra! Sección 14

3 La rutina

30 Sección 1b
31 Sección 2
32 Sección 3a
33 Sección 4a
34 Sección 5a
35 Sección 9
36 Sección 12a
37 Sección 13
38 Sección 14a
39 ¡Extra! Sección 15b

4 El tiempo libre

40 Sección 1
41 Sección 2a
42 Sección 3b
43 Sección 5a
44 Sección 6
45 Sección 9
46 Sección 10
47 Sección 12
48 Sección 14
49 ¡Extra! Sección 17a
50 ¡Extra! Sección 17b
51 ¡Extra! Sección 17c

5 El dinero

52 Sección 1a
53 Sección 2a
54 Sección 4
55 Sección 5
56 Sección 10: 1
57 Sección 10: 2
58 Sección 10: 3
59 Sección 12
60 Sección 14
61 Sección 16a
62 Sección 17
63 ¡Extra! Sección 20

6 En la ciudad

64 Sección 1
65 Sección 2a: 1
66 Sección 2a: 2
67 Sección 2a: 3
68 Sección 2a: 4
69 Sección 4a
70 Sección 6a
71 Sección 7
72 Sección 10a: 1
73 Sección 10a: 2
74 Sección 10a: 3
75 Sección 12
76 Sección 13a
77 Extra! Sección 14

CD Track List

CD2

7 En el futuro

01 Sección 2a
02 Sección 3a
03 Sección 4a
04 Sección 6a
05 Sección 7
06 Sección 9
07 Sección 11a
08 Sección 12
09 Sección 13
10 ¡Extra! Sección 15

8 Trabajo de verano

11 Sección 1a
12 Sección 6
13 Sección 7
14 Sección 9b
15 Sección 14b
16 ¡Extra! Sección 16b

9 ¿Dónde estuviste ayer?

17 Sección 1
18 Sección 2
19 Sección 6b
20 Sección 11: Fernando
21 Sección 11: Maribel
22 Sección 11: Itziar
23 Sección 11: Enrique
24 Sección 14
25 ¡Extra! Sección 16b

10 Repaso

26 Sección 1a
27 Sección 4a
28 Sección 7a
29 Sección 9: 1
30 Sección 9: 2
31 Sección 9: 3
32 Sección 9: 4
33 Sección 12
34 Sección 17a

Más Práctica

1 Tú y los demás

35 Sección 1
36 Sección 3
37 Sección 4
38 Sección 6

2 La familia en casa

39 Sección 1
40 Sección 3
41 Sección 5

3 La rutina

42 Sección 1
43 Sección 4
44 Sección 5

4 El tiempo libre

45 Sección 1
46 Sección 5
47 Sección 6: 1
48 Sección 6: 2
49 Sección 6: 3

5 El dinero

50 Sección 1d
51 Sección 1e
52 Sección 1f
53 Sección 1g

6 En la ciudad

54 Sección 1a
55 Sección 1b
56 Sección 4

7 En el futuro

57 Sección 3
58 Sección 4
59 Sección 6

8 Trabajo de verano

60 Sección 1
61 Sección 3b

9 ¿Dónde estuviste ayer?

62 Sección 2: 1
63 Sección 2: 2
64 Sección 2: 3
65 Sección 3

10 Repaso

66 Sección 2

INDEX